Elizabeth Speller's other books include *Granta City Guides: Rome* and *Athens*. She lives in Gloucestershire, and is currently a Visiting Scholar at Lucy Cavendish College, Cambridge.

The Sunlight *on the* Garden

A *family in love, war and madness*

Elizabeth Speller

Granta Books
London

Granta Publications, 2/3 Hanover Yard, Noel Road, London N1 8BE
First published in Great Britain by Granta Books 2006
This edition published by Granta Books, 2007

A CIP catalogue record for this book is available
from the British Library.

1 3 5 7 9 10 8 6 4 2

Typeset by M Rules

Printed and bound in Great Britain by
Bookmarque Ltd, Croydon, Surrey

For my mother, Ann Gyllian Howard Moore (1928–1993),
my daughters, Miranda and Abigail,
and my granddaughter, Tabitha

The Sunlight on the Garden

The sunlight on the garden
Hardens and grows cold,
We cannot cage the minute
Within its nets of gold;
When all is told
We cannot beg for pardon.

Our freedom as free lances
Advances towards its end;
The earth compels, upon it
Sonnets and birds descend;
And soon, my friend,
We shall have no time for dances.

The sky was good for flying
Defying the church bells
And every evil iron
Siren and what it tells:
The earth compels,
We are dying, Egypt, dying

And not expecting pardon,
Hardened in heart anew,
But glad to have sat under
Thunder and rain with you,
And grateful too
For sunlight on the garden.

Louis MacNeice (1939)

Contents

Introduction *Nice, Baie des Anges 1963*   1

1   *Lausanne. Fin de Siècle*   7

2   *London 1950s*   32

3   *Paris. England*   51

4   *Brittany 1950s and 1960s*   67

5   *War. 1940s*   84

6   *Gloucestershire 1960–1970s*   107

7   *England 1940s*   133

8   *Berlin*   154

9   *Peterborough 1980s*   180

10 *Lincolnshire 1980–1990*   202

11 *Home*   213

Epilogue   237

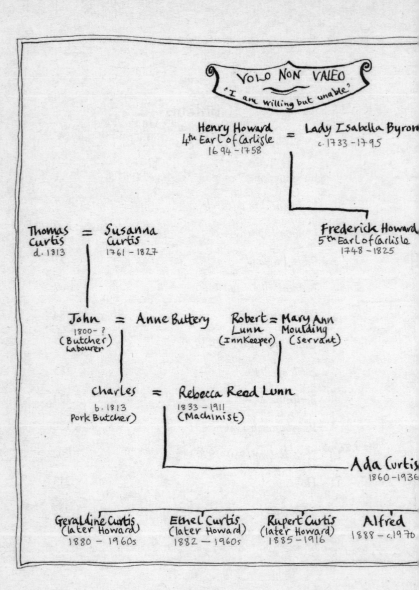

Family Tree ~ To the Author's

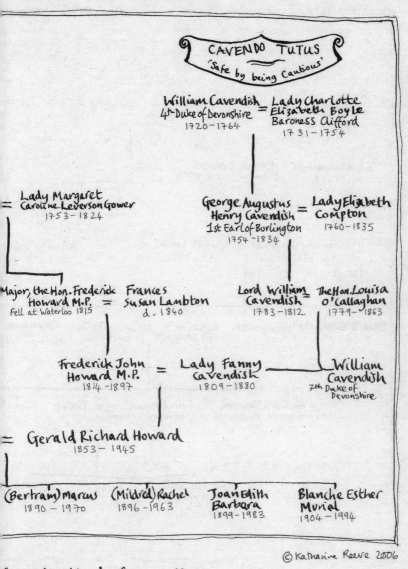

CAVENDO TUTUS
'Safe by being Cautious'

William Cavendish
4th Duke of Devonshire = Lady Charlotte
1720-1764   Elizabeth Boyle
Baroness Clifford
1731-1754

= Lady Margaret
Caroline Leverson Gower
1753-1824

George Augustus
Henry Cavendish = Lady Elizabeth
1st Earl of Burlington   Compton
1754-1834   1760-1835

Major, the Hon. Frederick   Frances
Howard M.P. = Susan Lambton
Fell at Waterloo 1815   d.-1840

Lord William
Cavendish = The Hon. Louisa
1783-1812   O'Callaghan
1779-1863

Frederick John
Howard M.P. = Lady Fanny
1814-1897   Cavendish
1809-1880

William
Cavendish
7th Duke of
Devonshire

= Gerald Richard Howard
1853-1945

(Bertram) Marcus   (Mildred) Rachel   Joan Edith   Blanche Esther
1890-1970   1896-1963   Barbara   Murial
1899-1983   1904-1994

© Katharine Reeve 2006

Grandmother's Generation

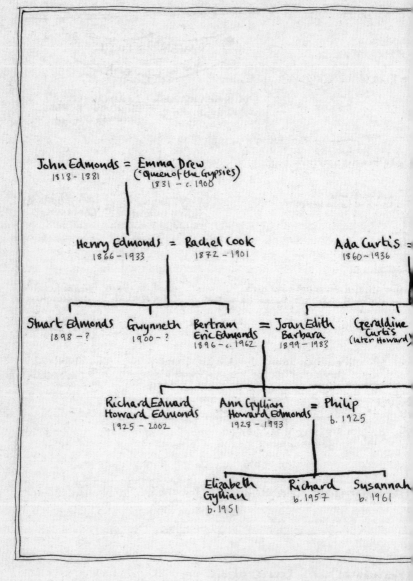

John Edmonds = Emma Drew
1818 – 1881   ('Queen of the Gypsies)
                1831 – c.1900

Henry Edmonds = Rachel Cook   Ada Curtis =
1866 – 1933   1872 – 1901   1860 – 1936

Stuart Edmonds   Gwynneth   Bertram = Joan Edith   Geraldine
1898 – ?   1900 – ?   Eric Edmonds Barbara   Curtis
                              1896 – c.1962 1899 – 1983 (later Howard)

Richard Edward   Ann Gyllian   = Philip
Howard Edmonds   Howard Edmonds   b. 1925
1925 – 2002   1928 – 1993

                    Elizabeth   Richard   Susannah
                    Gyllian   b. 1957   b. 1961
                    b. 1951

Family Tree ~ To

Lord William Cavendish = The Hon. Louisa O'Callaghan
1783 – 1812   1779 – 1863

Lady Fanny Cavendish   William Cavendish
1809 – 1880   7th Duke of Devonshire
                                        1808 – 1891

Gerald Richard Howard   Lord Frederick Cavendish = Lady Lucy
1853 – 1945   1836 – 1882   Lyttleton
                               (Murdered by Fenians   1841 – 1925
                               in Phoenix Park)

Ethel Curtis   Rupert Curtis   Alfred (Bertram) (Mildred) Blanche
(later Howard) (later Howard)   Marcus   Rachel   Esther Muriel

Mary St. Joan   = James Kennaway
Howard Edmonds   1928 – 1968
b. 1930

© Katharine Reeve 2006

the Author's Generation

Introduction

Nice, Baie des Anges 1963

I knew of Nice by family reputation, of course, so it was no surprise to receive my first serious proposition on one of its municipal benches. Every winter my divorced great-aunt Gwynneth went to Nice to gamble away the winter months. It was non-consummation my mother said sagely: while the man who was briefly my great-uncle and who was called Mr Peek toiled over great-aunt Gwynneth, she did the *Times* crossword, pausing – her not him – to ring a friend to complain about the tedium of marital obligation. 'Oh my God,' she drawled in popular family renditions, 'it's Barry, he's at it again.' When he eventually ran amok with a carving knife she had him and the marriage set aside. Such problems were unlikely to arise with her companion Sidney Alberga, with whom she went to the Hotel Negresco each November. They travelled as brother and sister: Gwynneth a relic of the 1920s, signing the cheques, and Sidney, his white face, dyed red hair, smudged eyes and fur coat conferring considerable glamour on the two of them.

Nice was also the place where my parents had been happy, as undergraduates abroad, after the war. For years I treasured a photograph of them just *being* happy. My father, slim yet strong, with a lock of light brown hair falling in his eyes is controlling a small boat which he is inducing my mother to board. She, still on shore, in a patterned cotton bathing costume and with her dark curls wet; has her back to the camera, but I recognise and love her freckly shoulders and can almost smell her: one of the best smells of childhood summer; her hot skin and *Ambre Solaire*. My father is looking up, persuading, reassuring; it is probably the sun shining in his eyes, but he looks as if he is gazing up at her into radiance. Apart from the boat, the landscape is hot white; sand, rock and water. I worked out when this must have been taken, because I am obviously not yet born, and they had very little time without me. It had to be the south of France where people lived lives quite different from home.

That summer my grandfather and his mistress had invited my newly engaged parents to travel with them. My grandfather took his Rolls Royce which he drove very slowly. On reaching his superior hotel, he was alarmed to discover the cost of putting up my parents as well, so he gave them a modest amount of money and the Rolls. They drove around, *fast*, my mother related with triumph, and found a pension in the Alpes Maritimes. My mother, who was reading French at Oxford, asked for two rooms; the patronne had only one, 'mais c'est un grand lit', she said to my mother, and my mother repeated it to me many times in her life. This chaste protestation was something of a misrepresentation; my parents had been living in part-time sin in Oxford for ages. Perhaps it was that my mother foresaw a tussle with the Catholic Church as represented by the owner of the guest house, or that she simply wanted to explain to her child that things were different abroad, morally, sexually and pragmatically.

All the weight of their desire and love and hope I placed on this photograph. I had a vested interest in the evidence it presented, especially as I was apparently about to be conceived. It was decades until I realised that in this cameo of absolute intimacy, where the shade and the heat were captured in black and white, there must have been a third party; someone to hold the camera. Someone to watch. Someone else to encourage her to get in the boat. Right at the end of her life, my mother told me the photograph had been taken at a picnic on one of my grandfather's newly excavated gravel pits in Gloucestershire.

So that was Nice, alluring, deceiving and more than a little unwholesome.

One summer day in 1963, my uncle crossed over the border from Italy to France and roared along the corniche in his white sports car. It was not the sports car in which he was to die one winter's night at Slough, five years later, but the spirit of the car was much the same. And we were four months short of that other, more fateful, car ride, when an assassin's bullet would seem to change the world. It was just a hot, innocent day abroad. My uncle – an uncle only, and more excitingly, by marriage – was Scottish, dark-haired, mercurial and drove too fast. On that morning in 1963, he was thirty-five years old, a novelist, a successful screenplay writer, and we were late.

I had spent a month with him and my aunt and their four children in a villa above Alassio. When I arrived they telegrammed my parents 'Lolita has landed.' This seemed to cause general amusement, although most people called me Libby. In the afternoon they took a siesta. Sometimes when they were rising we children would tumble in. He would be lying under a rumpled sheet with his arms up and his hands behind his head, his dark armpits a startling counterpoint to his wavy head of hair, and she would be half naked, slipping back into a cotton frock, and the light through the shutters would stripe them both with shadow. Now it was time to catch a plane home. We sat in a jam at Ventimiglia while my uncle explained the plot of *Irma la Douce* in some detail. But by the time we reached the airport west of Nice, he was anxiously looking at his watch. There was obviously a further rendezvous, one perhaps which explained the willingness with which he had brought me on this long and tiring journey. I only had a single case and a cheese for my parents, which in the June heat was beginning to deliquesce, its liquor running out of its balsa box, and the slightly smoky, acrid scent filling the car. 'You can do the rest, can't you, Libby,' he said. 'You're quite grown up now – and thing is it's hell parking here, as you can see, and you can go straight through, s-o-o.'

He leaned over and opened the door. The back of his neck was burned pink by the sun.

I hopped out of the car. He roared away. I dragged my heavy case into the departure halls and found the flight desk. The flight was eight hours late. Eight hours; long enough to go back and forward to England three times at least. The airline took my luggage, but I kept my cheese. I went up to the most formal of the two restaurants overlooking the runway, and ordered lunch. I was treated with every seriousness. A middle-aged waiter showed me to the table and I ordered: terrine de lapin, poulet, pommes frites, and salade verte. I had a starched white napkin and I read my book. Then I ordered une tarte de groseilles. Unfortunately when I had finished, only an hour had passed. I tipped ten per cent and went out to sit in the sun.

In front of the airport were some benches set between whitewashed raised beds of controlled exuberance. Rose of Sharon, geraniums, roses, bougainvillea. Shade was provided by tamarind trees, and pink and white oleander bushes marked the incoming and outgoing roads. Cars came and went, especially Citroëns, which I loved because they rose under you like living creatures as they started up. Sparse and weary grass grew from cracked earth and there was the hazy buzz of cicadas. I chose a bench under a palm tree: it was everything that England was not. I put my cheese beside me.

In 1963 twelve-year-old English girls were rarely in control of their day to day lives. On this bench I had half a day to myself. I had fallen into a time hole; nobody knew I was missing and nobody knew where to find me if they did. I could do anything. I had a white cotton piqué shift dress, with navy lines on the collar and armholes. It was totally unsuitable for travelling but I had bought it in Italy and I wanted my mother to see the new sophisticated me when I stepped off the plane. It had four little buttons down the front which were open in the heat and I was wearing a pendant that I had bought my mother, in a sort of enamel of liquid swirling greens like a cat's eye. It was almost the same colour as my own eyes and I had put it on to travel in as it looked so good glowing against my brown skin. My hair was very short – it had been head lice, I think – but the effect was foreign and pleasing. My legs were long and tanned, against my slightly grubby white sandals, another impractical purchase which, strangely, my mother had been induced to make on my behalf, back in England. Perhaps she too yearned to leave the green orderliness of Wimbledon and sensible shoes, for the south. My toenails were pink, and there were small, pale scars on my brown knees where I'd slipped while walking on the rough stone wall that surrounded the vineyard at the villa. I liked the effect very much.

I got out my book; started to read, and then a man invaded my kingdom and sat down on my bench. I gave him a look; there were three other empty benches. But then I realised that only my bench had shade. He nodded back. He had a grey suit on and a white shirt, but it was open at the neck and he didn't have a tie. He did have a briefcase and he put it on his far side. Then he opened a plastic bottle and drank from it. I watched, a bit enviously. I hadn't thought to buy a drink, and it was a long walk back to the terminal, and someone would steal my shade. He saw me and after a moment's hesitation offered me the bottle. I declined. I pretended to read my book, and he gazed into space with his eyes crinkled.

After a bit he asked me in French if I was English. I said yes. Then he asked me if I was waiting to meet someone, and I explained about my aeroplane. He said he was in the wine business and had come to pick up a ticket. He complimented me on my French, but I was used to that and I told him what I told everybody, that my grandmother was fluent in French and Polish because she'd been to school in Switzerland and lived in Paris, and my mother had started speaking it to me when I was a baby. She'd had to leave university to have me and often she would say poems or sing lullabies to me in French. I didn't understand them then, of course, but I think it started me off. Then he told me I looked very hot and was I sure I didn't want a drink. As we knew each other a little by now, I said 'yes, I would' and he smiled. He had a really lovely smile. The water was warm and fizzy – almost salty. I took too much in and some of it fell back in the bottle, then he drank, and I thought he must be drinking the water that had been in my mouth, but he didn't seem to care.

After a bit more, he said my colouring was very unusual with my hair almost red when my head moved into the sunlight; that's how he guessed I was English. I was a bit disappointed because I hoped I looked Italian at the very least. He said English women dressed very badly but were much more beautiful than French women and it was because of the rain and the perpetual fog. I had, he said, very soft skin because of all the moisture in England. I said thank you. He laughed and said I had gone red. He said he expected men told me all the time that I was rather beautiful. I agreed that they did (though it wasn't true). After a lot of silence he moved up the bench a bit. He said how pretty my necklace was and when I said I'd just bought it, he asked me how much it was and could he have a closer look as he had a brother who was in the jewellery business and he thought it might be worth more than I'd paid for it. I reached round the back of my neck to unclasp it but he just reached forward to lift it up from inside my collar. He moved closer and his leg was next to my leg. He fumbled a bit and his face came quite close. I could even smell him; quite a nice smell. He had dark brown – not English brown, but almost black, eyes, and dark stubble and a little sweat made his rough chin shine. He held the green pendant and in the V of his shirt was a vest, even though it was so hot, and curly dark hairs came up to the hollow at the bottom of his throat. He had dark hairs on his hands too, and when he blew softly on the pendant and buffed it with his sleeve, I could feel his breath on my neck and it made me jump. His breath smelled like he had been eating sweets. Then without saying anything about the value of the necklace, he suddenly said as it was so hot why didn't we go to a hotel, and when I said I didn't really have time, he said we could take a taxi. And that too was Nice.

Chapter 1

Lausanne. Fin de Siècle

I have a rendezvous with Death
At some disputed barricade,
When Spring comes back with rustling shade
And apple-blossoms fill the air—
I have a rendezvous with Death
When Spring brings back blue days and fair.

Alan Seeger 1888–1916

Midwinter and the stars are shining on the icy crust of Switzerland and on Lausanne, set like a jewel at the centre of Europe. A thousand lights mark out the shore of Lake Geneva, the boats at anchor and the steep-roofed houses. Rising above the little city the cathedral is a dark silhouette against the night sky. Women in furs and boots and men in vicuña coats hurry to friends and restaurants, to pleasure and excess; to watch the weary old year die and a new year full of opportunities and novelty come in. Icicles hang from the fountain rim and from time to time tiny avalanches of snow slide off the roof tops, and the women squeal and laugh and clutch harder at their companions' arms. There are the town band booming in the Place de la Palud, its members' are slightly impeded by their feathered hats, heavy capes and mufflers, and inside the better restaurants there are trios and quartets playing the year in. The tails of the musicians' black coats hang over the seats of their chairs, their collars are stiff under faces already pink and sweating as they fiddle and blow. The ladies and gentlemen in the new and opulent Hotel de la Paix can be seen through a haze of condensation, greeting each other, eating, bowing, dancing, climbing the broad stairs to the loggia or passing under the illuminated diamond shards of the great chandelier. 'Eleven o'clock and all's well,' shouts the night watchman from the cathedral bell tower.

Just above the town, at Villa de Giez, there are candles burning and a dinner of goose and chestnuts and thick cherry cake dusted with icing sugar, followed by dried fruit and mountain cheeses, and the girls have planned a play and games and have strung lanterns across the salon. Along the wall are portrait silhouettes which each schoolgirl had done the week before in Lausanne. They have not been here long and are still struggling to understand each other's languages and fighting off homesickness.

Clarisse d'Apathy tries not to think of her little dog Bibi and the forests of her home near Kosice in Hungary. Maria and Veta Peterej feel if anything more homesick in winter because the snow reminds them of winter in St Petersburg; Bora Kostiruva thinks more than she would have expected of her three tall brothers in Bohemia; three brothers who in reality teased her all the time and only talked about hunting. Berthe Schoss thinks her teacher, Fraulein Edith von Känel, reminds her a bit of her dead mother, and wishes she were as beautiful as Edith; while Lilly Schaff wishes there were another girl from Czechoslovakia but hopes the tall, pale, Finnish Marguerite might be her friend. Six English girls: Ruth, Winifred, Dolly and the three Noake sisters, talk to each other in English, which is normally forbidden but, after all, it is a party; and the Greek girl, Stefanie, tries to join my grandmother, Joan, and her second best friend Helene Palme, from Austria, who are struggling in French, which is the official language of Villa de Giez.

Mina Baumeister is supposed to be sitting next to Rose at dinner, but Rose is scarily aloof and Mina is wondering if she could change the name cards round. Not much of a New Year to begin it not being spoken to. Kelly Jacobs is new, and her father is a Jew, Mina's mother says, but she too is German and she has some lovely clothes and is probably the same size as Mina. Charlotte Neubeck is German too, but is fat.

Rose Beauregard has a considerable advantage here in *being* French, a fact that the other girls both use and resent but which makes her one of Madame de Giez's favourites (another is, obviously, the Polish girl Krystina). But poor Rose has always been inclined to melancholy and has a calendar above her bed with every day between her arrival in October and her departure in twenty-two months' time, set out. The crossings-out do not seem to have covered many boxes, and the square empty days stretch out forever, it seems to Rose, who longs to be back home in the flatness of northern France or to sit in her dark room overlooking the canal and read one of her many books.

In three years' time they will all leave fluent in French and the ways of the world, or at least the world as understood by Madame de Giez and Lausanne society (in which they are rarely allowed to move freely, so untrusting is Madame de Giez of the gentlemen of the town and so certain is she of her charges' absolute naïveté when it comes to *les seduisants*).

Krystina is my grandmother's best friend, but Krystina has a quinsy, which is a poor way to begin a New Year, and is upstairs in bed. Krystina lives in a castle in Poland or at least, her family *own* one; she actually lives in Paris. Her family are descended from someone who was a prince and a hero in the twelfth century. They have servants – too many to count – who wear blue and silver livery on special occasions. They don't seem to have a country. Faced with a map Krystina is vague about the whereabouts of the castle but finds the river it stands on. Krystina's family, like all well-bred Poles, speak French, but Krystina is teaching my grandmother the forbidden delights of Polish. This knowledge will later alter the course of my grandmother's life.

My grandmother is less homesick than many of the others because she has too many brothers and sisters back in England. Later she will say her childhood was unhappy, but perhaps this thought has not crystallised yet. She is the youngest but one in this large family and at home has to share a room with Blanche who is four years younger, pretty but clingy. Rachel, who is older than Blanche and my grandmother, and has a room to herself at home, is her father's favourite, which is largely not, or in this case not, a blessing. For a while the whole family lived out here but now they are back at home. My grandmother thinks herself lucky to be far away in Switzerland – her older brothers had been at Schorne College which was only in Buckinghamshire. For a minute she does feel a tiny bit homesick thinking of the silly jokes they made about its name. But who would not swap life in an improvident family – my grandmother knows they are improvident because she read it in a letter from her father's cousin which she found when she was exploring her father's desk – with sharing a room with a girl who sometimes lived in a castle?

Madame de Giez has let the girls buy pretty dresses for New Year and they have been fitted in Lausanne, and the bills sent to their papas – those who have papas (Rose does not). My grandmother's is forest green crêpe with a velvet band round the hem the neckline and the waist. Scattered round the skirt are tiny rectangular beads which catch the light. She hopes her father will pay the bill this time. She had never had new clothes before she came to Lausanne; they were always cut-downs from Rachel, who is much bigger than she is. Momentarily guilty as she takes off the little gold cross and chain that was a goodbye present from her eldest sister, Geraldine, she is swiftly diverted by her reflection in the looking glass. She thinks she looks quite fine and she is right; she is sixteen and losing her childhood plumpness, and her wavy hair is dark brown shot through with copper. She has a sweet smile, and men are already noticing her as she is shepherded through the streets of Lausanne.

And then the party begins. There are three local musicians, the doctor – who has nipped upstairs to examine the sick Krystina and pronounced her improving but not well enough to come down – his wife, and some of Madame de Giez's friends from the town who may go on later. Six of the girls are going to change into Swiss costume and sing folksongs.

So, Lausanne, on 31st December 1913.

My family. Always travelling. Always getting away.

In 1913 my grandfather was far away in America, seeking his fortune. The routines of my grandmother's life altered very little after the outbreak of war, but the man who was later to be her husband was to have a very different experience. Conscription was to call him home and then deposit him in France, 300 miles to the north-west of his future wife.

There was always one element of my grandfather's war, which puzzled me. Where did he get his scissors and glue? Did he take it with him in case somebody on the western front needed some sticking done? Or were such commodities still readily available locally in the months after the Somme? A quarter of the male population of Britain fought in the Great War and, like many men of his age and class, my grandfather spent the years from 1916 to 1918 as a subaltern in France. In his case he passed the time in cutting up the copious and sexually charged love letters from his girlfriend, Mollie, and pasting them into a small leather-bound book of poetry called *The Open Road*. It was in many ways an apposite title. Here Mollie, of Ballyhooly, County Cork, seethed and promised and recollected amid the sea ditties and the pastoral sonnets. My grandfather also stuck in extra poems in French by Baudelaire, which added a certain sophisticated piquancy to Mollie's spectacular self-absorption. 'I am a gambolling, dancing wanton elf', announces Mollie. A lock of her dark auburn hair, tied in a disintegrating crimson ribbon, is still tucked into a tiny envelope with a mummified flower. Mollie herself is revealed posing in a newspaper cutting, statuesque and dramatic (but decidedly not elfin) in a toque and long fur-trimmed cape above the caption: 'Miss Clancy is of Irish-Spanish parentage and has all the vivacity, verve and charm one associates with that blend of nationalities.' The photograph has been modified to suit my grandfather's artistic sensibilities, or perhaps the frustrations of service: although the pose is obviously of her standing, *sweeping* even, he has stuck her half lying down, like a fallen mannequin, across two pages.

I do not think Mollie Clancy was a nice girl any more than my grandfather was in a crack frontline regiment. He was a vainglorious raconteur, although often with considerable wit, and if any war heroism was to be gleaned from his service, he would have gleaned it. His silence, I am certain, did not cover undisclosed valour and an MC, as was the case with my other grandfather, or even a capacity for endurance and good fortune like his own brother, Stuart. (Stuart was another storyteller but claimed, plausibly, to be the longest surviving gunner officer on the Ypres Salient, was injured twice and spent his time off in Paris.)

By 1916 the address on Miss Clancy's envelopes to my grandfather indicates his posting at a military vehicle depot near Dijon, which, though less heroic, must have kept him safely away from the more demanding part of the action while he snipped and pasted. Then he engineers an attachment as liaison officer with the French Alpine troops. Skiing is one thing he genuinely enjoys.

Mollie's written style is in a league of its own, though she has read her Yeats and Joyce. 'Bertrand o Bertrand, cher ami' she improvises (one of my grandfather's names was Bertram, but I never heard anyone else call him anything but Eric. Perhaps Eric's Viking stolidity was too uncompromising for a Romantic or – less likely – too German for a patriot?). 'Come to me as you did with the moon and the big silence. I yearn now for the Beautiful Impossible.' Mollie's Ballyhooly war is more anguished, more explosive, than my grandfather's. Perhaps she injected a little excitement to those long military days. 'I shall lie awake thinking of you until I slip into the mists – meet me there', she implores.

'Come to me when the night is dark and the wind howls, the fire roars. I am mournful, Bertrand, and I . . .', and then, invariably, the page is neatly censored with a sharp pair of scissors.

Mollie Clancy, 1915

'It is pleasant to desire as much to . . .' *snip snip.*

'Milton's definition of poetry might serve as one for my inner nature; it is "single, sensuous and passionate" when you nourish my soul with such delights as . . .' *snip.*

Little letterbox excisions pattern Mollie's correspondence. The letters are increasingly impatient with the exigencies of war. 'Hurry, sweet Bertrand, I await you', she demands as if he were held up finding a cuff link.

Her own daily life is full of danger; only the day before she had been almost knocked down by a bus and while hovering half unconscious with shock had been thinking of him and his . . . *snip snip*. Also there is a little matter of a 'safe' address; Mollie is not, it seems, a free woman. Letters must now go c/o Mrs Wilson at Kinsale. The recriminations build up as the pages turn.

By 1918 it is all coming to an end. Eric had a choice: War or Mollie. 'But Darling, you went away into Life, Real, coarse, sordid Life where there are no beautiful shadows only cold decided Actuality, Realism.'

No matter. He has always had speedy powers of recovery. Here, stuck in next to Mollie's letter in which she is 'worshipping' her sorrow, is my grandfather's pencilled draft of a note he is composing to an unknown girl he has spotted on a beach.

'*Mademoiselle*,

Vous ayant trois – no, he crosses *trois* out – too obsessively accurate – *deux ou trois fois a la plage et voulant faire votre connaissance je me permet de vous envoyer ces mots pour demander si vous permettez que je vien vous parlez* – mispelling but never mind – *un peu. Malheuresement je me trouve tout seul.*'

'*Tout seul*' – all alone. Indeed.

French is another skill that will stand him in good stead.

My grandmother had been keeping a little book in the war too. Where Eric had immortalised action with his Irish actress, between other men's poems and a few of his own parodies, Joan had used her friends to record life in her Swiss school in an autograph book.

The girls' parents' money has not been wasted. By summer 1916, life at Lausanne has become familiar, and the girls are becoming more sophisticated. Life outside Switzerland turns stranger by the day.

My grandmother had intended to return to England in the summer, and her papa had said he would visit her one spring, maybe even bringing Blanche with him, but that is not how it has turned out. Anyway, he would probably have spent all his time with Rachel who is at Neuchâtel. Her eldest brother, Rupert, far away in age as well as geography, has joined up.

'*Rien n'est bon que aimer, n'est vrai que souffrir*' (nothing is good but love, nothing true but suffering), Lilly from Czechoslovakia had written in a perfect hand just weeks before Archduke Ferdinand was assassinated in Sarajevo, and the world tumbled into war. At that point the girls knew far less than they wished of love or suffering. They, and their world, were to learn fast.

Some time in June 1916 the girls go on a picnic up in the mountains. There are still some spring flowers, it seems, because they all have their photographs taken; their smiling eyes are screwed up to the Alpine sun, and they are wearing little black straw hats, white blouses and long dark skirts and carrying bunches of wilting blossoms. Each has taken her coloured inks and carefully drawn her national flag next to her tiny photograph. Bora Kostiruva from Bohemia and Lilly have the same flag: the colours of the proud Austro-Hungarian Empire. Russian Maria and Marguerite from Finland both draw their allegiance to the Russian flag. '*Zur freundlichen Erinnerung an deine, Helene*', signs the Austrian girl (who has, regrettably, now become everybody's friend, not just my grandmother's). Her flag matches Bora's and Lilly's.

When they get home from their day out Berthe Schoss draws a picture of Villa de Giez, on the mountainside in Indian ink shining like dark varnish. But things are changing at the villa. Days later, on 1st July, the opening offensive of the Battle of the Somme brings an era to an end and sets still unbroken records. There are around 58,000 British casualties on the first day. A few weeks later Marguerite Schaff is recalled home. Marguerite is something of a realist, '*Oubliera jamais meme si nous ne nous revoyons pas*'. Winifred Milton-Ellis had left long ago – on 12th August 1914, only ten months after her arrival and a week after Britain declared war on Germany. She never really picked up French although she liked to look on the bright side of things: '*To our next meeting in happier (i.e. international) circumstances*', she writes, with the exactitude she will later pride herself upon, shades of the home counties matron she will become. Winifred's stoic qualities will stand her in better stead than French when, in another war, she loses two sons, both naval officers, in the north Atlantic within the same month.

For Rose, life's pain has been translated into poetry. '*O ma France, o ma patrie, o ma terre natale*', begins one of her longer works. Above, in tiny, unhappy writing, she records a German reversal in northern France. She accompanies her own work with quotations from Victor Hugo and has acquired a purple signature stamp. She is now R. Beauregard. Her brother survived Verdun a few months earlier. One of the girls has drawn a caricature of the Kaiser with the words '*le plus grand imbecile du monde*'. She doesn't dare sign it in case the book falls into the hands of Madame de Giez. Still, mostly things go on the same. Maria's parents in Russia think she should stay in Switzerland for the present, Bora is not going back to Bohemia for a while, and nor is Hanna to Serbia. Clarisse d'Apathy's autograph is accompanied by the epithet '*Le Tragédie d'Homme*'. Krystina's brother is dead, but Krystina doesn't quite know how; he was in Poland, and she hasn't heard from the castle for months. Madame has let her have a puppy – an unheard of privilege – and Krystina spends much of her time playing with him in the garden.

A call to Madame de Giez's study has become a summons to be dreaded. In the autumn of 1916 it comes for my grandmother. There is news from home. The Somme has claimed one more victim: her brother Rupert. Later, Rachel tells her that on still mornings back home they could hear the guns booming all the way from France.

One of the girls, leaving for the wider and now trembling world quotes from a poem by Edmond Haraucourt: '*Partir, c'est mourir un peu*'. My grandmother takes this as her motto for the next seventy years.

Ruth is still there; she and Dolly talking English when Madame de Giez is out of earshot and sharing a crush on the Doctor's son. On 20th January 1918 it is Ruth, now back in England, who fills in the last Villa de Giez autograph in the book: a girl in white stands on a globe, her raised arms unfurling a Union Flag above her head. 'Send us Victorious Happy and Glorious', she writes.

Ten months later He does.

Four years later my grandfather is still pursuing difficult women. Here he is in a faded photograph. It is taken at the British Embassy in Paris on

My grandparents' wedding, 11th November 1922

11th November 1922. His hair glistens smoothly and he has a full, wide mouth under a thin moustache. He holds a homburg and is wearing a natty pair of spats. He is a tall man and here he is leaning protectively towards my grandmother as she stands beside him, still a little round and pretty and very young, half hidden under a cloche hat and the droopy sort of fashion that date the photograph as clearly as the ink on the back. My grandfather, also educated in Switzerland, then sent to America to make capital in the brave new world until the old world called him back to fight, pitched up in Paris as a journalist at the end of the war, drifted into copywriting and has been bringing Advertising and the Future to a fragmented continent ever since. But why did my grandparents choose Armistice Day, only four years after the end of hostilities, for their wedding? It was wonderfully, provocatively inauspicious.

In November 1922, thrown together by the war, two of its survivors are smiling as they face a new world together.

Was my grandmother a little mad already? Just waiting for my grandfather and fate to trigger its more full-blown manifestations? Was that half the attraction? Was she too a bit of a Mollie Clancy, wild and available? Or was she, as she seemed later, remote and markedly unavailable behind the pretty, now rather chic exterior? – a chic exterior funded by Eric. Was she a challenge and an opportunity? She was certainly unavailable in one very real sense, as she was head over heels in love at the time she married, only, sadly for her and Eric, with somebody else. Her first choice was a man her father Gerald would not countenance as a husband for his daughter. By comparison, Eric looked a reasonable match. If not love as my grandmother would have preferred, or rank, as her father would have chosen, then why not profit? Eric had access to his father's money.

The substantial attraction of my grandmother to her new husband – and indeed his father – was undoubtedly her blue blood. Though only a rather diluted shade of blue it was blue enough for Eric. In acquiring her he acquired the great-niece of a duke, the great-granddaughter of a couple of earls. Through her paternal grandmother, Lady Fanny Howard, née Cavendish, and her grandfather, Frederick Howard, a pride of other dukes, duchesses, earls, countesses, marquises and marquesses might credibly be claimed as relatives. Fanny gives her 'rank, profession or occupation' as 'Duke's daughter' on her census return. My grandmother's own grandfather was a Member of Parliament, her great-grandfather had been Prime Minister, one uncle was a colonel in a superior regiment, another a general. Her Aunt Louisa married the first Earl of Liverpool. Uncle Alfred won the daughter of Lord Gilbert Kennedy. Aunt Margaret had married the Hon. Frederick Ponsonby, reinforcing an existing blood tie. The family had a preference for marrying each other: cousin matches between Howards, Cavendishes and Leveson-Gowers. They had a murky but alluring distant past; lives that had quite often ended prematurely on Tower Hill, but in the last couple of centuries, everybody had done their bit. The inclination to duty felt by his wife's family appealed to my grandfather; indeed on the family tree in his possession he amended the details of the early death of Major the Hon. Frederick John Howard, his new bride's great-grandfather, from the accurate but prosaic 'killed' at Waterloo to 'fallen'. Anybody could be killed; it took breeding to fall.

Where one or two of the Howards turned out, on closer acquaintance, to be a bit odd, my grandfather's family, the Edmonds, were, in the matter of madness, of the sort that either provoked it in others or were attracted by it rather than exhibiting it themselves. For one reason or another, he and his siblings all married partners who ended up in mental hospitals. For mostly the same reason, they all ended up divorced.

Just before her wedding my grandmother returned to Switzerland to have an abortion. My paternal great-grandfather, Henry, did not want scandal to taint the advantageous match his son had engineered, and she herself knew better than most people the reach of illegitimacy.

The Paris embassy wedding was a quiet one. It was only five months since Eric's sister Beryl had succumbed to TB at the age of twenty-four.

His other sister, Gwynneth, came, passing through on her way to the south of France; Stuart, hid his current mistress, who was also along for the ride, in their hotel room, so that the old man wouldn't cut up about his allowance.

Gerald and Henry also turned up for the wedding. The small talk between the two fathers-in-law may not have been easy. Where Gerald was an idle, self-important, high-churchman, whose one skill was dancing and whose one passion was his own bloodline, Eric's father was energetically in trade, an atheist, a radical, at least in theory, who had written pamphlets promoting workers' rights and free love and had for a while an almost obsessive wish to bring about the destruction of the House of Lords. The House in which Gerald's cousins sat. In matters of free love the widowed Henry had at this point long advanced from theory into practice: although there would always be something about women which puzzled him even as he waxed his moustache in pursuit. Gerald has eight children. Henry has only three left. But despite all of this Eric's father holds the trump card. He is rich. He is *very* rich. Gerald feels poor; he cannot forget a remarkably irritating – a remarkably *impertinent* – letter from his cousin, the eighth duke, a man almost as po-faced as his father, professing himself puzzled by how Gerald cannot manage on the £900 per annum his Grace is providing for him. So much for family loyalty.

Henry receives nothing from anyone; what Henry wants he takes or buys. Born into a large family in a small village in Gloucestershire, he now presides over a small empire of London department stores and a couple of south-coast hotels, Russian colliery stock – not the best investment as it turned out – his wider share portfolios and land in the county of his birth. He has bought himself a gentleman's residence, some fishing rods and plenty of books, both classics and the avant-garde. His intellectual roots are pleasingly displayed on his shelves; along the neat spines one may read of a man who is as at home with the arts as he is exploring the issues of the day. He reads Freud and Yeats and Marx in good bound editions. His taste in gardening is for miniature plants; bonsai trees, tiny dolls' house roses, miniature oriental bridges and fine gravel paths which grow in shallow stone troughs and which are, like the family, easily controlled and always ultimately portable. They are still around, unchanged, a quarter of a century after his tiny secateurs pruned their last stunted branch.

Both fathers rule their families with a potent combination of fear and emotional blackmail and, in Henry's case, with money or the threat of its withdrawal. This Eric and Joan have in common. They defer.

If my grandmother's life was confused, it was about to become more so. Eric himself was in life, as on the battlefield, a cut and paste man; he was a ferocious acquirer of money, businesses, ideas and personalities. Out of fragments, and held together by selective charm, he built new selves. In 1922 he was probably being Scott Fitzgerald, while busy setting up the Paris office of Irwin Wacey, an American advertising agency. My grandfather was admirably suited for slogans and selling. My grandmother, with her fluency in languages, was suited to life in Paris and to advancing his career.

Later in life he was a country gentleman in shabby tweeds, buying farms in eastern Gloucestershire around the village from which his father had first wandered sixty years before and where distant relatives were still bedded in and had been for five hundred years. The years and acres between these two existences were easily elided to create a solid dynasty of gentry. Later still he was Freud, bearded, intense and intellectual or Churchill, standing at an easel, wearing an old hat, in his garden by the Thames. By this time the rural gentleman co-existed with the urban intellectual. Like his father, my grandfather asserted his left-wing credentials. Spain held little temptation – he was, after all, a married man and had done his bit in the Great War – but he had an order at the village shop for *The Daily Worker* and he sent his man in to fetch it, as well as *The Times*, each day. He claimed to be a capitalist communist. By this time he styled himself 'landowner'. Yet in the early days among the poetry and the lush Mollie Clancy outpourings in *The*

Open Road his true feelings for the country life seep through. In a chapter winsomely entitled 'A Little Company of Good Country People' is a pastoral ditty. It is not great poetry:

> *The Milkmaid*
> What a dainty life the milkmaid leads,
> When over the flowery meads,
> She dabbles in the dew
> And sings to her cow,
> And feels not the pain
> Of love or disdain!
> She sleeps in the night, though she toils in the day,
> And merrily passes her time away.

Underneath Eric, for whom the nuts and bolts of agriculture held little romantic appeal, has scrawled:

> What a bloody life the milkmaid leads
> Over the blasted weeds
> She dabbles in the mire
> Cursing like a liar
> She has no leisure
> For love or pleasure
> She sleeps in the night, has no time in the day
> And smells the vile cows 'til she passes away.

The Howard name was a major coup, a major *purchase*, for my grandfather. His new bride had a legitimate coat of arms. She had an incomplete but still impressive set of silver knives and forks engraved with the family crest, and some linen embroidered 'WC' for William Cavendish – one of the many satisfactory William Cavendishes in her family tree. She was a bit vague as to which. Through her my grandfather gained a place in Debrett for himself and his children to come.

My grandmother, 1902

But she was not quite the dynastic prize she seemed. There was no money, of course. Gerald was something of a black sheep. This branch of the Howards lived on annuities from their richer relations. She was certainly well connected; all Lady Fanny's older children had either joined the right regiments or entered politics or married where they should; my grandmother had the noblest cousins any upwardly mobile bridegroom could hope for in a wife; even the future queen, whom she strongly resembled, was some degree of cousin. But then there was Gerald, her father, Lady Fanny's troublesome last son, and, one day forty or so years earlier, Gerald had met Ada.

My great-grandmother Ada came from a bleak and narrow street in a Midlands city; her mother kept a taproom, her father was a butcher, as was his father before him. My grandmother's cousins on her maternal side were innkeepers, labourers, coopers and servants. Ada's sister was a machinist. Ada had become my grandfather's mistress in her teens. At nineteen she was returned home to produce a daughter in a backroom of her parents' house. She called her Geraldine, the feminine variant of her father's name, perhaps expressing Ada's hope for the relationship. Gerald was firm, and the baby was swiftly fostered out with a childless farm labourer and his wife in a Norfolk backwater. This was fairly standard procedure for a child of sin in 1880, 'a black lamb of a black sheep'. Geraldine thrived, unlike many other discarded Victorian babies.

But Gerald couldn't keep away from Ada and another illegitimate daughter, Ethel, followed a year or so later. This finally made them a family and Gerald retrieved his first born and set Ada and the girls up in Brixton. There was nothing wrong, nothing unusual, with a well-born man keeping a mistress in the second half of the nineteenth century.

In 1885, as the year drew to its end, Lady Fanny died, reproachfully, at Compton Place, the Cavendish estate in Eastbourne, and her body was taken back to be buried among her ancestors, in Edensor churchyard, at Chatsworth. While Gerald was to-ing and fro-ing from his mother's deathbed and watching her coffin lowered into the hard earth of a Derbyshire January day, Ada was pregnant again.

Into the vacuum caused by Fanny's death, came God, equally uncompromising and disappointed with Gerald and his meaningless life, telling him exactly what to do. What God wanted, in absolute and surprising opposition to Lady Fanny, was for Gerald to make an honest woman of

William Cavendish, 7th Duke of Devonshire, Gerald's uncle, 1886

Ada. God was backed up, as always, by Gerald's uncle, the 7th Duke. He was, Gerald thought, an insufferable and interfering prig: it came of not re-marrying after his wife had died young. But the Duke had also lost a son, Gerald's cousin, murdered in Dublin by the Fenians, three years before, and he was willing to support Gerald if Gerald married the mother of his children. Finally, in August 1886, Gerald and Ada left their now shared house at 12 Trinity Square, Brixton, and were married at Lambeth Register Office. Gerald's stern parliamentarian father, Frederick, did not attend. Nor did the duke. Nor did Charles the butcher.

Around this time, Gerald and Ada produced their first son, Rupert. Apparently fortunate child of the 1880s, Gerald's heir, Fanny and Frederick's grandson, was born into the British Empire at its pinnacle of power and into a cadet branch of one of the most illustrious families in England. He would live for thirty-one years, dying in northern France in 1916.

When I look at the only picture I have of Ada, long into her respectability, I see a plump middle-aged face with hooded, calculating eyes. On her head she wears a galleon of a hat and attached to it a badge of the coat of arms of the Earl of Carlisle, given to every female descendant of the Howard family at the time of Queen Victoria's diamond jubilee and the first and last real recognition of her marriage by the family.

On the whole the Howards and the Cavendishes coped with Ada by pretending she didn't exist. Even after his marriage, Gerald continued to live the life of an aristocratic bachelor. He spent weekends at Chatsworth, Compton Place, Blenheim and Holker Hall. Although he disliked shooting, he was renowned for his skill on the dance floor and sought after in this respect, and possibly others, in the greatest houses of the land. This also enabled him to petition his better placed relatives for increases in financial assistance. Meanwhile Ada kept having babies. Just once, early on after Gerald had finally married her, she did go to a society dinner. She was a handsome woman, and Gerald splashed out on a fashionable dress and but at the last minute Ada pinned a corsage of roses to her train. It was, murmured those who whispered around her, rather what one might expect from a butcher's daughter.

In Victorian England, Gerald and Ada had created a problem. It echoed down the generations. It was a time of tremendous sensitivity to class and rank, and the stigma of illegitimacy was inerasable, so although all their subsequent children, including the penultimate child who was my grandmother, were legitimate, a shadow lay over the family's reputation. The older children were social outcasts: unable to marry at a level their father would contemplate, unable to support themselves in the professions. Their lesser status was reinforced even in the details. The legitimate children had several names apiece; all had at least one Christian name that was a traditional Howard family name. The others had only one Christian name on their birth certificates. Much more damagingly they had no surname, no legal identity and, until well into the following century, nothing could ever rectify this. There was huge social shame in illegitimacy whatever station you were born into and there was huge disparity in families where some children were illegitimate and others, born after their parents' marriage, had all the freedoms and rights of the law. In this family the name from which Geraldine and Ethel were excluded was also an old and renowned one in a society that revered such things. The family took off to live near Dover. Not too far from but not too close to Compton Place. They lived in a house called Compton Lodge. There was a Compton Lodge on the estate, but this one does not seem to have been it. Refused a grace and favour home, Gerald simply renamed the one he rented to clarify the connection.

For a long time Geraldine and Ethel made up for deficiencies in staff caused by Gerald's lack of money. 'Assisting at home', Gerald writes of their status on the 1901 census return. He himself is styled 'living on means'. Both Geraldine and Ethel had tried to be lady-probationers – trainee nurses – and all had gone well until they were asked to produce their birth certificates, then their places were withdrawn. Ethel eventually consigned herself to God's more forgiving love and entered a convent.

Little Geraldine, the first born, looked to the empire for salvation and went to be a governess, like so many inconvenient Victorian daughters, first to Sevenoaks and then to nicely remote Bulawayo.

Many decades later, when her charges had grown up, and she was returned redundant to a kinder England, she had become an angular, self-mortified old lady, controlled by hairgrips, thick stockings, button shoes, regular habits and a profound sensibility for social etiquette. She surrounded herself with pictures and magazine cuttings of the royal family; a particular favourite was a colour-washed, curly-haired toddler Princess Elizabeth.

Oh fortunate royal family whose lineage was brilliant and unsullied; oh royal family who were so nearly her own family; oh kindly maternal queen and decent, sexually continent king and their two tidy daughters.

Geraldine did a lot of covering up. Her other handicrafts included making muslin jug protectors trimmed with beadwork, initialled bookmarks and tapestry spectacle cases and, combining her practical skills with her religious fervour, making oil-cloth wrappers for her bibles, prayer books and volumes of consolation, all trimmed with raffia blanket stitch. Heaven too was a nicely ordered place – the Old Testament was firm on lineage; woman begat man begat man with a comforting inexorability, and even in the bureaucracy of sanctity angels, archangels, seraphim and cherubim all knew their place. Geraldine too had a little book. She, like her more fortunate finishing-school sister (no finishing school for bastards), and her entrepreneurial brother-in-law, wrote down her thoughts in a book already written by others.

None of them ever claimed an entitlement to a little book of their own. Perhaps clean pages were just too daunting.

Where my grandmother filled her Swiss schoolbook with autographs and photographs and sketches and poems and declarations of undying friendship from girls whose families and countries were dying in a more literal sense, and Eric/Bertrand stuck his mistress's nocturnal fretting on top of the works of minor Georgian poets, Geraldine wrote out her life for more than sixty years in the margins of the same small book of prayers and uplifting religious texts, in tight little sentences of faith and loss and respectability. Round and round and round she went again, a martyr to thrift. Geraldine, fathered in passion on the teenage daughter of a sausage-maker, was always condemned to the edge of the page. The book was called *The Cloud of Witness*. To witness was Geraldine's only role. On the fly-leaf is her new name: Geraldine Howard.

Communion is one of Geraldine's particular concerns. *To the pure all things are pure*, is the first text for the day. She underlines it deeply. 'Anniversary of my Confirmation Day 1905. Put clocks on tonight'.

Death is another abiding interest.

'Mr Rainsford died'.

'The night little Margaret Hudson died aged 4. Nov 14th 1915'.

'Mrs Hunt and I had our last communion together. Her son knelt at her bedside' (texts: *The Destined Unity*).

'Mrs Hunt was buried today, Nov 24th 1945. A & M. Hymns 135 and 27, Psalm 23. A beautiful service'.

She lists all her Easter communions, confirmations of siblings, friends and her charges in Rhodesia. A scattering of world events punctuates the spiritual agenda:

'The Armistice signed 11.11.11.18. went to Shelbourne Church to Thanksgiving Service'.

'End of the general Strike. May 12th 1926' (the theme of the day is *Work*, the text from Carlyle: 'Effect? Influence? Utility? Let a man do his Work; the fruit of it is the care of Another than he').

'Surrender of Germany in Italy, May 2nd 1945'.

Occasionally there is drama: 'Terrible thunderstorm, Mrs Hunt taken to hospital. Maurice Lancaster preached on Railway Mission', but mostly it is God and the king who provide the news:

'This is the day after King George and Q. Mary were crowned Jan 25th 1911, we saw their progress through the city'.

'Princess Mary's Wedding Day, 28.II. 22' (strangely the theme is *Penitence*).

'Saw the King and Queen at Bulawayo', she loops tidily.

'Eclipse of the sun August 7th'. Text: *The Risen Life*.

She carefully records a last meeting in 1907 with her twenty-year-old brother Alfred whose response to the contradictions of Howard family life is also to exile himself to another distant part of the empire. He emigrates and joins the Mounties in Canada. She meets her brother Rupert's wife for the first and last time. He too is vanishing abroad.

Only once does the genteel composure break: when she receives news of him again. 'Sept. 2nd 1916. Our darling Rupert killed, he died a glorious death "a soldier and a gentleman".' She makes a mess of the date. In disarray she writes the news again on the facing page. 'Sept. 2nd. Dear Rupert was killed in France. 11.45 p.m.' She is more sanguine when one of her cousins is killed, 'Dear Cecil killed in action, Aug. 16th 1917'. Theme: *Sympathy*. She keeps a photograph of a uniformed Rupert, a poppy stuck in its frame, by her bed for the rest of her life.

At an age when she should have been having her own children, Geraldine notes the birth of yet another child to her parents in 1904 (theme for the day: *Spirit of Peace*). Her youngest sister is named Blanche. The name Blanche has numerous Howard antecedents. All the most-loved (though also invariably short-lived, which may have affected their posthumous reputation) Howard girls have been called Blanche. This little Blanche will defy family tradition and live into her 90s. Geraldine is still recording when my brother, her great-nephew, is born in 1957. King George VI, she notes, died on the same day, only five years earlier. She is very keen on coincidences. Later the same year her sister Ethel dies. Ethel, the other illegitimate daughter of Gerald and Ada, has found Jesus to be the one accepting bridegroom. She has become a nun. A lay nun, but a *Catholic* one. 'Ethel passed on this day. God bless her soul', reports Geraldine, tersely. It is her last entry.

When Geraldine eventually dies, without having to face what would have been, for her, the considerable challenges of the 1960s, she has been reunited with family. She spends her last years living with my grandmother, eighteen years her junior. It is in its way more of a mother–daughter relationship. They have a thatched cottage in

Buckinghamshire; my grandmother gardens and cooks, and Geraldine sews and cares for their souls.

Geraldine has a wonderful sewing basket. It is filled with treasures: a dozen wooden cotton reels, the coloured ends of the thread neatly tucked away. She has bias binding in pink and black and fawn and white; tiny black and silver hooks and eyes, neatly engaged on cardboard strips; poppers, popped tidily; rickrack; pins arranged in a lilac pin cushion; needles regimented in size along the padded saffron silk lining of the basket. She has a bodkin, a wooden mushroom for darning, and wools in various colours in a range from beige to grey to navy, some of it crinkly where she has unravelled old jumpers, and in every ply. She has velvet ribbon with a luscious pile for hair-bands and pink satin ribbon for underwear. She has elastic: shirring and knicker. Then there is her button box: a heavy, rattling toffee tin, full of cannibalised tortoiseshell, mother of pearl and bone off long-lost garments. In a drawer she has snippets of dresses she has made herself, her sisters, her nieces and great-nieces and pupils, over decades. She can remember and describe every one. She should: she has hemmed and unpicked, altered and repaired and re-cut them all. When she dies I inherit this box. I cannot sew a stitch, of course. I have never had to make do. I am a lily of the field.

The sisters are regarded with some affection in the village. Two harmless Englishwomen and two dachshunds, with strange Polish names, have reached a kind of contentment, and on their shelves are the autograph book from Lausanne and *The Cloud of Witness*. But the century has many journeys and tribulations in store before they are to find this measure of peace.

Chapter 2

London 1950s

I never liked magic. There was a picture of fairy revels hanging on my wall; elves, goblins and woodland creatures grinned as they danced in a ring around a fire, while all around them trees were leering from the darkness. This scared me so much that I had to sleep with my head under my eiderdown and this in turn gave me bad dreams. I couldn't understand other children's fascination with spells and wands; if magic was the process by which things turned into other things or were not quite as they appeared to be, then I came into the world with quite enough magic around me. I never wanted the Marvo the Magician Set with a cardboard roll covered in red foil and feathers hidden in a stick. But I got one just the same. Later I was horrified even by an illusion of women being cut in half or of live creatures being crushed in clenched hands or large silk scarves, before being freed to fly or hop about.

Once I'd come across *The Lion, the Witch and the Wardrobe* I did tunnel into the back of cupboards hoping there was a doorway to another, quite different place but I was always fastidious in my efforts not to wipe, or indeed touch, any brassware in case a genie materialised. This included the neat fire tools at my paternal grandparents' and the knocker on our front door in the shape of a galleon. Even this might be not quite as solid as it seemed. I would look at it closely with my hands behind my back because in tiny, dirty writing underneath it said:

One ship goes east, another west
By the selfsame winds
that blow.
'Tis the set of the sail,
and not the gale
That determines the way they go.

Like the winds of the sea are the
winds of fate
As we voyage through life.
'Tis the set of the soul that decides
the goal
And not the calm or the strife.

I hated the dark, in which I could hear the house breathing and faintly pick out the sinister shape of my dressing gown on the door peg. The flickering nightlight my mother provided only revealed the malign eyes, distorted bark features and beckoning branches of fairyland. Night was generally a problem. If I got out of my high bed it was to drop onto a small mat, which invariably skidded away across the lino, or onto my already full potty. The nightlight was a candle in a saucer of water. By the time I was five I knew what I really wanted was a mouse grotto electric nightlight, where mummy mouse in a gingham dress, cooking, and daddy mouse bent over his workbench, consorted with various infant mice in a strange, but illuminated, porcelain termite hill. When the candle set fire to the books on the mantelpiece, I thought I might get one, but it never happened. Probably it was common.

I was already having trouble with words and turning them over and over – *fairy*, which had wings and *furry*, which was what a moth's body and mice and cats were like, was one pair which confused me. *Bough*, from which babies, incomprehensibly abandoned up trees in cradles, fell, and *bow*, which dogs said in books but not in real life, was another. When my mother wanted to turn the curtains from pale brown to dark blue she used *dye* in a boiling vat on the cooker, but I thought she was making the old colour *die* in the scalding, strange-smelling water. When I went for an interview to go to my first (short-lived) school, the teacher asked me to give her two meanings for 'place', two for 'band' and two for 'tap'. I could do this instantly; it was how words worked.

I could read in bits; I picked off words on food packets and individual letters that I recognised off billboards. Clement Attlee was CAT. I looked at the big sign with Greater London Council on it. 'That says EAT like the troll and the billy goat', I announced. 'Don't be silly,' my mother said, 'it's too big for eat.'

But I could not read harder things and kept words I wanted in my head by making my parents recite them, wearily and resentfully, again and again. When I remember them they are still prefixed with 'oh for heaven's sake'. But my father told me tales from his own childhood, a childhood precarious in the extreme. There was the time he went to stay with his wicked uncle and was sent up a tower in the dark to find a chest of gold, but lightening forking through the sky saved him from falling to his death at a spot where the stairs had crumbled away; and the time he was trapped in a vault between the coffins of long dead pirates and found a secret map, and the time he hid in an apple barrel and overheard a ship's crew planning mutiny. There were various other close shaves involving Red Indians, wrecks and swordfights. I had to accept that all this had happened despite the protection of his parents who had spent almost all their lives in a green suburb of Birmingham, where my grandfather was the Director of Education and a governor of the university.

'*Birmingham*', said my mother, blending contempt with resentment, as if she had been deceived. Yet she loved her father-in-law unequivocally for being everything her own father was not and, above all, for being the *same* thing, day in, day out.

My mother read me poems every night. Mostly the same poems. I was unbending. Three occupied the uneasy landscape of my imagination:

Whenever the moon and stars are set,
Whenever the wind is high,
All night long in the dark and wet,
A man goes riding by.

This produced a magical frisson of terror every time, although my mother added her own drama by letting her voice rise as the horseman galloped towards me. She had once got a place at drama school, but my grandfather had said there was quite enough melodrama in the family without anyone being specially trained for it. So she went to Oxford instead and then she had me.

In the silence after my parents had perplexingly, and despite my best efforts, gone to sleep and ceased their vigilance, I would listen out for horsemen clattering wetly through the London streets. I also liked a poem called *Disobedience*. It was the tale of James James Morrison Morrison Wetherby George Dupree aged three, and his gadabout mother. Even then I thought you could tell she was not quite concentrating on being a mother, naming him the same thing twice. Despite James James's best efforts at controlling her he managed to lose her – for *ever* – when she put on her golden gown and went right down to the end of the town. I made my mother tell me it over and over again, hoping for another ending. It was worrying. But the saddest poem I knew was *The Dormouse and the Doctor*.

There once was a Dormouse who lived in a bed
Of delphiniums (blue) and geraniums (red),
And all the day long he'd a wonderful view
Of geraniums (red) and delphiniums (blue).

A Doctor came hurrying round, and he said:
'Tut-tut, I am sorry to find you in bed.
Just say "Ninety-nine" while I look at your chest . . .
Don't you find that chrysanthemums answer the best?'

The Dormouse looked round at the view and replied
(When he'd said 'Ninety-nine') that he'd tried and he'd tried,
And much the most answering things that he knew
Were geraniums (red) and delphiniums (blue).

The outcome is inevitable. Soon they are digging up the Dormouse's
beloved delphiniums and geraniums and replacing them with a chrysan-
themum bed. But the dejected little Dormouse prevails in the end.

The Dormouse lay there with his paws to his eyes,
And imagined himself such a pleasant surprise:
'I'll pretend the chrysanthemums turn to a bed
Of delphiniums (blue) and geraniums (red)!'

I began by shutting out the picture of the scary wood on my wall, with
my eyes so tight that I could really believe it had gone. But later I would
work at creating a scene in a unknown place just outside my closed eyes
and my pillow, until I was as near as could be convinced of it and then
open my eyes to relish my own surprise and relief at the same old bedroom. Later still, years and decades later, I would lie in unfamiliar beds,
in unwelcome houses and strange places and re-create home in the
darkness. All my life I suffered from homesickness and the Dormouse
was a paean to homesickness and how it might be survived.

I was not just my parents' first child but also the first child of a
generation. My physical characteristics, and later my psychological
ones, were allotted by my mother to different lines of the family. The
desirable ones were Howard: duty and nobility. The rest, in descend-
ing order, were Edmonds: whose features implied determination,

artistic talent and a certain ruthless, but manly strength; Moore: decency and brains; and Curtis: fecundity and cunning. Then there was my great-great-grandmother Emma Drew who had been a famous gypsy. The Queen of the Gypsies it was said. Obviously she had contributed mystical powers to the mix, and the thick dark hair and brown eyes which my mother had inherited. I was a genetic jigsaw. Howards, allegedly, had a delicate touch of neurosis and fine-boned thin feet – as might be expected. I was imaginative but my feet were square and plump: my maternal grandfather's rural tramping feet. I had wavy hair like my mother's family but blue eyes like my father's: the Moores. Howards also had soft double chins – a sign of breeding my mother said – and she claimed to see these emerging contours – or rather lack of them, in my infant jaw. My mother hoped, when my father was out of earshot, that I would not have his mother's jaw or his nose. In fact his family were an attractive lot but my mother liked to claim a greater share of me for her own superior bloodstock. I was widely said to look like *her* mother or, when she was in a bad mood, poor great-aunt Geraldine who had teeth which came out, and thin – though wavy – hair in a little net. Her jaw, Howard or not, was pointed and whiskery. Many years later I found a picture of my grandmother and her sisters, including Geraldine, when they were young Edwardians, in high lacy-necked blouses and huge hats, heavy with flowers and I did indeed look like this desiccated, angular old lady when she was young and had hopes and before Jesus had found her and she had found the Princesses Elizabeth and dear little Margaret Rose.

My mother's curves were already softening into fat. The only bones she had left were her fingers. She struggled into corsets every morning, and she ate chocolate when my father wasn't looking. I loved sharing a bath with her; it was a treat if I was good, the water all milky with soap, and the tiles running with wetness, but when she got out the bath gulped and the waters sank by several inches, leaving scum on the sides and my skinny body exposed to the unheated bathroom.

Geraldine, c.1898

Sometimes at Easter or at Whitsun, when I was a little older, we would go away to a cottage in Dorset. It was set in a cleft of a steep valley which ran down to the sea through wild and empty countryside. The valley came out at a bleak cove called Winspit where the waves battered the limestone slabs with a resonant boom, and the salty breeze was always wet even in summer. But here the name suited the place, unlike the next outcrop which had the somehow uneasy name of Dancing Ledge. At Winspit you simply had to endure the sea's malice (although there was a memorial on the height of the cliff to a young man drowned there); at Dancing Ledge the elements conspired to trick you into making a false step and waltzing straight off the edge.

Still, man had had his day here and triumphed against the landscape. Behind Winspit were galleries and caverns, where generations had excavated stone and where square rough columns were left to hold up the roof. But all over the area were enclaves of furtive, exciting ground, circled by barbed wire. Thick gorse and scrub made the purpose of these imperceptible, but a skull and crossbones surmounted the words **MOD. Danger. Unexploded shells!!** My parents, too, frequently held forth on the care required when encountering shells. My cousin Simon and I were attracted by the skull and crossbones and the strong possibility of pirates or smugglers. *Moonfleet* was our favourite book and Winspit seemed to hold obvious advantages for wreckers. We imagined the shells were like the vast fossilised ammonites which came to the surface in Dorset after cliff falls, or possibly like Japanese clams which you put in water and which opened to reveal pastel paper fronds. We made dens inside the barbed wire where basins and humps of earth were eroded by rabbit warrens. We lay on our backs where the rabbit droppings smelled like hay, where yellow broom or blue scabious was shrouded in fine cobwebs, and we whistled secret signals to each other with blades of grass caught between our thumbs. We dared each other to wee on ants. Not a soul could see us or hear us or find us. There were larks and sometimes hawks riding thermals down the valley. It was obvious the earth had been disturbed and periodically we dug, using old cans as spades but although we turned over thousands of weightless rodent bones and minuscule conical sea shells, there was no pirate treasure and no great fossils exploded or otherwise.

Similar misinformation made our home life in London both exciting and terrifying. Until I was seven or so, by which time the war had been over for thirteen years, I believed every aeroplane which flew over carried bombs for dropping. Nobody ever explained this to me nor understood why I screamed when my cousin and I were taken to an air-display and perched on a car boot to watch the aerobatics. We lived in flats and there was a well-locked communal air-raid shelter in our square. In friends' gardens these seductive, smelly rooms, with the humped roofs and bottled jam or deck chairs, over-wintering tubers or broken bicycles inside, were a part of the landscape. Some had started to evolve into rockeries. But where were the keys to ours? Nobody seemed as concerned as I was. Aeroplanes criss-crossed the sky, at a distance it is true, but you could hear their drone, and yet the shelter doors remained closed. Air-raid sirens were still tested, undulating mournfully across the streets, but apart from me, scarcely daring to look upwards through my fingers, nobody was vigilant. Night and day I was ready to go. I kept my knickers on under my nightie.

And so I grew up, unaware that I nestled in that soft pocket of certainty of the 1950s and 60s, one of the later baby boomers, the children who had it all, somewhere between bombing past (as in 'that was during the bombing' or 'let's go and explore the bomb site') and '*the* Bomb' yet to come which was to make my mother cry.

German bombs had turned London into a city that went downwards as well as upwards and laid bare cross-sections of lives interrupted by war. You could see the different decoration of four or five rooms where a house had been demolished, shortening a terrace. Their imprint was edged with the mortar of old floors and dividing walls, like the marzipan of a Battenberg cake with yellow, dull pink and old green plaster in a rubble heap beside it and with the dark sooty Y of a long-gone chimney rising to the sky. Floral bedroom wallpaper, brown varnish. Sometimes a bath was stranded on black and white tiles on an upper floor, its pipes severed, or a gossamer rag of curtain was still caught in the fragment of a window. Real flowers: buddleia and elder thrived in these ghost houses.

Roofless churches with empty, gothic eyes, punctuated the square mile of the City of London. But craters created by high explosive or in subsequent demolition, or simply in the eruption of new construction, revealed older lives and buildings. Ancient masonry, old pavements, city walls, graves and market places, under street names which had always kept faith with what once went on below; Byward Street, Cheapside, Falcon Street, Ironmonger Lane. Poultry, Cornhill, Sea Coal Lane and Milk and Bread Street. We had been to the Tower of London where the changed course of the river had left the traitors and their gate behind but that was official history, on show. Now incomprehensible and far more thrilling secrets were coming to the surface.

My father was excited by a Roman temple which had been unearthed at Walbrook. His reports of its progress to the light punctuated breakfasts which were usually a slightly tense matter of incorrectly boiled eggs, un-cooled toast, or inadequately chunky marmalade. One morning we got up early; it must have been a weekend as the city was empty of people and cars, or perhaps the cars melted away in all the excitement. After some years the temple was finally on show. It was decades later that I discovered that the Roman god Mithras, venerated there, had been worshipped underground in his first life. Indeed in the spirit of post-war rehousing, his temple was moved some distance from its original uncongenial location. Mithras resurrected and relocated was contained in neat paths, edged with salvia and roses.

When we moved from a flat to a house in the suburbs our neighbour had a German wife. Her hair was always up in plaits and at Christmas they had real candles on the Christmas tree. Neither it, nor the family, nor their house ever burned to ashes despite my mother's annual prophecy. While my mother pegged sheets on the line we could hear Christa calling her entirely English sons lost to her in a small plain English garden, in tones of accelerating panic: 'Teemothy, Jeffrey, komm'; 'Wo bist du Timmy? Lunchie ist here'. My mother and I laughed a bit, nastily, but only quietly. Her husband was thin and seldom smiled but he had 'been in Intelligence' my father said. He still wore glasses. On the other side was an Irish family whose house looked the same as ours but which had seven grown-up children in it. They had beautiful names: Angela, Gabriel, Brigid, Michael, Desmond and Deidre. One was called Bernadette and she was my babysitter and pretty and she had a fiancé called Bernard.

My parents had tried sending me to school – ideals of post-war unity had named it the Universal Kindergarten – and I screamed all the way there while my father tried to drown out my sobs with jolly improvised songs. 'We're going to schoooool, hooray hooraaaaay. It will soon be the . . . Libby, you'll make yourself sick . . . end of the daaaay.' I was so homesick that even six hours away from home was misery. I was thus far an only child, as my mother had assured me I would remain. I was not very good at mixing and I had three characteristics that made me stand out. I had a pronounced lisp which meant that I was plunged straight away into elocution lessons. I already had a fear of blood, since my uncle's dog bit me for trying to ride it like a horse, and was inclined to faint, blood or no blood. Finally, I was an excellent reader, but this was no advantage; it simply singled me out from the rest as trotted out aged four I lisped fluently to the ahs of collected parents. I read my way through one of the readings for the festival of Seven Carols and collapsed. I had nightmares, my speech deteriorated to a point where I was having to attend Great Ormond Street paediatric outpatients. I told them my bad dreams were of men with spears chasing me. My mother would later become a psychotherapist and was already reading up; she sat, red in the face, shaking her head. After a bit they simply gave up. I stayed at home.

One day a man knocks on the door. He has a brown gabardine raincoat with a belt and a brown briefcase. He asks me how old I am. I tell him, including quarters. He asks if I am at school. I am not. He asks to speak to my mother.

Faced with the authorities, my parents find a governess. Why was I not at school? I have no idea. Why did they still not send me? Why do I go to school later? Who knows.

I share the governess with two other small girls. One of the little girls has a second governess whom she shares with Princess Anne. This as good as elevates me to court circles. My governess is very good at nature walks: we draw horse chestnuts and skeleton leaves, we collect frogspawn, grow beans in a jar with blotting paper until the jar fills up with their tentacles, and for science we grow sugar crystals from threads of cotton over another jar. We do tables and get stars, but arithmetic is not her forte. I will never catch up. We do a lot of French and poetry. My reading leaps ahead. I can read anything and I do, from the Bible to the *Reader's Digest* condensed books. My father brings back comic book versions of the great classics in his bag: *Kidnapped, The Last of the Mohicans, Black Beauty*. When I get to *Kidnapped* I find that the hero has almost the same experience with his uncle as my father. He too is tricked by his wicked relative into climbing a ruined tower in the stormy darkness and again only a flash of lightening stops him falling to his death. I am wary in my encounters with my uncles from then on.

I flourish. My father teaches me codes. Every night I have to decode a different message. Sometimes they are just left on my pillow. Mostly they are warnings. These are dangerous times. I am really good at codes.

I like to listen to *Sparky's Magic Piano*, *The Three Trolls* and *Tubby the Tuba*, especially the bullfrog. I hate *The Laughing Policeman* and *How Much Is That Doggy in the Window*? I especially like it when my mother cleans the house singing 'honey in the morning honey in the evening honey at supper time, be my little honey and love me all the time'.

At weekends we go to Gloucestershire. My grandfather has gravel.

They dig out his fields and make white hills of it next to the water which fills the holes in the ground. The oldest pools have become surrounded by trees and the heaps have turned into green hills. On the most beautiful one my grandfather has built a low boathouse to keep his punts in and it has islands you can boat out to with a picnic of 7UP and a ham sandwich. You'd hardly know the lake was not real except that everywhere else in the area is flat and occasionally bits of metal hawser stick out of the slopes. In the pits still being dug, the water is murky and dangerous and we can't go near the edge. But next to the digging the heaps of fine stone hold thousands of tiny fossils. There are ones like sections of clay pipe, only dark brown, there are ones like giants' toenails, horny and deformed, and there are perfect little fan-shaped stone shells. Tiny beetles and stinging ants colonise the heaps and if the gravel is left too long sand martins nest in it and flowers start to grow at the sides. My grandfather bumps down the track in the Rolls Royce to look at the gravel. The car is covered in pale gouts of mud. He pokes the stones with his stick. He says they can write off the heap with the nests. I'm glad he is kind to the birds but later my father says it's because the gravel is ruined. When the birds have gone, we slide up and down the hill in a rattle of stones.

My grandfather has shelves of books. There are books that I dare myself to look at with pictures of the war or car crashes. There are books in leather with swirling oily endpapers, whose page edges are gold and with engravings protected by tissue paper. I like and dread Edgar Allen Poe and I love the smell of the *Rubáiyát of Omar Khayyám* but my favourite is the book of the *Ingoldsby Legends*, illustrated, which in due course I steal.

I can never remember seeing him read one, but a whole wall of his house was books. Later on I understood what people meant when they said he bought his books by the yard and that it was meant to be a criticism. It had been said of his father, too, but even if it was true, those random purchases created a magically unsuitable library for a child.

Me, fishing at the Round House, Lechlade, 1955

My other grandfather, near Birmingham, often reads books. He has fewer of them but they are so precious they are locked up behind glass. He walks to the case, unlocks it, searches for the precise one he wants, picks it out without hesitation and locks the case behind him. Quite a lot are about Greek wars. Some of the books in his cases had belonged to my father and his sister when they were young. I am allowed to look at my favourites – about a schoolgirl called Dimpsey – if I am good.

Now my grandfather is gone, but my father reads every evening. He has a book by his bed with a bookmark, next to the Teasmade, and he gets more books from the library every week. They have some shelves in the sitting room but the only volumes I can remember us owning are Winston Churchill's *History of the English-Speaking Peoples* and a book about the Fuchs expedition to Antarctica. One of my mother's cousins

was part of the expedition and here were the photographs of somewhere so strange that it was hard and frightening to believe it was
earth. Oranges and blues, purples and white – a collection of shapes, of
vast vistas, only given meaning by the tiny lines of men, deep in their
arctic wear, traversing the ice. I was eighteen when a man walked on
the moon, but that landfall seemed a poor thing compared to the fear
and alien places of our own frozen planet.

I don't remember my grandmother ever reading or my mother
ever reading for fun, and Geraldine only read picture books of her
Little Princesses (even after they had become middle-aged women) or
religious tracts. Reading occupied a strange and evolving place in
my life. To start with, the fact I could read so young made me clever
and what my mother called 'a credit'. Reading was power to such an
extent that if I had a thought I wanted to put forward for serious
consideration I would say, 'I read it in a book', so that it could have
the status of fact. Then it became naughty, mostly when I read when
I was supposed to be going to sleep. Then very naughty if I used
a torch or turned on the light when it had been switched off by a
higher authority. Being caught with a torch – going equipped for
reading – was bad by association. At boarding school it became a sign
of anti-social behaviour. I was hit, hard, with a ruler just for not hearing a teacher come into a room where I was deep in *King Solomon's
Mines*. Then there were books as things. Precious books – *Puck of
Pook's Hill* and the *Poetry of John Donne*, which had both been my
father's and the set of 1962 *Children's Britannica* in red cloth with
gilt binding that I got for passing my eleven plus. I still have it, or all
but Volume D. It was a time of confident declaration: '**F. FAMILY**.
With us the father usually works and earns a living, while the mother
looks after the home and brings up the children . . . Men are usually
masters of the family even though women may have great influence
inside it.' And there were the ivory-covered Bible and prayer book
that I got for being a bridesmaid and was never allowed to handle
again and the disintegrating *Journal of Marie Bashkirtseff*, that Helen,

Helen, née Nelly Fox, suffragette, communist, in old age

my great-grandfather's mistress and co-conspirator, had given me. It was the rousing story of a nineteenth-century feminist painter, writer, linguist and fighter against convention and had been the most precious book Helen owned. Marie was dead by twenty-five but she was, Helen said, an example.

Where Helen intended me to read tales of woman triumphant my mother wanted me to read about wholesome adventurers. Her favourite of these was *Swallows and Amazons*; she bought me the whole set of books, and *Hiawatha*. It was all to do with our houses in Gloucestershire being by water. Not that the Thames at a point where it was scarcely more than a stream or newly dug gravel pits were redolent of either the Norfolk Broads Lake Gitchee-Gummee. 'Why don't you go and play at Swallows and Amazons?' my mother would suggest, hopefully, on long, cool summer days gesturing towards the horse flies hovering over the mud. Once she started reciting *Hiawatha* nothing could divert her. The metre drove her on with a fixed look in her eye as she dreamed of being the lissom Indian maid Minnie Ha-Ha. There were only two books she told me not to read and that was much later. One was *Peyton Place* and the other was *Sophie's Choice*. I spent a lot of time poring over *Peyton Place* trying to work out what she wanted to protect me from. When I grew up she admitted that it was the account of an enema that bothered her. When she had been sent to South Africa in the war, purges and enemas were part of the weekly routine. In *Sophie's Choice* it was, of course, the choice itself. Much later I realised that both, in their way, dealt with families gone terribly wrong.

In 1955 polio was in London and panic in homes. My mother kept me in, out of contagion's path. I wasn't allowed to go to see *Aladdin on Ice* at Wembley. I screamed. I couldn't go to the zoo. More screaming. Ponds in London were drained. One hot afternoon I developed a stiff neck. Polio was diagnosed the next day, and I was in bed for a long time. It was probably then that I began to associate being ill and being cared for with reading. Having a book with me at all times came to make me feel safe. There was always a way out.

I get better, but my mother is pregnant. She cries sometimes, not because she is having a baby but because of the wireless. Sitting on a stool in the kitchen with her head on the counter. The walls have cross-sections of giant onions and tomatoes in a trellis. The surface is slightly shiny and slightly rough and the cabinets are cream and glazed and open downwards on little chains which I am scared will give way so that they smash against the wall and send spikes of starry glass into people. A baby is inside her and things in the world a long way away are hanging heavily over them both.

Things are not straightforward at home. We live in a maisonette in Notting Hill. It is right at the top of the building. *The Laughing Cavalier* guards the bottom of the stairs which lead to my parents' bedroom on a separate floor. This is a bower of red wallpaper roses, even on the ceiling. My father has been very ill and in hospital having an operation and he is often in bed. The bed is downstairs when he is ill. We don't have very much money. My grandfather could give us some but he doesn't. My mother and I go for a walk every afternoon. Plane tree leaves have left shadowy imprints on the pavements, and the slides and swings in Holland Park are slimy. When my father is better but still not at work my mother has to rest, and he takes me out to see a St Trinians film. Then we go to Lyons Corner Shop and have cake and then we walk home through London glistening with rain and cars and Christmas lights. He stops at a brazier glowing with coals and buys me a bag of chestnuts which he peels and hands to me, seared crunchy on the outside, sweet and pasty inside and then he buys me a big black furry spider from a stall. It has red eyes and bounces at the end of a long piece of black elastic. 'You mustn't put it near Mummy or it will make the baby come.' I don't want the baby to come. It is moths which really frighten my mother. If a moth comes into the hall, she will stay in a room all day rather than confront it. She is scared of their furry bodies, their powdered, iridescent wings, their fragility and their incessant beat. In Africa, in the war, she had been trapped with big fat moths inside the mosquito nets that shrouded her bed.

My brother is born in winter. He is big and noisy with soft hair and comes home wrapped in a shawl with silver threads. It is beautiful, and I am jealous.

Four years later she is pregnant and crying again. Last time it was the Suez Crisis. This time it is the Bay of Pigs. I have nightmares about these pigs, baying, every night. The night she comes out of hospital with my little sister the temperature of the Cold War becomes glacial. Overnight the Russians erect a wall in Berlin cutting other families in half. Babies are held up over the wire to relatives in the now far off west. Years later, when my own children are grown up, I am on holiday with Khrushchev's great-granddaughter – a fair, handsome young woman; a clever St Paul's girl with political ambitions. I marvel that her great-grandfather could have made my strong, stoic mother so frightened.

Sunny lemontina.

My mother sings me French nursery rhymes and recites poems to me in French. They are a lacy spell of words. Sounds with no meaning. When I am little I sing 'sunny lemontina' which I think is a drink and 'sollapon davinon' which is about curtseying. When I whinge she laughs and says 'Ariane sur les rochers en contant ses injustices'. My mother loves France. On our first family holiday abroad, she slips out of the hotel at dawn with my baby brother and his shouting and climbs onto the ramparts of Dinan. My mother has a white and yellow shirt-waister with a wide cotton skirt, a wide fabric belt, and she is covered all over with its pattern of golden keys. She holds the hand of her wriggling boy and her skin is freckled and she walks in and out of the rays of the rising sun as she laughs along the ramparts and when the light hits her it turns her hair bronze.

Chapter 3

Paris. England

Gentlemen are expected to salute a lady before she bows to them, and, in speaking to her, to remain uncovered until requested to resume their hats. The hat is also raised to any lady passed on a stair of a flat and when a funeral is passed in the streets. Evening dress is essential at the Opera and usual at dinner in the first-class hotels and restaurants. The afternoon (after 3.30) is the proper time for formal calls and for the presentation of letters of intro-duction, which should never be sent by post.

Findlay Muirhead and Marcel Monmarche (eds.), *The Blue Guides: Paris and its Environs* (1921)

My grandparents married into the photographic age and entered pos-terity on a mountainside. Somewhere in Austria, Germany or their beloved Switzerland. Climbing up, skiing down, posing with their guide, always in plus fours, woolly socks, wooden skis, leather bindings and Fair Isle jumpers. Little figures in enormous vistas of snow. The odd fir tree or chalet; they could all be decorations on a large iced cake. But they do look dashing and quite happy. Both my grandparents are tremendous skiers, and mountains remain the one thing they have in common until the accident which will change everything. Skiing has the great advantage that it renders conversation impossible, and exhaustion follows a day on the slopes.

Life abroad suits my grandmother. They live in Paris; the company flat in the rue de Berri is quite a large one; when her father comes to stay he is impressed, although he doesn't approve of republics as a

My grandparents, Switzerland, 1922

matter of principle. When he leaves, Eric slips him some money. As my grandmother enjoys her morning cigarette, she leans from the window taking in the view of green lead roofs, wrought-iron balconies and children with their nurses strolling in a little park. She listens to the pigeons scrabble and coo above her. She has escaped. It is all going to be alright.

Europe is beginning to understand the advertising business as explained to them by my grandfather; he reaps the accounts of Frigidaire, Colston and Ford. One night my grandmother thinks she sees Rose Beauregard across a restaurant, dark and intense under a deep hat, with a much older man beside her, but she isn't sure and besides, what could one say? Allied guns had pounded Rose's town into the mud by 1917. Her mother and brother died of Spanish flu the year after. There is no tall purple brick house by the canal to return to, no gloomy, loved bedroom with its heavy lace curtains and its books. The canal, which was green and mysterious, if slightly smelly in summer, was, for a while, clogged with the stinking bodies of men and horses. Not that my grandmother knows that. She does know that other girls from Villa de Giez had worse luck. Even she lost poor Rupert. But still, she can't think what she would say to Rose, if it was Rose, which it probably wasn't. Rose, always a little distant, a little superior, was never really her friend anyway. And my grandmother is busy. Her husband is an executive and Irwin Wacey expect their executives' wives to entertain. My grandmother takes the wives of American executives shopping. The fashion houses are recovering from the war with speed, the restaurants flourish again, the rich prosper. Fabric which was put away in 1914 is unrolled and cut. My grandmother has pretty dresses and permanent indigestion from the entertaining and she is getting plump. What on earth, she wonders, would she look like if she had a baby?

They decide to go skiing.

But when they get back. Disaster.

The old man – Henry – Eric's father, whose labours have oiled the way for his children's leisure, who has controlled every aspect of their lives, thoughts, hopes, productivity, exacts his price for the years of ease. His health has taken a turn for the worse. Eric is summoned home from the glamorous life as an advertising man in the rue de Berri to take over his father's businesses. Under supervision. Among which is a department store – in Watford.

He distances himself from his new life by writing short stories. They owe quite a lot to Somerset Maugham.

My great-grandfather had tired of the grand house – the stage on which he created his effects – and was living in smart hotels. He had built a large flat on top of the shop to keep an eye on things, now, more specifically, on his son. Soon my grandfather is showing that he has inherited a way with money and has started another little book, itemising every penny and every mercantile hope, fear, battle, victory and defeat:

October 11th 1926. Visited Alexandra Palace Exhibition and saw Barton's show. Not as good as last year. Was pleased at my ability to price an eight guinea garment to a penny and a thirty-shilling Macintosh within sixpence. I am more than ever convinced that we did the right thing in not exhibiting at the Palace. Wireless received on loan from G.E.C. 10 o'clock.

October 12th. Newell discovered holding cash. Suggested he be relieved of his duties and Cuffs notified.

October 15th. Transferred Miss McColl from Flowers to Lace. Put Miss Wilkinson in Millinery and Miss Sams in Juveniles. Transferred Miss Gamlin to Gents' Hose for the day but shall have to pack her up tonight. G.N. said the wireless was no good owing to the buzzing from the station.

October 17th. Fairly busy in spite of the fact that people keep telling us the Alexandra Palace Exhibition was packed. Received letter from Mrs. McColl protesting at transference of her daughter from Flowers to Lace. In reply as to whether this was necessary I stated that Miss McColl originally started in Underclothing; did not get on very well with Miss Judges, so I transferred her to Miss Russell. However Miss Russell feels she can spare her – in fact she is nobody's darling. Incidentally, this apprentice was not engaged by me.

Miss White started in Babylinen as first hand. Living in, salary 22/6 a week.

Miss Robinson started as temporary assistant and is taking first sales in gloves at the rate of 5/– a day.

October 20th. Attended staff dance in the evening. Spoke regarding success of Cricket Season. Congratulated Cannon and his Committee and expressed Mr Denham's regrets at his inability to be present pointing out that there was no part of our organisation in which he took greater interest than the social side. Sent Mr Billee and Doreen in my car to Euston – and so to bed.

It is ten years and a lifetime since Mollie Clancy and the war and Baudelaire.

My grandmother surrenders too and provides him with babies. By 1930 they have three children: a boy, then my mother, then another girl. Soon there are pictures of sun-hatted, plump, dark toddlers in the album. I do not think my grandmother took to motherhood in any instinctive sense. But perhaps I am judging her in the light of what followed. In my mother's case all the care and love came from the two short, square sisters who were brought from the Alps to life in Watford and a river plain in the Cotswolds. Alice and Margaret who came into the household to be cook and nanny. Margaret retained her thick Swiss accent, garnished with west country, for the rest of her life and was, in time, interred with the rest of the family in Gloucestershire soil.

My mother was born at home on a hot September 1st in 1928. My grandfather remarks on the day: 'The weather has been simply perfect. I had a chat with Mr Sanders of Cawdell's yesterday and he told me that Cawdell's Blanket Club is a great success and practically advised us to go in for the same thing.'

My grandparents' first child, 1925

My grandmother told me that she looked out of the window and saw and smelled gillyflowers – wallflowers – growing in the bed below and named her first daughter Gyll. I hope it is true. Even in naming children, there was a certain amount of re-invention and complication in the family. The second daughter, the one who would one day marry the dashing Scottish writer, had rather more to live up to than a cheerful and fragrant garden flower; she was called St Joan as my grandfather claimed to have been much taken by Shaw's play. But, was not little St Joan who would one day burn like her namesake; it was her mother. For now, where my grandmother was Joan, her daughter was the beatified version. Gyll and St Joan, which it was soon declared was pronounced Susie, were what the girls were actually *called*, although on their birth certificates, their first names were Ann and Mary. Later in life that youngest child would also call her favourite doll, Joan, and then as an adult, her dog Joan. All the children were provided with the additional name of Howard to smooth their path into the world.

My grandmother took a while to recover from childbirth. Nerves, the doctor said. A sherry or two of an evening would settle her. She is rarely seen without her Craven A.

I have no pictures of Gyll and Susie and their elder brother, Dick, with both their parents, but then middle-class English children of the 1930s were often in the care of nannies. There are some photographs of my grandmother deep in a swing-chair in the garden with her cluster of children at her feet, one of them invariably picking its nose, some with her on a picnic blanket, but none of her holding them in her arms. Even the garden she sits in looks tired and bare. There are others on English beaches where Ada, the children's grandmother, now seventy, sits in her hat, a vast presence blocking out the beach cabins, while to one side is the grasshopper-like Geraldine on home leave from Africa, and on the other, Margaret the maid grinning through her pebble glasses. Not all of my grandmother, furthest to the left, is included within the picture frame.

My grandmother, Margaret the nanny, Ada (centre),
Geraldine (far right) 1931

Stuart has been evading wives and his father, travelling in France with a troubled but brilliant artist, Bernard Meninsky, and staying with Vanessa Bell and the Leonard Woolfs at Cassis. But he comes back to England and stays for a couple of weeks at the end of the winter. He was always larger than life but is now also, quite simply, large. He looks larger perhaps because he has brought his new woman along. The current attraction is a writer of some acclaim – eventually to become a wife – whose slender, blonde sex appeal owes more than a little to heroin. She calls this indispensable aid to creativity her bazooka. For my grandmother life has settled into predictable and comfortable cycles, where everybody knows what is expected of them, and even if it is not very exciting; even if she sometimes wonders if this is all there is, with the years rolling over before her, calm and already known; even if sometimes she envies Stuart and his Helen closeted in their bedroom for hours or walking in the dark their cigarette tips glowing, or sitting up until two with their Scotch and a dying fire, she thinks it is probably enough to be out of harm's way.

My grandfather takes her to Germany for a holiday, and my grandmother makes half-hearted attempts to track down her school-friends. The Jacobs family have a large town house but so much time has passed since the girls picked flowers together in Lausanne, and anyway what etiquette encompasses your country having been at war with your host's? She knows her neighbours in England think the trip is unpatriotic. They would have been more perturbed if they could have heard her chatting in German or seeing her face as they drive down Unter den Linden in Berlin. Later she thinks this is what happiness is like. The sticky lime leaves, the shining cars, the parasols, although it is only April, and the cafés. In the evening they go, well-wrapped, to the opera and she is surprised by how elegant the women are.

This holiday is an exception. The family usually spent their holidays in Gloucestershire, in their country cottage, with its small tower and acres of wild countryside on the banks of the narrow Thames at Lechlade, the cottage standing at the highest navigable point on the

river. It was somehow appropriate: it was not a place of no return
but a place from which you could go no further. A backs-to-the-wall
sort of a place. It had been built as a smithy and warehouse for the
Thames–Severn canal and converted around 1910. It was to serve
the family well. Generations would use it for clandestine rendezvous,
for loud parties, for quiet, if illicit, indulgences, for recovering from
ill-judged emotional excursions. Here they amused their London
friends, seduced their wives (the tower was strangely aphrodisiac in
this respect; something about the disorienting lack of corners or the
three rooms piled up on top of each other, or the almost vertical stairs
between floors which had their prey trembling and gasping at the wide
view of the river, the water meadows and the distant spire of Lechlade
church from the top floor, where the bed was; or simply at the all-
pervasive cold and damp which inclined visitors to stay under the
covers). At the Round House one escaped scenes. Where a trip abroad
could not be swiftly arranged, a trip to the cottage could be almost as
effective.

Stuart holed up there with Wife 2, his writer, while she was still,
inconveniently, but somehow alluringly, someone else's Wife 1. His
father had threatened to cut off his allowance (again) if he was named
in any divorce petition but for now there was no impediment to love.
She left her small son and bought sufficient bazookas to settle into
rural life with equanimity. They punted up stream. He caught a trout.
He painted her naked in the garden. It was the life. What more could
any man ask for?

England, oh England. Sheltered at first from economic and political
realities, everyone, well, everyone except for Geraldine, of course, back
in Rhodesia, and Alfred, trotting the beat on his horse in British
Columbia, and getting his man, was at home as the 30s sent them on a
new, and as yet invisible, journey. But the happy domestic scene remained
unruffled for a little while yet.

Stuart was playing cricket for Bledlow Gentlemen, in
Buckinghamshire *and* he had kept his allowance. He had married his

writer – who was busily mining his family's more extreme absurdities for her latest novel. The family, who had, as yet, only a vague idea of what it was about were fearfully pleased to be translated into fiction. Henry writes excitedly about it to Gwynneth: now they are in a book they will be more than real. The glamour of heroin addiction was beginning to wear a little thin – especially for Stuart, for whom the phrase 'for better, for worse' was never particularly compelling – but she was breeding bulldogs, and they adopted a dark, curly-haired little girl, Susanna. The bulldogs were more of a success than the child.

Gwynneth was ensconced within the muffled walls of her Chelsea flat with Sidney to bring her tea or sherry as appropriate or to transport their fur coats in and out of storage as the seasons turned.

Little Blanche had done rather well. She had found herself a count. He was an Italian count but still, another countess in the family was always welcome. He was also, it was widely agreed, extremely nice and, because educated in England, extremely *British*. Angelo had seen Blanche, more than twenty years his junior, while she was still a school-girl in Lausanne. He fell in love almost immediately and waited until she would agree to marry him. There was also the slightly knotty prob-lem in that he was already married to someone else but in the years after he first spotted his girl in the snow, an annulment freed the pair to marry in Switzerland. It was the one happy marriage that the family produced.

My great-grandfather Howard's declining years were mellowed by the contemplation of his daughter's title. When Angelo was in the party there was always someone to talk to about the old days, the problems of country estates, of possessions, marriages and connections. My grand-mother's response was a little more equivocal: vague in most matters, she was at pains to explain the all-encompassing range of the Italian nobility, where, to hear her tell it, conventions of descent meant that almost every Roman or Florentine was titled. All quite different from the standards of our own, discriminating peerage.

In the white mission church in Bulawayo Geraldine prayed for black babies and her rather plain white charges in the heat of the African plateau. It was a good thing in the matter of Blanche's fiancé that Geraldine was abroad and had her thoughts elsewhere, as the price of the Noble Angelo was Catholicism.

* * *

It is 1936; my grandparents are holding a party. They have just returned from skiing at Wengen. She had wondered if it was bad form to go ahead with the arrangements, after all, the king had just died, but my grandfather insisted such notions were old-fashioned. Anyway, his sympathies are currently republican. There are worrying developments in Europe, but he knows plenty of Italians and Germans; the former are too excitable and the latter too disciplined for any of it to come to anything. Bluff. Says he. One of the first weapons of business, and what is international politics but big business?

My grandmother is not very interested in politics, or indeed business. Tonight she is soft and happy; a little fragility has only added to her appeal. She has a dress of lace and taffeta; a long black and pink dress with a fishtail, on which scattered sequins pick up the candlelight and the flicker of flames. It is spring but the evening is cool, and they have banked up a good fire. She moves, laughing, flirting, from one group to another.

Then, as she squeezes between a group of guests and the fire, smiling back over her shoulder, suddenly something is wrong. She knows it a second later than the nearest guests. She knows it from their faces. Others look up, others step away, some have their hands to their mouths. Or that is how she sees it replayed for years to come when she tries to put the events in sequence. A tableau of frozen images seared on her mind. Her first thought is embarrassment, she has done something awful. Eric will be cross. Then a noise: a whisper first, then a spattering crackle, and a pain in her leg. The smell, the rustling, the sound like wind, her ears are singing, her heart is crashing, missing beats and all the time someone is screaming. She is moving, she is backing away, her lovely dress, her lovely, lovely dress. Flames are engulfing one side of it. She beats it with one hand, the other keeps hold of her champagne glass. She is a candle, melting. Whatever is Eric doing? Is he mad? Drunk? He is pulling at the curtains, but they won't come down. Another man knocks her to the ground, he rolls her in the stiff old rug – she tries to tell him not to, the rug is valuable – Eric bought it in Paris. He beats her chest and legs with his flat hands, her head bangs against a table, the glass shatters in her hand, cutting her palm. Then Eric is there wrapping her in thick material. People are shouting. Eric is crying. His hands are black. She doesn't understand. She can't breathe. She feels very cold.

She is in hospital for more than a year. Her children are not allowed to see her and she refuses to see most other people. Her skin is tight, hot, sometimes numb, sometimes being torn from her bones. She is demented with itching, her muscles contract, her scars infect. She is feverish, she is in delirium, she is all too conscious, she weeps and weeps with dry tears. The drugs make her sick and confused, and the room smells sweetly of ether and rottenness. Demons taunt her. While the doctors and nurses struggle to save her and local congregations in churches in Watford and Gloucestershire pray for her, she wishes she were dead.

It is, in fact, Ada, her mother, who dies this year, but this passes as a dream. Even Geraldine, chronicler of death, does not record it. Ada had gone quite peculiar, shuffling around in a black shawl; as embarrassingly eye-catching in old age as she once was in youth. For now there is some relief that much about Ada can be forgotten and she can, quite simply, be remembered with affection. Ada Howard, wife and mother, RIP.

Sometimes my grandmother makes herself follow the path through the meadows that leads from Villa de Giez upwards to the mountains. She crushes gentians and violets underfoot. She breathes deeply on the cool air as it gets thinner and thinner and her lungs no longer hurt. Beyond her the peaks are pink above thin clouds.

She thinks she cannot bear any more, but she is treated by the plastic surgeon Archibald McIndoe who will soon find himself honing his techniques on more burned and mutilated patients than he ever dreamed possible. He is a winner; the best you can get. A year and a bit later, she returns home. She moves into her own bedroom. She is thin. Her face is as pretty as ever. One arm is burned, one is untouched. Her other physical scars are mostly hidden under clothes. She takes painkillers by day and barbiturates by night. She never really comes back. Eric too is scarred. His hands and arms bear the marks of his attempts to save his wife.

My grandmother and her children, before her accident, 1935

My mother's eleventh birthday fell in 1939 at the end of a fine summer. There was the table, the jug of squash, the jellies and the cake made by cook with my mother's name in silver balls and a flower that was supposed to be a gillyflower. The grass is cut neatly: croquet for the grown-ups and hoop-la for the girls, all set out on the lawn, the gladi-oli and dahlias fine and bright, her little plot of nasturtiums flickering like flames. On 1st September she puts on her blue dress but nobody comes. Far away, in Scotland, three destroyers are sailing up the Firth of Forth. They are OORP *Blyskawica* (Lightning), *Grom* (Thunder) and *Burza* (Tempest) – ships of the Republic of Poland. They have come from Gdynia, a Baltic port, escaping the German invasion and they will form the nucleus of the Polish Navy in exile. The Polish flag and the flag of St Andrew are raised together for the first time.

While my mother still waits and hopes, her friends' mothers and fathers are, as her own are, listening to the radio; waiting. Two days later they are told that Herr Hitler has given no assurances to Mr Chamberlain that he will withdraw from Poland, and my mother's childhood, like her birthday, is swept away.

O Valiant Hearts they sing that November as they form up and lay their poppies. They sing it with some gusto as it is war again. War which will send the sons of those who went through the first war (those who are not lying tranquil, their knightly virtue proved) back into combat. War which is officially terrible but is, in some ways, to some people, quite exciting. War that will seek out courage and cowardice in strange places.

Stuart's third marriage has just broken up. The writer is currently in an asylum having tried to kill herself. He feels bad about this although it is obviously the bazookas not him; not entirely, anyway. He had tried his damnedest to get her treated. He loved her. It is not all loss, though. The writer will emerge to write her best ever work on the fruits of this breakdown. Stuart just wants a peaceful life. He is seeing a new woman, a nice, uncreative sort. A trip abroad appears to be in order and then – bingo! – war breaks out. It seems meant. He goes off to see about joining up as an officer. He is over forty now but his service in the last war was long and commendable and he is rather surprised to be asked what he has been doing in the interim (only the interviewing captain, too young to have seen just how bloody, how gruelling it was in the trenches, who has – obviously – never had lice or maggots or dysentery, or even worn a filthy, stinking uniform for days on end, says *interval*, not interim, as if it were all just one long play).

Stuart has not been doing a lot, though he has been busy. Oh yes. What with cricket – serious cricket – women, painting – he won the Slade prize and some critics agree he is by now an exceptional painter – the bulldogs, France, lending a hand with the family business and so on. They turn him down but perhaps it is just as well; he has tried harder than anyone realises to forget the Ypres Salient. He has a son aged thirteen. He hopes this war will not drag on like the last one.

Blanche is happy with her two daughters. One day my grandmother tells my mother and sister that a countess is coming to tea, but when she turns up it is only Auntie Blanche without a hat; no jewels or furs or coaches or anything, just her wet-nosed, snuffling peke. Still, Margaret curtsies when she brings in the sandwiches. Blanche's husband, an antiquarian bookseller, is in fragile health and her war will be spent nursing him. He will not live to see the end of it, dying as the Allies push up towards Rome, a week before they liberate it from the Germans. His death leaves Blanche to half a century of widowhood.

Gwynneth and Sidney are not much bothered by the outbreak of war – or indeed anything outside Chelsea, though Sidney's foreign surname will sometimes cause problems with the ignorant. In fact Sidney is Jewish but as he seems to have sprung up exquisitely formed and made up with just the hint of a middle-European accent, no one ever knows if he has family in more unhappy parts of Europe.

Far away, Geraldine prays that war will be over soon. She watches a parade of the South African Rifles, feeling very proud, and the Archdeacon of Bulawayo – she calls him the Arch – gives a stirring sermon and they pray for the king and queen and the princesses.

Geraldine is still recovering from the shock of the abdication. *That woman*. So handsome, the Duke of Windsor; she still feels sorry for Queen Mary.

She is glad that everyone she knows is either too old or too young to go into action this time. She says an extra prayer for her brother Rupert whose photograph fades a little in the African heat.

She is now nearly sixty years old and he is still thirty-one.

Chapter 4

Brittany 1950s and 1960s

Until I was six I had two grandfathers and two grandmothers. The Birmingham ones were like everyone else's grandparents, only nicer. They had high beds, beef olives on Sunday, an Airwick to push up and down in the lavatory, shiny glazed red tiles to slide on and a bomb site at the end of the garden. They never had scenes. My grandfather made trains from logs of wood which my cousin and I could pull along the paths. He had been to Cambridge University, had been a hero in the war, mowed the grass a lot and smoked a pipe.

> *sing something simple*
> > *as time*
> > > *goes by . . .*

My maternal grandfather, Eric, however, lived with his secretary Beryl. By the time I was born they mostly lived in Gloucestershire in the Round House. Later he would build a house on the most beautiful of his gravel pits, which he had landscaped and planted into a fifteen-acre lake. It was called Thornhill after the field it had turned to water. We would go to the Round House at weekends, driving around Hanger Lane where my father got cross, to narrow roads through Slough,

My grandfather, Eric, 1960

Maidenhead, Henley, Wallingford, Wantage. We would stop for breakfast on the way at an old inn at Hurley. My mother said this was a place
where people came to get out of London for dirty weekends. A couple
who sat, perfectly clean, and talking quietly in the corner of the dining

room, seemed to take her attention. 'See', she said. Once, at Hurley, my mother said I was old enough for just a touch of lipstick, so she reached over and applied it out of a gold case, and put a dab of scent behind my ears, and I came out of the ladies excited by the transformation not just of my lips but of the world. Her lipsticks were worn flat across the top whereas mine, when I got my own, were worn into a point.

On the way back to London, I'd be given a car sickness pill, semi-submerged in a spoonful of bitter raspberry jam. It blighted my appreciation of jam for life. We would play I Spy until my mother's irritation at my cheating and the sedative effect of the drug left me drifting in and out of sleep on the back seat. Snatches of my parents' conversation and *Sing Something Simple* or *Your Hundred Best Tunes* playing soothingly on the radio were broken only by my father occasionally cursing at another motorist. Sometimes coming out of sleep I would hear a man talking of Leopoldville and Elisabethville and nuns and massacres. I woke up, because it was funny to hear my name as a place. If my parents saw that I was conscious at this point, they would turn the radio off.

The Round House was wonderful and it was scary. It had a tower and a cottage which stood so close to the Thames that you could fish out of the downstairs window or jump in. If you were a man, it was supposedly possible to pee out of the upstairs window and hit a duck. Lots of people had done it. Everyone else went in the basin because the lavatory was so far away downstairs in the coldest part of the unheated house. On the way you had to go under a huge head of a pike with an open mouth and teeth mounted on the wall. Two Jewish friends of my grandfather now rented the tower. All their family had died in the war, my mother said. By day the cottage was the most peaceful place in the world, by night it was soothingly mournful. It was never quiet in the darkness: if it rained, the drops pattered on the water and the tall trees always roared in the breezes coming off the river. Poplar trees had been planted to mark the births of my grandfather and his brother and two sisters, and they had been planted for my mother and her siblings and

The Round House, Lechlade, 1960

now they were planting a new generation of saplings. Mine was the oldest and my name was on a belt round the trunk, and as it started to grow, my grandfather's generation of trees crashed to the ground in a series of summer storms.

In early evening my grandfather or my uncle or my father or their friends, or much later, my brother, would wander off to fish in a haze of midges and cow parsley. When they left the house it was always a ripe summer's day, and various children would tag along until they got bored, but by the time the anglers returned they were reduced to unidentifiable silhouettes coming alone along the river bank under a darkening sky. In the evening flights of duck and geese honked as they returned to roost in fields by the water. Somebody told me their cry was the baying of the Gabriel hounds, foretelling misfortune hovering over the occupants of the house below. I never considered the misfortune might be allotted to me so they simply seemed harbingers of a dangerous parallel existence from which I, under my blankets, was protected.

The Round House was a damp, green world where water was more evident than earth. Even the sounds were wet: dripping, splashing, ducks skimming to a landing, oars cutting into the Thames, rain falling in tiny circles on the water's surface. The house stood at the confluence of three waterways. The derelict Thames–Severn canal crossed the garden and another river – quite different from the muddy eddies of the Thames – joined it here. The Coln was the loveli-est river in the world. It was shallow and the gravel on the bottom reflected the sunlight. Long strands of soft weed trailed in the current like mermaid hair. Willows hung over it and every so often tore away with a cracking noise and fell into the stream, making a leafy perch for moorhen and duck. Every year angry swans nested on a steep bend and water rats plopped in and out at the river margin and occasionally there were kingfishers. Under the old wooden bridge the water was deeper and swirled around the stone stanchions. Here lived the wili-est of trout, long and thick – a dark shadow of alert inertia. On the shallower bends, a flickering shoal of tiny fish would scatter if a leaf fluttered down to the water. Here cows turned the sides to mud where they came down to drink and on July days, rust-brown flies hovered and had a nasty bite, but we could swim here too. The gravel was firm and not slimy under foot. We would strip off and step unsteadily down the bank. However hot the day, the water was always shockingly cold.

We had always swum without anything on in the Coln – it was only us, and it was often impromptu – but my grandfather's gravel pits were another matter. Nude swimming was one of the ideas he had got off his father. He would no more have swum, naked or clothed, himself, but he had made my mother and now he made me. I was the embodiment of his anti-bourgeois principles. He could come it with the car and his chauffeur, with his shooting parties and his fishing cronies, and I could go naked to show his heart was in the right place. This meant I had to swim bare when everyone else – all the friends, the old reactionaries who came to visit – swam in their costumes. By the time I was eleven I noticed this included boys. Normally, like everyone else, there was only one place I would enter the water: where the sandy side sloped very gradually, and frequent use kept the bottom free of weed and there was a small island not far from land to swim to. Now I was forced to get in anywhere as long as it was away from the others. Down steep stony banks where red ants stung my bottom; into shady coves, the water thick with rotting leaves, where I had to leap in to avoid putting a foot on the slimy bottom; too near the sunken boat and mass of dead willow trees in the middle, where everybody knew it was possible to be bitten by a pike or entangled in underwater horrors and drown. Then I had to stay in until I was purple-grey and wrinkled as a corpse and only when everyone else had had their fill of swimming could I emerge muddy and unnoticed.

There were other more basic communication problems with my grandfather. I had, finally, been sent to a proper school. I was still the best silent reader in the class, but my speech was becoming worse. This school was very keen on clarity and order. They had different speech therapy sessions for stammerers, for 'r' girls, who said wobin and weally and pwobably, but came out trilling 'brrr brr brrr brr' like a telephone, and for 's' girls, who hissed like asps in the session but still went around saying thorry. Twice a week I was pulled out of regular classes for every category but stammering. It was my mother who stammered especially on m's, which was unfortunate as marrying had turned her into Mrs Moore. I would ring up for her: 'Please may I make an appointment for Mrs Moore on Monday', and she successfully taught me to say 'the grey green greasy Limpopo river'. My problem, as well as s's and r's was speed. I talked three times as fast as anyone else and half as intelligibly. I had so much to say but conversations were always a disappointment; however exciting my news, it was greeted with 'just say it again, s-l-o-w-l-y'. I could say it again five times, and my grandfather would simply comment, irritably, 'can't understand a word the girl says'. He would say it to the dog if no one else was listening.

Some days we would go on patrol, hunting down trespassers, armed with a shooting stick. Sharman, the chauffeur, who had been a sergeant in the war and was tough, would drive and we would bump across fields to comfortably concealed glades or riverbanks. Once we came across a couple rolling about on a rug. The Rolls purred so low, and they were so engrossed that they didn't notice until we were practically upon them. You could see the woman's pink suspenders. Their car was parked nearby and they had a small picnic. The number plate proved an inspiration for my grandfather; the three letters spelled WHY.

'Why?' said my grandfather, pointing oratorically at the car. 'Why, indeed?', sorrowfully. '*Why* are you are on my land, and *why* should I tolerate it and *what* do I propose to do about it?' By this time the couple were throwing their picnic, rug and some of her clothes into the car. Clearly they thought they had fallen into the hands of a madman.

When my grandfather wasn't in Gloucestershire, he still had his father's flat over the Watford department store. To get there you had to go up to the top floor in a lift like a cage, through school uniforms, past the staff canteen, out on to the leads of a flat roof, and into a door on the far side. If there had been a fire he would have been sizzled or had to jump out, probably to his death, over the illuminated lettering of his shop frontage.

Inside, the flat was larger than seemed possible from the space it occupied on the roof. A long, dark corridor with a vaulted ceiling stretched away. It was papered all over, even the ceiling, with maps and then layers of varnish so that seas and continents could only just be seen under the surface. When a door was opened at the far end it glistened brown like a sea cave.

Beryl, my grandfather's secretary, went everywhere with him. My mother said she was 'petite' in a tone which suggested some sort of inadequacy. Beryl was the same age as my mother, was very small, very pretty and very neat. She was kind and she had an inlaid cigarette box,

which opened to reveal moulded cedar wood tiers which held her cigarettes, and she had a jewellery box which played a tune while a tiny
ballerina pirouetted slowly and unevenly while her reflection copied
every jerk in the mirror behind. I knew exactly what my mother would
think of this. Beryl had a red silk dressing gown with a great dragon
crouching on the back and a swansdown powder puff, which was contained in a crystal bowl. She had a green Morris Minor estate car with
indicators which popped out of the side like small wings, a spaniel
called Skipper and a bad-tempered Jack Russell called Penny, but
what she mostly did was sew. She made me a garden of dresses: a
white sundress with large yellow poppies, a red gingham summer
dress with a white collar and shiny buttons, a party dress from a
bolt of Nottingham lace with a lilac velvet sash. My mother despised
women who sewed or knitted. I explored wishing Beryl was my
mother to see how guilty I felt. Sometimes when she was bathing me
I'd call her 'granny' as a tease. The results were always gratifying: 'No,
you absolutely mustn't call me granny', she said. 'I'm not joking,
Libby, that would be a very *bad* thing if you did that.' Years later my
grandfather married her, perhaps when he realised that my grandmother really wasn't coming back, but I never did call Beryl granny
for real. She died a grim death when she was forty-two and left me two
beaded cocktail dresses and a Norwegian cardigan with silver buttons,
and a Meninsky painting of a woman with a bowed head, facing away
from the viewer. I loved the cocktail dresses although by the time I
could get anyone interested in offering me cocktails I had grown out
of them.

I did know she was called a mistress, although I was vague about the
implications, and that I shouldn't talk about mistresses in my school
friends' houses.

Helen was a more traditionally granny-looking figure; slightly
hag-like with a grey bob and glasses, she lived first of all in a cottage
next to my grandfather's house and then in Valence-en-Brie near
Paris. She too had been a mistress, both to my great-grandfather

My grandfather finally marries Beryl, c.1960

Henry and his son, my great-uncle Stuart, although she had eventually got married and was retired now and lived in a house with iron gates and a courtyard and lime trees and books and old theatre posters everywhere. She had started her association with the family when she became Henry's housekeeper when his wife died leaving him with the four small children. Just as there was something lazy in the repeated pattern of father and son sharing women, there was an equally pragmatic spirit in the way my male forebears converted their employees into lovers and, on occasions, vice versa. Stuart's father had once told him to seduce an extremely competent accounts' clerk who was on the point of leaving the business. Stuart was an obliging man and anyway he always did what his father said, and so the clerk stayed for a working and adoring lifetime. Decades later they were complaining about having to give her a pension, but this time there was no easy way out.

Helen was as argumentative and untidy as Beryl was biddable and ostensibly respectable. Both were loving and energetic and fun. Neither had had children. Helen told me about cooking, the communists who came round for meetings, her dead husband who had been a principal actor with the Comédie Française; she had a photograph of him playing Dorante in *Le Bourgeois Gentilhomme* and Valere in *The Miser*. She had been a suffragette and a lesbian, as well as Henry's mistress, my mother said with a degree of respect. I never asked her what that meant.

Many years later I learned one of Dorante's monologues for A Level. It was called *The Shopkeeper Turned Gentleman*.

My real granny, Joan, my flesh and blood granny, just couldn't compete. She had no substance compared to Beryl and Helen, although we saw her a lot and she telephoned a lot more, usually in the middle of meals when my father would sigh and my mother would make faces while she nodded down the receiver. Though quiet, she was always somehow a nuisance. When I was younger she lived with her sister Geraldine, at the seaside. She had a clear, rather high voice and two interesting dogs. Geraldine made covers for milk so that flies couldn't go in, and green and red beads weighted the edges down. I can only see Joan in bits: in her greenhouse which smelled of tomatoes and dark earth, in her garden which had pebble paths, chalky snail shells and big blooms so heavy the plants had tumbled to grow on the ground, or peeling peas next to me on a step. One of the three things she told me was that fresh peas were better than tinned or frozen ones. Another was that it was a relief when you stopped being interested in sex, and the third was that when my mother was born she'd called her Gyll because of the gillyflowers.

Several people said I was a lot like my grandmother. My mother said that this meant I was like how she was a long time ago when she had been pretty. Now she had flat grey wavy hair, fine broken veins in her soft cheeks, some puckered skin on her arm, and pale eyes which watered all the time. She wore shapeless clothes: old corduroy trousers in the garden and a navy blue dress for best and she always clutched a crumpled white handkerchief to mop her eyes as she had shingles. Her bath had crouched legs, like animal feet, and a horrible dark, crooked space underneath, from which I always expected a tentacle to shoot out and curl round my ankle or that there might be something dead and decaying in there. I would avert my eyes as I spanned the widest possible distance from the cork mat to the water. Helen had a picture of a man called Marat in his bath; strangely he was wearing a sheet and a turban, but he had also been stabbed and was white with blood loss. The stabber was just a girl, she said, nodding her head in approval. Afterwards she was sent to the guillotine. But after seeing Marat I had started to have problems with the best of baths and this one, deep in the Buckinghamshire countryside, was all too redolent of the washing arrangements in revolutionary Paris. At night I would listen to the two old ladies snoring and tiptoe down to try and make long-distance calls home and cry.

My other real granny, my father's mother, the one who had her hair done every week, wore a hairnet at night, had played violin for her school in Harrogate, hockey for her county, and bridge for her golf-club, accompanied us on our first family holidays abroad. She removed the key from the cabinet of my late grandfather's books, put the hose in the shed (a post-war housing estate crawling over the former bomb site towards her house threatened her sense of inviolability) and cancelled the milk. Newly widowed and dressed in neat navy or lilac figured shirt-waisters with matching belt and white gloves, she was the spirit of Englishness against whom abroad could be measured. She was armoured against the continent and its seductions.

* * *

When it was that my mother's family hit on travel as the answer to any problem or inconvenience, it is hard to ascertain. Perhaps it really was the adventuring Howard blood of centuries. *Bad blood*, my father liked to maintain, mostly with a certain pride, as if his own Cumbrian platelets and plasma, of livestock auctioneering, of school-masters and clerics, had finally managed to invigorate and cleanse my mother's unfortunate heritage and produce robust stock who would neither paint nor write nor loll nor lie nor be taken in adultery. The words 'unearned income' would have been seen as a puzzle, not an opportunity, for my father's family; the earned element might even have been more valuable than the income to them. Not so the cadet branch of the Howards who could scrounge as well as they could dance. 'The whole family: in-bred', my father would mutter with blended contempt and admiration. 'Weak chins', he would add. This ignored the fact of course that on my mother's side it was not in-breeding that was the problem but out-breeding – the strange and difficult heritage of children born to the house of Howard and the house of Curtis, Lincoln. In reality the last significant excursion made by any Howard before Gerald, the remittance man, was his own grandfather, the Honourable Frederick, who had made a one-way journey to Waterloo in 1815.

By the time my great-grandfather Gerald was proudly bearing the family name, he and Ada were travelling to avoid creditors, to live cheaply, and in obligation to Gerald's wider family. Promises had been extracted from him by those who had paid him an annuity, that he and his large and embarrassing family would take themselves off. They took themselves off to Brixton and then to a house near the Cavendish large Eastbourne estates. After a bit he was persuaded by the duke to take himself off further and he moved to Switzerland. After a bit longer he came back.

Eric – yet to meet Mollie Clancy or my grandmother – had also been coerced overseas early in life. After his cosmopolitan Swiss education *his* father gave him £100 and told him to go to America. America, Eric's father believed, was not fossilised by class. America and Eric were made for each other, and there he might well have stayed had not war intervened.

Not so my father's family for whom duty – battle or missionary work – had long been the only reason to contemplate the considerable sacrifice of leaving one's country or even, for centuries, their town. My Birmingham grandfather had been the one exception. Most years this grandfather went on a walking tour with a man friend, my grandmother being disinclined to adventure and unwilling to leave the children. He tramped through the Alps and along the fjords – places whose aesthetic effects were achieved by the hand of God not the hand of man; places that were never sensual but, rather, rigorous in their demands. He was a man of the north. An Apollonian.

Still, in matters of travel, and despite my father's happy memories of a decade of identical childhood holidays in a Criccieth boarding house, ended suddenly by war in 1939 – my mother's instincts prevailed. In 1957 we went south, to France, in a Sunbeam Rapier.

My father, as was often pointed out to him, had the misfortune of not having descended from a line of adventurers. His father's stout boots and medalled Alpenstock might stand in the deep recesses of the hall cupboard but they brought no whiff of abroad with them. My grandfather's trips took place in a discrete parallel existence that had no intersecting point with home.

My father's only experience of foreign travel was as a paratrooper subaltern over Norway, and even then they didn't jump out but returned home to East Anglia, and in Palestine, where both sides wanted to kill him, and in the south of France before his marriage, with my mother and her father and his mistress and the Rolls Royce which was, in its way, like taking England with you. Nor could he speak French. My mother had – she said – very good conversational French but wouldn't converse. Unlike my mother who blossomed, silently but comprehendingly when abroad, my father, who was later to become a passionate traveller, floundered at first, trying to find a new role that did not involve being armed. Nevertheless he sensibly assumed a degree of hostility on the part of foreigners. He took a pillow – he had experienced the French tendency to bolster in his post-war excursion with my mother. He also took butter on the long journey through the dairy farms and lush landscape of Normandy. He was vindicated at our hotel when we had croissants, a very odd way of starting the day we all agreed, with only apricot jam to eat with them. My grandmother was content to have prejudices confirmed by the French expectation that children would eat chocolate in their bread at breakfast and drink hot chocolate in excessively large cups. 'No wonder', she reflected firmly. There was no need to enquire further into the French character, conduct in the war, personal hygiene or religious practice.

As we journeyed my other grandmother was being taken into hospital again.

France was still a wounded country. A strange and wonderful land. My paternal grandmother was surprised that French marigolds, so dominant in her own planting schemes, were not more evident in their home country. The rest of us were surprised at everything. Fertile apple orchards and sweeps of farmland with black and white cows were deceptively like home, but there it ended. Political graffiti, priests in hats, children in blue school pinafores, fishermen in striped jumpers on the quays of Concarneau or Quimper, mending nets which used glass balls as floats, two generations of women in black; France in the 1950s was a foreign place. My father stood with tears in his eyes and surveyed the massive concrete defences and rusting iron stanchions along the northern beaches. The beaches had glittering names: Juno, Gold and Sword. Clean-cut new buildings rose among the ruins and the medieval survivals of the town of Caen.

War's hand had apparently not reached western Brittany where young nuns in coifs and cornets of white linen paddled in the shallow waters of long fine sand beaches. Tiny silver pink shells lay at the water line. My grandmother was openly dismissive but secretly, we could tell, envious, of French grandmères in the Sunday lace caps and white pinafores of their regional dress and in total charge of the family. It was not just breakfast which was odd. There was unfamiliar plumbing. Strange eating habits: at lunch, vegetables followed meat, cheese preceded pudding. Soft cheese, wrapped in slimy wet paper, was eaten with sugar. Children – though not us – drank a little wine in their water. They did not drink milk. A large motorised caravan toured the beaches offering free – free! – milkshakes to induce the children of France to drink up and grow strong bones for their country. 'So they can fight bloody wars in Algeria', said my father when my grandmother was out of earshot. I expanded my vocabulary: *fraise, banane, ananas, vanille, framboise.* I drank milkshakes from morning to night. I was an example to French children everywhere.

At home my maternal grandmother sat out the days at St Andrew's hospital, Northampton. She had contracted shingles. With her old burn scars and the irritation from the illness, she was being driven mad. It was not the first time. She dabbed her tender eye. Sometimes she rubbed her skin so hard it wept with her. The fine house looked out over beautiful parkland. I imagine my grandfather was paying the bill. The doctors and nurses were kind – they had been kind 125 years earlier when the hospital had been called the Northampton Asylum, and warders cared for the poet John Clare. They were, decades later, to be kind to me. He loved the countryside as my grandmother loved her garden. They both found themselves confined. But there were new drugs now, and new treatments, even since her last admission.

Alone and ill again, losing her looks as she moved towards sixty, it was perhaps inevitable that she made a suicide attempt. Again it was not the first time. She was discovered. They put her on new drugs, they started ECT. This too was not the first time. It was no longer the brutal, scarcely more than experimental, experience she had endured a decade before, but the memory of it was more terrifying than any comfort brought by talk of recent refinements. The electric shocks which sent convulsions through her body shattered her memory. She was still unhappy but now she couldn't always exactly remember why. With her defences down some unwanted memories slipped back in. The fire. A ship. U-Boats and, finally, a man. Wotzek. The sadness that had been kept outside her was now inside, and outside was just a mesh of tingling, itching nerve ends.

France was something of a success. Every evening my other granny sat up and did her tapestry (chrysanthemums) by lamplight just as she did back home. My mother got her freckles, and in the evenings my parents drank a lot and stayed up late in cafés arguing about de Gaulle. My father had found his voice. My little brother was adored by the nuns and the grandmères. The things which frightened me at home were miles away.

When my mother returned to England it was to a meeting with my grandmother's psychiatrist. They were considering a pre-frontal leucotomy. It was not the depression she had endured for so long, or not only that, but the shingles that made such an intervention a possibility. For once the doctors agreed with my grandmother that her life was not worth living. They proposed to sever the connection between the cortex and the frontal lobes of her brain. On this occasion they held back, but the idea was on her file.

My mother was fighting the flab. It was a heroic battle. Her first effort had been at school when she'd swallowed capsules of tape worm eggs in the hope that the worm would hatch and devour her from inside out. Now there were diets and gadgets: glutinous frothy drinks, rolls with the texture of wasps nests. She lay on benches in beauty salons, with electrodes strapped to her thighs and stomach; she had colonic enemas. Sometimes they saved up, and she went off to a Health Farm. My father would do before and after photos. For a while she had a set of pink plastic bloomers and matching long-sleeved top. The plastic was thin and soft, almost like human skin, and smelled of talcum powder. It was gathered at the waist, wrists and ankles. She would get into this at night and then, the idea was, sweat away the pounds. She lay on towels in case the pounds leaked into the mattress. From time to time she laid claim, rather vaguely, to a metabolic disorder, but it was not one that seemed to be susceptible to treatment although around this time one of her doctors prescribed her amphetamines. All her life my friends remarked on her incredible energy. But she was never moody or emotional. Any sign of family instability appeared to have passed her by. Only the eating remained.

For her thirty-fifth birthday my father came back with a mysterious box, from Fortnum and Mason, tied with ribbon. We'd all seen the box as it was whisked upstairs but that morning it was laid on the bed in front of her. She untied the ribbon, opened the box, peeled away the layers of tissue paper and there in voluptuous folds of black and peach, trimmed with lace, was a negligee. It was beautiful. My mother was silent. Two days later she exchanged it for a pair of very good walking shoes.

Chapter 5

War. 1940s

Hamlet: *Goes it against the main of Poland, sir,*
Or for some frontier?

Captain: *Truly to speak, and with no addition,*
We go to gain a little patch of ground
That hath in it no profit but the name.

(*Hamlet*, Act IV)

Britain battles with the weather rather than the Germans in the winter months of 1939/1940. Blizzards immobilise the whole country. The temperature continues to fall after Christmas and record figures of more than twenty degrees below freezing are recorded in the last week of January. An ice storm shrouds the west; the Mersey, Humber and Severn freeze over, and the Grand Union Canal is solid all the way from Birmingham to London. The sea freezes at Bognor, the harbour mouths of Southampton and Folkestone are impassable and the Thames turns to ice for eight miles between Teddington and Sunbury.

At the Round House the whole world is white and still. Frost glazes the inside of the windows and, outside, the Thames, almost at its source, is motionless under the crystallised branches of overhanging willows. The burden of ice causes telegraph wires to snap and birds, unable to fly, die in the hedgerows. Beyond the river snow-covered pasture fades into a misty horizon and when the sun sets the fields, river and sky are lit with a fire that is without heat.

Serious floods follow when the snow eventually thaws, and in April another record is set, this time for rainfall. Only in May and June does warm sunny weather return the country to what would in other years be normality. East, the chauffeur, drives my grandmother and the girls to Harrods to buy new summer hats.

During that wet April Denmark falls to the Germans and Belgium and Holland surrender in May. In June the Italians declare war on Britain, and Allied troops are eventually evacuated from Norway, while King Haakon VII leaves for London to form a government in exile. At 7.00 am on 14th June the victorious Germans enter Paris and raise a swastika on the Arc de Triomphe. Joan cries as much for the country as for the French. Not again, she thinks, and wonders briefly how Rose Beauregard will get along. In the evening, once the children are in bed, she and my grandfather make serious plans.

Helen, stuck in a village just a few miles from the French capital, hopes that she will survive the occupation as a free woman. She has been French to all intents and purposes for twenty years; she looks and feels and sounds French, but her birth certificate still reveals her as a Londoner. She is also a communist. Fortunately she is a resourceful woman.

High summer in England and the girls have their hats and dolls and are waving at the crowd on the quayside, almost as if someone there were waving back at them. Almost as if they were departing on a cruise. The great liner *Capetown Castle* can carry nearly 800 passengers and is leaving Liverpool, bound for South Africa. Now its huge engines start to pull its vast bulk from the quayside. The band strikes up *Finlandia*. In front of them the deck railings vibrate, then a dark chasm opens up between the ship and the dock, with black water far below, then more sea, and the land moves slowly away with the crowds on land crying and calling out and holding babies up, while armed soldiers stand by impassively. As the ship pulls smoothly towards open sea to join her convoy, a breeze gets up and a few seagulls circle, crying, over the wake.

Far under the Atlantic German U-boats are silently tracking ships leaving British ports. The first attack on a passenger liner had occurred on the opening day of the war, 3rd September 1939, when nine children were among the casualties of SS *Athenia*, sunk while sailing from Liverpool to Canada. Some people, including Winston Churchill, argue that it is defeatist and, indeed, unsafe to send Britain's children abroad; it is enough that they be evacuated to the countryside. In the last respect he will be proved right and official overseas evacuations will only continue for a year.

As *Capetown Castle* clears Liverpool docks that June, the threat is very real. 1940 is a bad year for British shipping: over five hundred ships are lost. *Capetown Castle* will zigzag much of the way to South Africa, changing course every nine minutes, which will turn life on board into a hell of seasickness, even in the comfortable first-class cabins occupied by my mother, her sister and my grandmother.

The war calls for sacrifices. My grandmother, never very brave or confident, has rarely travelled alone nor made any decisions for herself and, since her accident four years before, she has been sedated with pain-killers, barbiturates and Martini. Among many acts of wartime courage, hers is to give up all these for the duration of the three-week journey. She sits up, watching over her daughters in case a torpedo comes out of the dark. By day she sits on deck, wrapped in her black lamb coat, scanning the waves for periscopes. In this way she brings her daughters safely to Africa.

They have lifeboat practice and drills in which they are, terrifyingly, battened down below decks. One afternoon, in the middle of tea, they hit something large and solid and all the china comes crashing to the floor and some people scream, but it is only a whale they are told. On Sundays they sing 'Eternal Father strong to save, whose arm doth bind the restless wave. Oh hear us when we cry to thee for those in peril on the sea.' My mother cannot sing this again for the rest of her life.

In July they finally see the Cape, with long breakers rolling the sea into shore and the green slopes of South Africa rising gently from the water. Dominating it all is Table Mountain. My grandmother assures the girls that they will just be staying for six months after which, Hitler having been routed, they will be brought home. In fact nobody ever summons them back, and it will be four years until they decide on their own to set out for England, and by then their home will be long gone.

On the way to Bulawayo they pass a group of soldiers in Nazi uniform on a station, and my grandmother tells the girls not to look. They stare long and hard at the handsome men in tan, red, black and white.

Geraldine is in Bulawayo. She is governess to a family she has known for decades and they have agreed to take in her nieces for what they still term 'the duration'. Meaning a period of months at most. My grandmother spends a few weeks settling the girls with her sister and the family but in reality she abdicates her maternal role almost immediately. Soon she is merely an observer in her perfect *maquillage*, her fine straw hat and pretty tea dresses in lawn and crêpe de Chine, all of which are a little too refined for the hearty colonials. There is so much to absorb: black servants who must be ignored; God, who is omnipresent; bowel movements which are central to a healthy life – all the children have to take Epsom salts on Fridays – fat insects which must be repelled. Everything is bright and dry in Africa. The earth is russet brown, the flowers pink and fiery red, the plants spiky, the distant mountains purple, the trees crooked and dense with thorns. Cows are thin and fly-covered and crows are large and aggressive. Eventually and with some relief my grandmother leaves the girls and turns for home. A fragile kiss, all face powder and Tabac Blonde and she walks down the path, through the gate to the car, is driven to the train to Cape Town. She does not look back.

This time she is really alone. All her life somebody has been there to tell her what to do and how to do it. Her father, Gerald, when she was growing up at Compton Lodge, Geraldine and Ethel and Rachel in the nursery, Madame de Giez at school in Lausanne, Eric, and indeed *his* father, in her marriage. Even in hospital month after month, the doctors and Sister Vickery ordered her daily regime. Now she boards the ship for England, lost but free.

Fears have become a reality in the weeks since her outward journey. Just weeks after *Capetown Castle* completes her successful voyage south, U-60 fires a torpedo at the *Volendam*, carrying evacuees bound for Canada, in a convoy of thirty-two ships. The torpedo passes straight through the ship. Astonishingly only the purser is killed. But much greater disaster follows. In September convoy OB213 is also heading for Canada. It is being followed, patiently, by U-boat 48. Six hundred miles off the coast of Ireland the convoy escorts are called off to support two incoming ships. The lead ship in the outward convey, making slow progress in bad weather, is now the *City of Benares* with four hundred passengers, including ninety children, on board. Her captain has stopped zigzagging – the pattern adopted to confuse submarines – in order to make progress in high seas. At about 10.00 pm at night, Kapitanleutnant Heinrich Bleichrodt, believing he is attacking a troop ship, gives the order to fire. The first torpedo is a direct hit on the *City of Benares* and she begins to sink almost immediately. The order is given to abandon ship and the other boats in the convey are instructed to disperse, leaving *Benares* and her passengers to their fate. It is dark and cold with winds blowing at five knots and many of the lifeboats capsize. It is the following afternoon before any help arrives. Over a week later one further lifeboat is found by HMS *Anthony*, but of all the children on board the *City of Benares* only thirteen survive.

On the way to South Africa my grandmother made herself stay awake, but now, thinking about U-boats, she cannot sleep. She is less sick this journey but has no appetite. She lies in her cabin, listening to the rumbling of distant engines, the clank of blows against pipes, the feet running in another part of the boat, sensing the regular change of course. She starts at any sudden noise but she is equally disturbed by silence.

My grandmother is not young any more but she is pretty and vulnerable, and a few days in she starts talking to a naval officer who is travelling home to take over a new ship. They only have brief periods together, but she has someone to think about when she is lying on her bed and she likes seeing Tom in his uniform and likes it when ratings salute him. Somehow having him for herself makes her feel that she has a better chance if they should be attacked. He tells her things she didn't know about boats and the war and speaks to her in Malay which he picked up in childhood, and she speaks back to him in French. To start with she sleeps with him because she is frightened of sleeping alone.

They lie in her cabin with his arm under her head. He inhales deeply on her cigarette. She makes him laugh. He makes her safe. She wanted the lights off and he agreed at first although she was still frightened that his fingertips would trace the puckered edges of her scars and they do but he kisses them, first with the lights off and then with the lights on. It is the first time she has let anyone touch her for four years and when he falls in love with her, she falls in love back, in gratitude.

They have to part at Liverpool; she to return to Eric, Tom to his new ship, but they are full of promises and plans. She has stopped taking her pills and feels an energy and clarity of thought that has been gone for a long time. In fact she can't ever remember feeling so alive – not since she was a girl in the mountains. She will write, he will write, they will be kind, they will make everything right at the end of the war, so she doesn't cry when her train pulls out. She does cry eight weeks later when she reads in *The Times* that his ship has been sunk with all hands. A few days later there is a small paragraph about Tom, who is described as a hero. She has to cry in private as she is home with Eric, in the Watford house; not that Eric doesn't know that something has happened but if nobody says anything then they can pretend it's just her and the fire and missing the girls. She still rubs cream in her scars because, on the whole, she does what she is told to do but she does so with her eyes shut trying not to feel what *he* felt. Some days she takes two pills when she wakes and then does not even bother to get dressed; sometimes she does not even bother to get *up*; sedated and despairing she is armoured against the Blitz: both the reality of bombs falling and the headlines in the paper. She doesn't care if a bomb drops right on top of them, in fact she wishes it would.

Deep inside, Eric has mixed feelings. He is a man who lost his mother when he was four and his sister in his twenties and he is terrified of losing his wife. He has of course already lost her in most ways, had done after the accident, but as things are he will always know where his sad, frail Joan is; she is upstairs. Eric starts to talk about moving permanently to Gloucestershire. Not to the Round House but to something a bit bigger. Further from the enemy. Something close to home. He means his father's home, of course, she thinks; in this family people always snatch up bits of other people's lives and soon believe they are their own. They can't tell where one of them ends and another begins.

But as autumn comes she finally wakes up. She is, in effect useless; the girls are on another continent, her son Richard is away at school. She can't get anyone to take her out in the car because petrol is restricted. Gardening is less appealing now she is being told to pull up her flowerbeds and sow vegetables, and the shadow of war falls over her cooking too: rationing is beginning to bite. Anyway, she has no one to cook for. In many of their acquaintances' houses all the help has been called up or gone to do more glamorous war work, but they have faithful Alice and Margaret, Swiss nationals, whose only loyalty is to them, so life goes on much the same. Eric has joined the Royal Observer Corps and is firing off letters trying to claim a medal for his war service in 1914–1918, to stick on his uniform.

It is Blanche who suggests she joins the FANYs, Blanche who, although a younger sister, always keeps an eye on her. Blanche has her own problems: since Italy declared war her kind, decent, thoroughly anglicised husband has the name of an enemy, but he is also, obviously, becoming less and less well. She is simultaneously terrified yet resigned to losing him.

My grandmother goes up to London by train despite my grandfather's protestations. He comes to see her off in his own new uniform. Sometimes it feels as if they are both acting parts in a play.

Bomb damage has halted trains on the southern networks, but her own journey is quick and easy. The train is streaked with grime outside; the autumn day seen through a veil of dirt on the window and the fabric of the seats is greasy. Although she keeps her gloves on, in a funny way tolerating this makes her feel part of it all. By late morning she is talking to two nice women in a shabby office near Hyde Park, who are pleased that she speaks French and she finds, at the end, that she has joined up on four months' probation and has a uniform allowance.

She had intended to go to one of the lunchtime concerts in the National Gallery; at home Eric has no great ear for music, but suddenly it is being alone in London, not organised, not *doing* anything that is immensely seductive. In the last months air attack has become the dominant face of war and since early September London has had air raids every night, but central London is busy despite the Blitz. Government offices are hidden behind sandbags, barrage balloons float, somehow unreal and theatrical, in a pale blue sky, and khaki and navy dot the moving patchwork of crowds. She expects to see Tom: a shadow glimpsed for a second in a passing officer; after all, months after her mother died she saw her everywhere. But Tom stays under the sea and to her surprise when a pair of laughing soldiers pass her, it is Rupert, dead for a quarter of a century, who is suddenly there in her head. What would he make of it all? He'd be surprised to see little Joan going to join up, that's for sure.

The papers say the smell of high explosive and burning lingers over the city by day, that and the sewage which has seeped from fractured drains, but it smells just the same to her. Coal fires, horse manure, people. She wanders up Piccadilly past Green Park, where couples are lying under the trees on the fallen leaves enjoying the late sun, just as they always did. The shops are all closing at 4.00 pm these days but she looks in the windows, criss-crossed with tape, as she goes by. She is feeling better than she has for months. Almost excited. She'd read that Lyons had been shut after bomb damage cut off its water supply, but when she reaches it, it has opened again so she goes in, all on her own, for tea and a scone. She pops in to Swan and Edgar too, not because she wants to buy anything but because she wants to see familiar things. Shop windows up Regent Street have been repaired but the grit in the gutter and between pavement slabs, sparkles with glass dust. She imagines the Watford shop after a direct hit: all plaster and dismembered mannequins, dusty sheets and smashed tea services.

It is only a week or so until she is off to do her preliminary training. Suddenly she is a part of it all, not just an observer. She is better than she thought she would be at truck driving and, having joined Eric shooting pheasant and duck around the Round House, finds her skills adapt quite easily to small arms. But it is her French that soon changes her life. Her French is fluent, her German is competent. Some of the girls with perfect languages are spirited off pretty quickly to unknown places for further training. Many of these will die as enemy agents when captured by the Germans. Because of her accident, my grandmother is unfit for such duties. Instead she is sent to help with the Polish forces based in Scotland.

The Poles and my grandmother might have been made for each other. Melancholy, lonely, rootless: her attachment to them is as inevitable as it will be catastrophic.

Thousands of Polish servicemen are arriving in Britain. Many of these have escaped over the borders of Hungary, Czechoslovakia, Latvia, Lithuania and Romania after first Germany then Russia invaded their homeland; 80,000 of them were fighting in France and half of those escaped to England after France fell. They are homesick, tired, angry, sad and determined.

Soon my grandmother travels north to Scotland. She is self-

My grandmother, posted to the Polish Forces, Scotland, 1942

conscious in her uniform, which doesn't fit very well. Winter is coming, and the colours of the north are purple and grey.

In Bulawayo the girls – my mother and my aunt – are trying to fit in. Geraldine's love and alliances have long been transferred to the family she is governess to and she, like them, welcomes the two girls more in a spirit of duty than blood loyalty. Everybody in the house hopes very much that the war will be over quite soon. My mother writes poetic laments. The first is called 'In the Absence of my Mother'. In bed at night the girls work themselves up to orgies of homesickness speculating on what their parents are doing back home and whether the dog is getting his favourite biscuits and whether their brother might be taking their toys. They miss Margaret and Alice but they can reduce themselves to tears considering how sad their mother must be.

* * *

Góral jak dziecko płacze;
Może ich już nie zobaczę?
I poszedł w dal mroczną zkosą,
W guńce starganej i boso.

You can hear the Poles before you see them. They sing in groups, they sing by themselves, they sing as they walk, they sing as they think, they sing, beautifully, when they have been drinking. But even the jolliest tune has something heart-rending about it. From all her time in Scotland it will be the cold and the singing she remembers most clearly.

The Poles are difficult. Relieved to have escaped both the Germans and the Russians, they nevertheless have to face the fact that their families are left behind, and rumours of Polish deaths at Soviet hands are relentless. The younger soldiers have parents, the older men have wives and children, all now trapped. She sees creased photograph after creased photograph of safe, compact families in stiff dress and pre-war sunshine. Jan, Basia, Jozef, Danuta, Antoni. Fingers touch tiny sepia faces and talk of family butchers' shops or a schoolmaster father, of a sister's marriage, of a grandmother who lived to one hundred, a cousin who played violin with the National Orchestra, a brother who was miraculously saved in a mining disaster. Some of the men seem little older than her own son; one has a photograph not of his parents but of his dog. After a few weeks he appears with a real dog; half-hidden at first but increasingly just a fact of life – a black and white collie cross which sleeps under the piano.

From 1939 the Scottish flag and the Polish Eagle have flown together. The Poles arrive at Lossiemouth, Cupar, Leven, Milnathort and Auchtermuchty, at Crawford, Biggar, Douglas, Duns, Kelso, Forres, Perth, Tayport, and Arbroath, Forfar and Carnoustie. They arrive in transports of three to five hundred men and they bolster the defence of Scotland after the loss of the 51st Highland Division in France. They are mostly soldiers and sailors, the Polish Airmen having gone to bases in southern England. My grandmother's official job is to care for these men and a few women; process their arrival, help them improve their English, check their health, and settle them into their new accommodation and into a new life. She also copes with more grief, anger and despair than she has ever encountered outside her own head. She sees the photographs, mementoes, letters and medals which they leave in small boxes when they go on operations. Boxes that are not always opened again. Some of the men speak French, and she soon picks up Polish – her ear for languages is good and recognizing the few words she learned at school in a mass of unfamiliar sounds, she feels more and more confident.

When did she first notice Wotzek? It was quite early on. He was older than most of the others, fair-haired, square shouldered, not a lot taller than her. He was an air force officer who had fought in the last battle for Poland and he rarely smiled. He was more contained: if he had photographs he kept them to himself at first. He had good manners and he spoke reasonable English. But he was angry in that barely suppressed way they all exhibited from time to time. The whole mood of the camp was edgy, excited, reckless. One night there had been too much drink. She was supposed to keep an eye on these things but what could you do. Sometimes it just slipped in minutes from being songs and stories and affable rowdiness, to shouting, fights and tears. A new arrival: a thin, dark boy had been hostile to everyone since he came. It was not surprising; he was a pilot whose plane had been hit by enemy fire and he'd parachuted out over Kent, suffering concussion when he landed. In his confusion he had called out for help in Polish. The villagers, hearing an unfamiliar language, had patriotically beaten him to within an inch of his life. His bones were mending, but he was still not fit to fly and was on attachment doing a routine desk job. That night one of the others had told him at least to be polite to the women who were only doing their best. The dark boy exploded with rage: here they were in Britain, when their families were God knows where and even their country had been gobbled up. Who knew when or even *if* they would ever see the people or the land they loved again. And they were supposed to feel grateful when every-body knew that if Britain and France had done something, had stood up to Hitler, if they had fulfilled the obligations of their own treaties, let alone of honour, they could have kept Poland out of the goddamn awful mess it was in now. They were in Britain because they had nowhere else to go. That was the only reason they were in fucking huts in the middle of nowhere being fucking polite. They fought with Britain because they wanted to fight the Germans. But the real ani-mals were the Russians, and to think Britain was worried about the Nazis – wait until the Russians arrived. He hoped they did. But increasingly his shouting became weeping. Wotzek came up to him, put his arm around his shoulders, and the boy only made a half-hearted attempt to shrug him off before being led away. 'We have been betrayed.' His words rebound from the corridor.

Christmas comes and they decorate the camp. Some of the locals bring in game or some unspeakable, almost certainly illegal, drink, a tree comes from the local landed estate, suddenly there are streamers and paper lanterns and the dog, Stan, has red ribbon round his neck. There is even holly and mistletoe and overnight a crèche appears with small wooden figures. The tree has no lights but on Christmas Eve two candles are lit either side of it and a silver star set on the top. The huts which had seemed so dreary a few weeks ago have been decorated with paintings by the Poles and the swirling colours and figures and forests, horses, eagles and warrior women seem richer and stranger in the candlelight. Home seems far away and not just to the Poles.

One of the boys takes control of the kitchen because they are going to have a Polish Christmas Eve dinner with twelve courses. Rationing means that some of the courses are more in spirit than substance but it is astonishing what ingenuity comes up with. Fortunately cabbage and beetroot seem to play a major part in the traditional feast. It's the same the next day when they have a British Christmas lunch. Some of the girls have even made crackers out of scraps. My grandmother plays the piano which needs tuning so badly that it is scarcely capable of doing more than keeping the rhythm going, and they hand out carol sheets: *Silent Night*, *The First Nowell*. She adds *The Holly and the Ivy* as its mood seems to match the paintings and someone else plays *O Come All Ye Faithful* and *O Little Town of Bethlehem*. For some reason, for them, not for her, this almost makes her cry. 'Yet in thy dark streets shineth the ever-lasting light' . . . she has never wanted to win the war so badly and see the men go home to their sepia wives.

Then Wotzek comes forward. He sits down at the piano and plays a few notes. Whatever he is playing is familiar to most of the others and they start to sing. In the second verse he joins them. She is still standing right by the piano and he looks up and sings, as it seems, to her. She has enough Polish now to know it is a lullaby.

Lulajże Jezuniu, moja perełko!
Lulaj ulubione me pieścidełko.

Lulajże, Jezuniu, lulajże, lulaj!
A Ty Go, Matulu, W płaczu utulaj.

Dam ja Ci słodkiego, Jezu, cukierku,
Rodzenków, migdatów co mam w pudetku.

Lulajże przyjema oczom Gwiazdeczko,
Lulaj najśliczniejsze świata Słoneczko.

[Sleep, little Jesus, my little pearl!
While Mama comforts you, tender, caressing!

Lullaby, little one, in loving arms lying,
Guarding my darling and stilling Thy crying!

When Thou awakenest, Jesus, my treasure,
Raisins and almonds I have for Thy pleasure.

High in the heavens a lovely star sees us,
But like the shining sun, my little Jesus.]

In Africa my mother is growing fast. She is a strapping girl with
dark eyes and curly hair and she is doing well at school. The grandfather of the house fumbles with her under the tablecloth and her
changing shape is an object of general hilarity and comment. It doesn't
help that she and her sister are usually kept in boys' clothes which only
accentuate their rounded figures. Eating becomes her principal comfort and will remain so all her life; her enthusiasm for food is a wonder
to her hosts. By Christmas 1941 they have been gone for eighteen
months. They have a sort of joke which they repeat. 'When they said
the war would be over by Christmas I think they forgot to mention
which Christmas they had in mind.' Letters from home are drying up
but they know that it must be hard for mail to get through. As clothes
are let down and out or handed on, they also have a feeling that *money*
may not be getting through and that duty is turning to be a longer and
more expensive commitment than their hosts had guessed.

My mother far left, Geraldine centre, my aunt far right,
South Africa 1943

Tensions have been building up in the east. The United States feels itself being drawn inexorably into war with Japan and there is an expectation that an attack on the Philippines or Malaya may be imminent. But two weeks before Christmas the Japanese Air Force turns east and makes a pre-emptive attack on Pearl Harbor to devastating effect. By mid-morning on 7th December America's fleet is sunk or sinking and more than 2,400 sailors and support staff are dead. Ships such as the *Oklahoma, West Virginia* and *California* have been blown apart by bombers flying off aircraft-carriers with names like *Happy Crane, Increased Joy* and *Green Dragon*. The hulls of the *Utah* and *Arizona* will be left at Pearl Harbor, part of the landscape, for ever.

On 8th December the United States declares war on Japan. On 11th December Italy and Germany declare war on the United States. Later that day the United States finally makes a declaration of war against Germany.

My mother and her sister are thrilled by all this because now the Americans are going to fight Hitler too and that must mean that they will be able to go home soon.

In Scotland they are all standing around, smoking, laughing, as 1941 turns into 1942. There is a tentative feeling of optimism, and it is not just that the Americans have finally come on board. The papers tell of terrible weather in Russia which has stopped the German advance on Moscow. The Poles are quite happy for the two sides to kill each other out there in the east. Wotzek describes hard Januaries as he knew them in Poland: nothing like they have ever known in Britain, he says. Cold they could not possibly imagine. It will be the old enemy, the eastern winter, which will do for Hitler's armies, not Soviet guns. Their blood will freeze in their veins; they will turn to ice soldiers. He laughs. Hitler should have asked Napoleon about tactics.

My grandmother likes the older officer's cleverness but later she is troubled by the vision of these fairytale armies, their hair frosted, their skin colourless, standing forever upright, halted between the forests and the snow.

Somewhere in the months between winter and spring she finds it is Wotzek she looks for when she comes into the mess, and his quiet, serious presence that she relies upon. She laughs at the jokes the others tell her but most of them are so young; she cries when sometimes she hears they are missing. She feels a bit guilty that she could probably have gone home on leave but she is needed here and she is not needed at home. Not really.

Occasionally, if their duty rotas coincide, she and Wotzek go for walks. He is not on active service as he has been ill, but he is longing to return to a fighting position. One day they take a picnic – not much of one really, but they have a hard-boiled egg – to a spot overlooking the sea. It is a day of hot and buzzing silence; there are swarms of mosquitoes. Slowly he begins to tell her a little more about his life. He talks of Poznan – the city where he was born. His father had a clothing business – two factories – and had become successful; his mother died when he was quite young. He has two sisters and he has an older brother who is an officer perhaps still in Poland and he has – *had* – he corrects himself, a younger brother. He is married and his wife is a teacher. My grandmother is shocked to find herself briefly disappointed by this. He also tells her he has a son who is nine years old. He has not heard from any of them since 1939, when he left the country to avoid the round-ups for labour camps. He was fighting and the Germans were between him and his home. As for the rest, he shrugs. His son is called Tadeusz and he keeps rabbits. Sometimes, although he is not allowed to, he brings one into the house and hides it down the bed with him at night. He has a badly damaged photograph of Tadeusz as a baby sitting on his mother's lap. Wotzek's wife has thick, dark hair and wears a high-necked patterned dress. The photograph is not in his wallet but in a drawer in his room. They go back to find it, and she notices that his few belongings are arranged with incredible neatness and although he said he no longer believed in God, there is a rosary and what looks like a Polish missal in the same drawer as the photograph. My grandmother thinks of this as his history drawer; as if everything that cannot be confronted in his old life has been packed away into this tiny space where he can keep it safe.

In return she shows him a photograph of her little girls, playing in the garden the month before they left England, and another of her son, Dick, in school uniform and, after a moment's thought, one of my grandfather and her skiing together before the war. She doesn't have any which show them all together. She has to think before telling him how old the girls are now.

One minute they are looking at the photographs, then there is silence, then they are both looking at each other and then, suddenly, he kisses her and tries to push her back on the bed. She hasn't told him about her accident so she pushes him off, and he is embarrassed and apologetic. She hasn't thought much about her scars over the last months; in winter it is so cold that she gets dressed in bed, and in summer there is rarely enough water to bath properly and it was always in the bath she was forced to confront the puckered and shining skin.

That night she has the dream again; the one where she and the girls are in the water, bobbing in a black slick of oil with flames flickering at its edge and she is trying, *trying* to keep them and herself afloat, but there is no sign of a ship or lifeboats just dead sailors floating in life-jackets, and when she looks upwards there is one clear star shining coldly on the water. She gets up at 2.00 am and takes a pill, knowing she will find it hard to wake up for her shift in the morning.

By winter my grandmother's Polish is fluent. Her friends tease her for her cheap and effective learning techniques. *La Méthode Polonaise*, they call it. A Polish lover gives her the edge. Not that she's the only one. Not that *he's* the only one. She had had others right at the beginning, but they were antidotes to loneliness, met and comforted in the dark. Not lovers so much as visitors, murmuring to themselves, as much as to her, in Polish. But now, with Wotzek, it is love. It is like nothing she has felt before for anybody. He removed her clothes slowly on a summer's evening in the clear northern light and smoothed her damaged flesh with his hands. With her eyes closed in case she might see any trace of disgust cross his face she can envisage his fingertips wiping the ridges away forever.

In spring she receives news that she will be transferred south again to different duties with the FANYs. She weeps in her room. Despite the tragedies which surround her she is incredibly happy in Scotland. As someone who has always been an outsider she feels more at home among these exiled foreigners than she ever did in her own family. Here she is finally needed.

Needed more than she realises, apparently, because to her astonishment just before her tour ends she is sent for by the commanding officer, who offers her a commission in the Polish army. She accepts; the FANYs release her, and a month later she has new insignia on her uniform. But she will still have to move. She is going to run a rest-house for Polish officers at Scarborough on the Yorkshire coast. A home for all the Poles who have no homes to go to on leave. Wotzek promises to visit.

One day will you marry me?

I will.

Zobrię to.

She travels south by train. She will see Dick at school and then explain how things are to Eric. When the war is over Wotzek, too, will get a divorce. It will be funny to have a surname that people won't be able to pronounce.

It all seems quite clear when they are together.

Only two barriers to happiness:

1) Her father. Despite his great age Gerald still takes a view on foreigners, Catholics and divorce. He might die, she supposes. She wonders if Wotzek has any aristocratic connections to ease the way.

2) Eric.

Eric is much more distressed than she has expected. He had been planning to put his foot down. To tell her that either she comes home on leave or promises to behave or he'll have to think about seeing his solicitor. He didn't intend to threaten divorce but let it hang in the air. Instead in she comes, trim in her uniform, a little nervous, patting her hair. Has hardly sat down when she says, 'I want a divorce' – just like that.

He gets very drunk that first evening after which further discussion is impossible. She leaves him slumped on the sofa clutching his glass of Scotch, but as the door closes the glass crashes and disintegrates on the wood behind her. The next day he thinks a lot about what his father would have said. She knows this because by the evening his mood is more resigned. He will give her a divorce. He will even give her an allowance. Henry's dead hand can be clearly seen in this. He was a great enthusiast for intervention whether abortion or legal separation or a take-over; Henry always said that a firm response concentrated the mind of the opposition.

Eric takes this to mean that if he lets her go now Joan might come back when she has tried being divorced. Everyone knows what these Poles are like.

He will take some tart to the sort of small hotel where they are ever alert to irregularities, and provide the evidence for a private detective. He gives my grandmother the name of a lawyer. Even in divorce she does what he suggests. In passing he makes it clear that he knows about all her lovers and would forgive her. If only forgiveness was what she was after.

She returns to Yorkshire with the very few things she cares about, to her small room in the Fairfield Hotel, now the Polish Rest Home. Eric proceeds with his plans for a family home. By summer 1942, he is a divorced man with an impressive, if uncompromising house in Fairford. It is a grey house in a county of cream stone, it has a heavy porch and slightly narrow windows. It says impregnable, it says well-secured, it says unbowed. It doesn't say all alone. He buys a blue leather-bound visitors' book in which the richness of his new life may be recorded. He engages a housekeeper. She is, supposedly, a widow, with a knowing face, dyed red hair and good legs.

Wotzek lies back on her little bed: his shirt is open, and the roughish wool of his unbuttoned uniform trousers makes her skin itch. His skin is surprisingly white and she likes the dark hair which climbs from his belly to his chest. She is propped up over him on one arm, while they share a cigarette. She holds it to his lips and sees a sheen of sweat on his face, and his short hair is damp around his ears. In this room, on this bed, in this coil of smoke is love and safety. She has never loved any-body or anything or wanted anybody or anything as much as she wants this man. She wants to be inside his skin; for her to make him better; for him to make her brave. She wants to be asked to die for him and for him to know her choice. She imagines them as partisans together, out-numbered, backs against a doorway, waiting for the end.

'So, Captain,' he says with his eyes half closed, 'how did you say you lost your uniform?'

In 1943 Captain Joan Edmonds is awarded the Polish Cross of Merit. Looking back she sees that as the last day of her happiness.

In mid-April terrible news filters through. The Germans in Poland have found the mass graves of 4,000 Polish officers in a forest near Smolensk. Thousands more are still missing. The Germans say the Russians executed them all in the summer. The Russians say the Germans perpetrated the horror during their winter occupation. The

The Manor House, Fairford, 1950s

bodies, trussed and gagged, each with a bullet through the skull turn out to have been clothed in summer uniforms. The pursuit of truth is swiftly stifled by the British and Americans. The Russians are their new ally; they need the Russians if they are to destroy the Germans. Churchill refuses to protest about this massacre and pressurises the Polish government in exile to withdraw its complaint. It is a triumph of realpolitik. It is the moment when even the most pragmatic Pole, even Wotzek, less hot-headed than the younger men, knows Poland and the Poles are of little consequence to Britain. They are, yet again, pawns in a much greater European game. It is the moment when my grandmother becomes clearly English in Wotzek's eyes. Horror and anger run through the Polish community but among the older men, there is little surprise. So many of them have friends and family who may now be rotting under the dark pines of the Katyn Forest that it is hard to know what to say or who to say it to. Wotzek, whose younger brother is an officer who remained in Poland, is almost silent. He still visits and sleeps in her bed but it as if she weren't there. His tension communicates itself to her and she lies unsleeping, hour after hour, hearing him awake beside her and miles and miles away.

In August the helicopter carrying General Sikorski, Prime Minister of the Poles in exile, who has pressed so hard for a Red Cross enquiry into the massacre, is killed when the helicopter returning him to London crashes on take-off at Gibraltar. Some of the Poles insist on seeing Churchill's hand in this. When my grandmother protests, Wotzek walks out of the room. He doesn't return to her for a fortnight but when he does he makes love to her with his eyes closed.

Chapter 6

Gloucestershire 1960–1970s

My great-uncle Stuart went to church in order to bear witness. At family weddings or funerals he would sit, relaxed and smiling, on a prominent gravestone watching the operation of superstition and convention. Geraldine would pass him with her eyes averted, her sensibilities detecting sulphur under the Trumper's *Eucris*, and pray urgently not to be contaminated before she gained the safety of the porch. On one of the many occasions I was taken out of church unconscious, a policeman who had carried me from the door set me down on the grass at Stuart's feet. Stuart looked down as he brushed the lichen dust off his trousers: 'See,' he said, 'it never did anyone any good.'

From then on I developed a church phobia; it was particularly bad around Easter when singing *There Is a Green Hill Far Away* would make my ears ring and black circles fill my sight almost immediately. So did *Let All Mortal Flesh Keep Silence*. The thought of either crucifixion or communion would reliably drop me to the floor. I knew all the details of crucifixion; exactly where the nails went in, what happened when the cross was raised upright, and how elevated arms created pressure which compressed the lungs. Wine that was really blood? It was decades before I could even drink red burgundy. White gloves, which I had worn to the wedding where I fainted, were implicated, incense too.

Yet churches as history I loved; it was all all right as long as there was nothing going on: the soothingly ancient smell of mould, furniture wax, Brasso and stale flower water. At the right time of day light filtered through stained glass windows, whose messages seemed to have little to do with the small mud-brown congregations huddled in the front pews under a gas heater. Then the pale arches and columns were magically transformed with a veil of colour. In the Fairford windows patrician angels and a persistent blue imp consorted with medieval peasants and red-robed ladies in a rather un-Cotswold scene of craggy mountains and pavilions. Perhaps this was heaven, but it was hard to see that Fairford's worshippers were going to feel very at home there.

My family's occasional forays into church started in the 1940s and were about something quite other than religious devotion. My grand-father started these outings as part of a general territorial imperative around the county of his social transformation. The house he had bought as Manor House Farm, was now called, by him at least, the Manor House. A manor house had a squire and squires went to church. He would go in last, sit at the front, ostentatiously put his watch by the Book of Common Prayer as the sermon began and claim to have told the vicar that if the homily overshot, he would walk out. At some point a suitably aged family bible was acquired and births, mar-riages and deaths were inscribed inside.

And then, as the new generation became adults, there was church as protest. My mother would come to the Remembrance Service, in a country coat with a white poppy. She would file out of the church, stand by the War Memorial while the names of the Fairford dead were read out and she would stick out like a sore thumb. As a child I was simultaneously proud and mortified. How I longed for a father old enough to have medals. How I wished to be a Girl Guide. *My* father was nowhere to be seen. But it was another thing 'we' did. What we did and what we believed was often reiterated by mother. We believed in pacifism, liberalism, education for women, looking after those less fortunate than us and social equality. We did not believe in apartheid or the Boy Scout movement, capital punishment or the Conservative party. My mother didn't believe in blue eye shadow, Gilbert and Sullivan, or heels with trousers either, and the vigour with which she expressed these antipathies was indiscernible from her horror at war.

We also, although this was less explicit, obviously believed that we were slightly cleverer and better connected than other people we knew. This was less evident in our new London life in leafy Wimbledon, my parents having fled Notting Hill Gate in fear of race riots, than in the country. In London my mother insisted that it was her education which set her aside from other wives, but even I could see that other wives were trim and wore make-up and deferred to their husbands' opinions in soft voices. But in Gloucestershire there was something about my family which made us not like other families in big houses with land. My grandfather was more obviously rich than anyone else in the two villages where he held sway. No one else had a Rolls Royce for a start. Nor a chauffeur in uniform. Nor a soda syphon and table napkins from the SS *Queen Mary*. Yet the people who shot with him were local farmers and imported London friends rather than the local gentry, and his poker cronies, who holed up with their whisky in the smoky reaches of The Bull in Fairford, were the local doctor, butcher and garage-owner. The barmaid came to dinner. Every evening he would listen for hints from the *Archers*; an everyday story of country folk. But it was never quite like that in real life. People were reasonably polite but the upper classes seemed oddly reluctant to recognise us as their own.

In old age my grandfather occasionally sat on a bench in Lechlade marketplace with Lord de Mauley, discussing better times, and my mother referred to our Ponsonby cousins every time we swept past a gatehouse and long drive on the Oxfordshire borders, but that was the limit of our aristocratic socialising. Just as she sometimes sat on beaches spotting children my age and insisting I go and make friends with them, she appeared to lay claim to almost anyone who looked or sounded as if they ought to be related to her. 'Oh look, Humphrey Lyttelton's on television; he's granny's cousin, of course.' Of course.

'Ours is a very old family', my mother said. As if other upstart families had sprung up newly made, their blood earth-red, somewhere around the turn of the century. 'And all shits', muttered my father. When I was nervous before a party, breathing into my cupped hands to check for bad breath (even your best friend won't tell you – but I simply longed for best friends, truthful in my interests or not) my mother attempted consolation: 'Never mind,' she said, 'you'll be the only girl there in Debrett.' When I burned for an impossibly handsome local landowner's son, she dismissed his apparent superiority, only half in jest: 'He's in the Baronetcy, we're in the Peerage.' *Pas de problème*. As my grandmother often observed.

The trouble was that she – my grandmother – the conduit of our blue blood – was elusive. Every couple of years a rice-paper thin copy of our entry in Debrett would arrive to be amended as required but of the woman herself only her silver, with a lion balancing on an earl's coronet, remained well-polished in the drawer. There was a family tree pinned on my grandfather's wall for a time. My grandmother's family tree, of course. Her departed substance had left only this skeleton of names, lines and tiny coats of arms. At the top were various kings and her family motto. *Volo non Valeo*. Willing but Unable.

Once I heard an old lady in the village whisper to a visiting friend that my grandmother was a 'bolter'. I had this image of her in some small house, vigorously locking herself in. In time, I suppose, I was a bolter too.

After she left my grandfather she always wrote her address as 'no fixed abode'. After the gas and the pills and her times in hospital she was unlikely to be employed again as anyone's housekeeper, which she had tried, briefly, after the war. Reliability was never her suit. For a while she had been stowed at the Round House. She was not the first or last troubled relative to be left in the house by the Thames. It was not an entirely suitable choice; the river ran swiftly under the bedroom window, and the whole house was run on gas. The tiny, delicate light mantles burned blue with flame and cast a uniquely bright but soft light. In winter the Thames, Coln and old canal rose and rose until finally they burst their banks and turned the fields to a sea spreading to the horizon. The only landmarks then were the telegraph poles, the upper curve of the old footbridge and, distantly, the spire of Lechlade church. When this happened the old house, its foundations scoured by violent eddies, creaked like a ship pulling at its moorings. But in spring fritillaries grew in the rich soil of the water meadows. It was where she and my grandfather had spent holidays with the children before the war, where they all ran wild with cousins and animals, in boats, on picnics. She had grown herbs outside the kitchen door, and my grandfather went out and caught trout for her to cook. She might have been happy there, I think.

Then Geraldine, that sad British institution, a redundant governess, returned to England and they set up home together on the south coast, at Bournemouth. Later, my grandfather moved them to Aston Clinton, a little village in Buckinghamshire. Did my grandmother have a view on these movings? She had no connection with any of the places she woke to find herself in and very few possessions. She had a piano which she played well and her two dachshunds. But by the cottage in Aston Clinton she made a wonderful garden. Cottage garden flowers grew in a tangled border, and wild violets and strawberries persevered on gravelled paths edged with flint. Scarlet flowers flamed on her runner bean canes and her decrepit old greenhouse smelled sweetly of tomatoes. Winter or summer her back door was always open and the garden-raffia, secateurs, and baskets of peas waiting to be husked, all spilled out. Again, possibly, she was happy. It was a funny union, two sisters, two decades apart in age, one having come to grief on the rocks of sex and passion and the other having never left the shore.

To get to Geraldine's room you had to walk through her sister's. My grandmother's room had a plump pink eiderdown and cut-glass scent bottles on a dressing table. Geraldine's had a perfectly made bed with

thin greyish blankets, a cross, a print of the young queen, and a photograph of a uniformed Rupert in a dark frame with a poppy. Even
when Geraldine was *in* the bed, it hardly made any difference to its
neatness; she scarcely raised a bump in the covers. My grandmother
had seed catalogues by her bed, Geraldine had – still – *The Cloud of
Witness* with a handmade bookmark. The church was just across the
road; she could gaze at its reassuring presence from her bedroom
window.

My own church-going continued to be problematic. At boarding
school it was compulsory and hierarchical; it had nothing to do with
belief, it was just something else to be learned properly like geography
or French. House sat with house: unfortunately I was in the second
worst one – Dorchester – and my house colours were a nasty shade of
mauve. Gloucester was at the bottom in desirability but at least you got
to wear flashes of red. I longed to be in Beaufort – terribly smart – or
Holford, slightly raffish, colours: *black*. In church the little ones sat in
clear sight of matron, sixth formers in corners behind pillars. Matron
would lean forward as the fancy took her in mid-devotion and hoick up
our skirts with her hymn book to check for the proscribed decadence
of petticoats. We were supposed to learn the collect for the day, and
sixth formers invested with frightening powers might pick on any
passing upper third or lower fourth girl and force them to recite it.
Morning Service was said without a girl lowering her eyes to her book
of Common Prayer. On the other hand, having a Psalter was quite pres-
tigious. All those tiny dots and slashes that only the acolytes of the
school choir understood.

Week after week I fell to the floor. Either in hymns which had connections, sometimes connections only I could see, with blood, or
sometimes in the psalms. More often I slipped into unconsciousness in
nauseated and clammy contemplation of martyrdom. It was not
enough that I wasn't a Catholic and that they didn't belong to me or me
to them; I was pursued by images of pierced flesh, severed breasts like
blancmanges on a tray, the hirsute head of St John, flayings, crushings,

severings, gridirons, spiked wheels. One year the calendar had us still at school on Good Friday. The last straw was the Seven Stations of the Cross. Interminable for others, quite short-lived for me.

Sometimes I'd fall awkwardly blocking a pew, sometimes sprawled over the black and red tiles, sometimes in the porch. Once I bit my lip as I went down and waking to see blood on my hand passed out cold again. They persevered for a term. '*Ride on Ride on in Majesteee, The wingèd squadrons of the sky, Look down with sad and wondering eyes, To see the approaching sacreeeefice*', they would sing, pulling my skirt down over my knickers, picking me up, hurrying me out, standing over me while I retched into a drain, before I was allowed not to go. I was a kind of heroine – the girl, the *only* girl, who had ever escaped church. Dissenters, Jewish girls, one Muslim, all had to bow their head to the inexorable rightness of middle-England Anglicanism. But I was now exempt and could read H. E. Bates in the library. I read it because bates and batey were the words of the moment at school. We used them wherever we could: 'don't get batey' meant don't get angry; 'she's in a bate' was simply she's sulking. I liked this word – its exclusivity to the world of school – so much, that I thought H. E. Bates was part of the title: a story about an angry man.

In time my phobia extended to the theatre or at least certain plays. *Macbeth* (Banquo's gory ghost), *Julius Caesar* (wounds oozing posthumously), *Richard III* (bloody ghosts of the vengeful slain). Some malign examiner selected all three for my GCE and A Level texts *and* they were put on in London so more notes had to be written exempting me from seeing them on stage.

It was also at boarding school that my insomnia really took hold. We slept in ornate and high-ceilinged mansion bedrooms. I would lie tormented by the deep, even breathing of sleeping girls around me, until morning light started to filter through the thin curtains. Some nights I would wander up and down the corridors, on others I would fall asleep for a while only to wake up with a start not knowing where I was. If I lay very still slowly the world would patch itself together again: above me hefty cherubs frolicked in peach clouds, and gilt fruit garlanded the doors, but there was always that horrible gap when I was simply adrift. The cherubs, bright pink, as if they had inhaled carbon monoxide, rather than ethereal vapour, were the kindly ones. How I knew their name I have no idea, but I dreaded seeing them, and tried not to look upwards. But when I couldn't sleep, the words 'kindly ones, kindly ones, kindly ones' refused to be extinguished. I could hear the words and see them written in my brain even with my eyes screwed shut.

The first few days of term were the worst when I was so ground down by homesickness that I struggled through the days exhausted. At night I cried hotly under the blankets for hours, sick at the absolute nature of my confinement, the weeks of term stretching ahead, the lack of privacy or escape, the teasing, the awfulness of games. Though not unpopular I was badly coordinated and always cold, and my peers sighed theatrically when the games mistress forced me on their team. Shortly before going to school I had my front teeth broken when I was hit with a rounders bat in a game on a beach so I was frightened of the greasy lacrosse sticks and I used to duck if the ball or other armed girls came in range. Above all there was a desperate longing for my mother and father and the dog and my room at home and knowing there was no appeal. At home were my little brother and my baby sister. At school was Miss Vanstone the games mistress.

I wasn't alone with my homesickness. A girl called Frances knew that you could kill yourself by hanging backwards over the bed until so much blood rushed into your head that your brain was crushed, and she was usually found upside down and scarlet faced. Janet, a thin, small sandy girl, was adopted and convinced every term that nobody would collect her at the end. When Kennedy was killed she cried, 'Now there'll be another war and your parents won't have any choice about getting you home but I'll just be left here and I'll have to cut my wrists with my sewing scissors.'

My grandmother too was sharing these thoughts. Strangely she had not developed many better techniques of suicide than us. She was in hospital again. However, pharmacologists had been making advances and there were, increasingly, new drugs for an old old illness: lithium, imipramine, largactil.

My sleeplessness was well known at school, but one night I was found sleepwalking and the school doctor put me on librium. It was suggested to my mother that I needed to see a psychiatrist. My mother decided, quite suddenly, that I should leave school: my grandmother looked to sodium amytal to provide the sleep which had eluded her for decades and the symptoms were too familiar. The prospect of a child on sedation or in psychiatric care defeated her. It all had a threatening inexorability. After all, she had done child guidance with me at Great Ormond Street and they had not really guided me anywhere I wasn't going already.

It was as easy as that. I was allowed home.

My mother had sent me to boarding school with a pack of sanitary towels. It was unthinkable that I should ever need them; my body was more like my brother's than my mother's extraordinary rolls and crevices, and I had a terror of the fact that I would bleed every month. I suspected it was too awful to be true and so far it didn't seem to be. After two years of transit backwards and forwards at the bottom of my trunk with my lacrosse boots, the packet was the least sanitary item I possessed. We'd used a couple to stop the door banging in the dorm. But others were noticing changes. Not all good. We were only allowed to wash our hair once a fortnight and until we were twelve years old matron had to do it. One day as she was tipping my head over the basin she said 'Tell your mother you need a bra and some deodorant.' This was it.

At home I stood in front of my parents' looking glass in my pyjama bottoms and there, particularly if I turned three-quarters on, were breasts, small but unmistakeable. When my father came home with a new code to break, I was waiting with them in the hall.

My mother went to Harrods. *We* went to Harrods, where she announced loudly to the whole department that I needed a bra.

Probably the entire shop heard and gazed at my incipient breasts. She had bought me two and sent me back to school. In the first two years at school we had to wear short-sleeved woollen vests in winter and for a year I put my bra on over the top.

At home walking around stark naked was something 'we' did, although as my mother's body ran out of control, after having my sister, she hated anyone watching her in the moment of transformation from clothed to naked, or vice versa: her flesh falling out of her dresses as she unbuttoned or wresting her all-in-one into place in the mornings and bending stiffly over this palisade of bones and wire to fasten her suspenders. Hung, pinkly, over the rack to dry the all-in-one retained the shape of her body. Cuddling her, when she let you, was always strange as her body was so compressed underneath that the tension made her springily resilient. My mother was still young, but she was always sore where the unforgiving fabric rubbed her talcum-powdered skin. But she was never that bothered about being completely naked despite the strange lines and welts that were the impressions of the bones.

However once I went away to school, and particularly after my breasts arrived, we covered up. At least my father did and from then on the bathroom door was shut.

That summer I discovered sex, or at least the faint promise of it, which, for a while, proved quite a therapeutic diversion. I went to stay with my aunt and uncle in Alassio, where there were lizards and bright red beetles, lemon trees and afternoon siestas. I ran around in faded shorts in the garden and often no top at all. But occasionally I would catch a glance of myself in a window pane and feel excited at the me who was emerging. We used to pay to go on a beach where the sands were tidied each night and well-ordered wooden chaises longues stood in rows under green umbrellas. At the top of these were a row of slatted changing cabins. One day getting out of my damp costume, I heard a scratching noise outside and looking through a gap in the boards, saw a boy – a little older than me – trying to peer in. A few

My sister and me, France, 1963

months earlier I would have put this down to the incomprehensible nastiness of boys, now, suddenly, I knew it was something else.

On the way home instead of a boy, it was the Frenchman at Nice airport who was interested. My main feeling was not fear or disgust but curiosity and an astonishing sensation of power. When I got home I would day-dream a quite different scenario where I didn't stay sitting on the bench with my cheese. I was still hazy on the details. The following summer I was thirteen and with my family on holiday at the Round House. My grandfather had built a small swimming pool next to the river to celebrate me passing my eleven-plus. On the far side of the river were the locals. This summer I suddenly noticed that these were not a generic group who might as well have been forty miles as forty feet away, but that among them were young men and a radio.

Have I the right to hold you? You know I've always told you
That we must never ever part oh ooh ooh oh

Have I the right to kiss you? You know I'll always miss you
I've loved you from the very start

Come right back I just can't bear it
I've got this love and I long to share it
Come right back I'll show my love is strong

No poetry had ever been so full of promise. I walked up and down my bank in my swimming costume while they roared out the chorus and drummed on their thighs and shouted for me to swim over. At night I lay awake making fantasy crossings of the small bridge to the other side of the river where I could send those shivers running down their spines – ooh ooh – and they could in return show me that their love was strong. Yeah.

But it wasn't just boys. It was, much more interestingly, men. Old men. The man in Nice had introduced me to the possibilities and my favourite song was *Milord* on my grandfather's record of Edith Piaf. That Christmas one of my parents' friends kissed me under the mistletoe and put his tongue in my mouth. Hanging around friends' fathers or my uncle's gardener or simply men on buses or in shops, I could sense their discomfort and their interest. Nice men would leave the room if they found themselves alone with me. Less nice ones would follow me in. It was all much more compelling than the beery fumblings of adolescent boys round the back of the tennis club. Nevertheless it was the local GP's son a year or so later who filled in some of the details for me. He found a film in his father's desk, took the family projector and came round to my house with some friends. My mother was out. The only clear white space we could find in an era of lively wallpaper was my bedroom wall and door, so we sat on my bed and pretended to be blasé and unaffected by the hard-core pornography being projected rather unevenly six feet away. We had seen it all twice and were experimenting. One of the boys had made it run backwards. Suddenly the door was flung open and there stood my mother, filling the space, while, unknown to her, ejaculate shot back off a woman's breast and up the man's penis all over my mother's pale-clad torso.

My first official older man was my brother's prep school headmaster. Grey-haired, clever, smooth and Aston Martin owning. He was forty-nine years old, divorced with three wives down and one to go when we met. I was now just seventeen. By lying to my parents I arranged to stay at his house. We had a wonderful dinner and then he settled me in the spare room. In the middle of the night I wandered through and slipped in beside him. He was saintly in resistance. 'This is all wrong', he said as he indulged himself to a degree that lay easily with his conscience. 'I'm old enough to be your father.' 'Oh you're much older than my father,' I replied comfortingly, 'my father's only forty-two.' Yet although I longed to sleep with him, or rather him to sleep with me, what I really loved was his sophistication. His wall of

books, his being able to speak – not just write but *speak* – Latin and
Greek: even reading Latin love poetry to me, and his knowledge of
Norman churches. I also loved his fast red car. We'd drive around,
stopping off at villages or pacing the cool aisles of city cathedrals, while
he talked of gothic tracery, corbels, lancets and misericords, or showed
me sinners stewing away in cauldrons on doom wall-paintings or talked
about the Reformation. On the way home we'd stop in a field gate and
grapple enthusiastically before he dropped me off at a corner near my
house. My parents weren't supposed to know. Soon my brother was
made a prefect.

My grandmother was long past such excitements. She was less
agitated now. There was no longer the violent turbulence of desire and
betrayal. The manic part of what I now knew was her manic depression seemed to have flitted away, not that I had ever seen her manic
or even mildly enthusiastic, and there was something washed out
and collapsed about her in her shapeless clothes and her limp waves
held out off her face with a hair-grip. Her eyes were filmy, perhaps
because of the shingles which came to torment her and never left
her. For a woman whose physical characteristics had been eagerly
sought by and perceived within her descendants, and whose flesh had
been, apparently, enjoyed by various lovers, her disintegrating body
was remarkably unattractive.

She finally had her pre-frontal leucotomy when I was in my early
teens. We went to see her on a long Victorian ward at the Atkinson
Morely in Wimbledon. The windows were high and she looked very
small, reduced in her bed. After that she never tried killing herself
again – it was if she had lost all will to die – but she continued to dab
at her shingles. She was, suddenly, an old lady.

Geraldine, on the other hand, had always been an old lady. She had
a life-long commitment to correct form. Looking glass not mirror, bedspread not coverlet, writing paper not notepaper, bathing costume not
swimsuit, drawing room not lounge and so on endlessly in a thin trail
of respectability. It was apparently the mark of a lady with time on her

lips never to use one word where two would do. In her eighties eccentricity and neurosis finally turned into dementia and she had to be removed to a Home for Retired Governesses, where as she approached death she became increasingly foul-mouthed, one of a chorus of disappointed spinsters who railed at Jesus as one might at a betraying lover.

Great-Uncle Alfred, Mountie, 1920s

The lives of the grandchildren of Lady Fanny Cavendish and Frederick Howard, MP, and of Rebecca and Charles Curtis, the butcher of Lincoln, were drawing to an end. Rupert had been gone for half a century and lay in northern France. Ethel the nun took to drink and became enormously fat. Eventually the convent put her out, and she lodged briefly in the real world – an affable if occasionally rowdy visitor in the homes of her nieces and nephews – and died of diabetic complications a year or so later. In Canada Alfred took off his Mounties uniform and got off his horse for the last time; Rachel, who had only married as she approached her forties, when her father, Gerald, had apparently relinquished his hold on her, died alone. Rachel's marriage was quite a statement. She married a butler, which must have provided a useful outlet for her kleptomania, my mother said, and, as a domestic couple, they had occasionally waited on the grand dinners where her father was enjoying country house weekends with one aristocratic relative or another. Marcus died genteelly in Mousehole. Now only the two youngest Howard children: the widowed Blanche and the divorced Joan, were left.

When Geraldine died, my grandmother was shifted back to Fairford. My grandfather had expired some time before, and his second wife, Beryl, although thirty years his junior, had scarcely outlived him. She had died at forty-two. Stuart too had died and Gwynneth soon followed. Sidney wept over her coffin: coloured tears stained with hair dye and mascara ran down into his collar. Everyone moved on. In my family this really meant that everyone moved on a *house*. My aunt now lived in the Manor House. Beryl had left Thornhill, the one on the lake, to my small brother, but my parents were living in it for their lifetimes, and we went there at weekends and in the holidays. Helen the ex-mistress had been living in the ancient and dark cottage next to the Manor House, where my parents had lived when I was born, as an honorary grandmother, but when she moved back to France my real grandmother was tucked up there. This time she scarcely bothered to do the tiny garden, but she still grew tomatoes and, inadvertently, cannabis. Somebody had given her the seeds, expecting her to relinquish the seedlings, but soon the thicket of foliage pressed out against every pane, like some science fiction plant about to burst free and rampage through the countryside. She believed it was tea and refused to part with her flourishing progeny. When the vicar came to visit she showed him her crop with pride.

My uncle and aunt, James and Susie Kennaway, Fairford, 1966

When distant relatives still commented on how much I looked like her in her youth it was simply impossible to believe, but I hated it when they said 'she's so *like* her grandmother'. The one I really wanted to be like was my aunt, who was chic and sexy and had lots of clothes. Although I knew by a process of family osmosis, about my grandmother's lovers and the suicide attempts and the stays in hospital, and I observed that the love I felt for my mother bore no relation to the distant exasperation my mother felt for hers, it was only when I was growing up that I first overheard somebody describe my grandmother's condition as manic depression. This was telling in itself because my mother used to run through a litany of her aunts and their pathologies. Rachel, kleptomaniac, Geraldine and Ethel, religious maniacs. Among other things. 'My uncle's a diplomat', said my friend Melanie at school. 'My great-aunt Ethel's a dipsomaniac', I replied to be one up. Ada, my great-grandmother, was, by inference, a sex maniac. That's how she ensnared Gerald, although she was not the sort of sex maniac who left murdered children in woods, was hanged and had headlines two inches high that I was not allowed to read. My grandmother had been a sex maniac as well. Yet the real variety of mania that afflicted my grandmother, and probably the others, was never articulated. Now it seemed quite likely that when I grew up I would be sex-mad – which was the up-to-date version of sex maniac – too.

After leaving boarding school I had gone to my local direct grant grammar school. It was a place of academic rigour and austerity. The uniform was an unappealing combination of navy and citric green. Apples figured largely in the school foundation myth. So keen were our Victorian forebears to learn despite the vigorous efforts of men, who wished to keep them cooking and having babies, that they sat on apple barrels when no chairs were provided. It was hard to imagine suburban Wimbledon as a place of leafy orchards or this particular shade of green deriving from any natural pigment. Summer dresses in the green check were cut as plain shifts to skim the problem contours of the adolescent girl and turn her skin tones to putty. My mother discovered some school by-law which permitted fabric to be bought and made up in a design of choice. So I arrived in a skirt with fitting bodice, fully gathered skirt and white Peter Pan collar. It was all very New Look; the trouble was that it was 1965.

But perhaps for the first time ever I was really well taught. I loved history, French and art and I was used to being in the bottom division in maths by now and, anyway, the fun bad girls were down there too. I started Latin and liked it. But it was the first time I had really been exposed to science, and chemistry and physics were two hours each twice a week of misery and incomprehension. English, which I had always been strong at, was overshadowed by this school's demand for recitation. Every week the class had to learn a poem and on Monday one of us was chosen at random to recite it. By Sunday evening I felt sick. One day my moment came. It was Tennyson. In the first lines were two s's and two r's but also some traps – th and w to lure me away from clean cut pronunciation. *On either side the river lie long fields of barley and of rye that clothe the wold and meet the sky and through the field the road runs by*, I stopped to take a deep breath and collapsed into nervous giggles. As did everybody else. I was then frozen, exposed and simply unable to carry on. I remember the poem to this day. The teacher had a mean look in her eye, 'I can see we shall have to come back to you', she said.

But it was games that were the real hell. I hated the cold, the mud, the ugly, itchy games skirts, the communal showers. The plump flesh on my inner knees was always chapped. I was always put in goal, both on the hockey pitch and as defender in netball, probably simply because I was tall and in the lack of any sporting ability could at least serve as a physical barrier. But of course I ducked. Somewhere around the middle of my first term, I hung behind in the changing rooms. When the other girls had gone up to the netball pitches I put my clothes back on and walked out of school. It was frightening and exhilarating. Nobody noticed my absence. Truancy was off their radar.

I took off again one Monday when *Kubla Khan* had been set as poetry learning; it was a nightmare of sibilance. Nobody noticed. A few weeks later I woke up feeling sick. It was chemistry. I'd got 6% in the exams. A 'wake-up call' said the chemistry mistress, stoutly, but it felt like the sort of wake-up call that preceded a meeting with a firing squad at dawn. I left the house went to the station and took the tube into London and sat in Green Park where my school uniform couldn't identify me, reading poetry. I returned home at 4.30, wrote myself a sick note, added my mother's signature and began a life of truanting. I learned what every truant learns, that the more you miss the more you have to miss. I was soon way beyond what could be caught up and, of course, if I took the whole day off I missed lessons I liked and was good at too. Every time I returned some new fiction had to be developed. Notes came and went mostly from my mother to school but sometimes from my school ostensibly for my mother. I replied in concerned tones. I was of course alert to the problems my daughter faced; it was indeed a pity that such a potentially bright, if unpredictable, girl was a martyr to ill health. She was under the doctor. I started taking home clothes to change into in public lavatories so that I could stay in my own area without being interrogated by old ladies, and then I found the Kenco coffee bar where boys who were also escapees seemed glad to see me.

At night I couldn't sleep. I had developed a fear of choking on my own tongue. In fact it was more likely I would suffocate on my pillow as I had to lie face down so that my tongue would fall out of my mouth rather than snake down my throat. I put a book either side to stop my head rolling into a potentially lethal position. There were other books propping up my bed. My mother had always told me that if I sat on the bed to read it would break. Lolling with the bedspread on was particularly suspect; in her world beds were for sleeping, supine, under the covers. When the leg fell off I always suspected she had sabotaged it just to prove a point. Only *Debrett* was wide enough and robust enough to support the head of the bed. Later on – a surprisingly long time later, despite my efforts – it supported me losing my virginity. No other legs fell off.

My chemistry teacher had already thrown me out of the class, but in the summer of 1967 I failed physics, maths, and biology O Level. I got A grades in French, the two English exams and Art, and a B in history. The spring term before I took them was hot and while others sat in their revision classes, I had escaped to London and, short of money, had hung around Victoria station. I met two nice Frenchmen who bought me coffee and chatted a while. Then they suggested I would make a very good model: one of them was a photographer they explained. We went off to St James's Park and took some shots. Then they ran out of film and so we hauled back to a neglected apartment near the station. The silence and the lack of furniture started to alarm me. One disappeared and the other tried first seduction, then coercion and finally a knife to get me into bed, or rather on to floorboards. I could see no way that, having raped me, an unknown girl in an unknown place, he would not kill me. As I took my clothes off it was only my incessant wailing and runny nose that finally deterred him. I ran into the street naked under my dress with my underwear stuffed in my bag.

I went home to discover that nemesis had struck there too and done so with a certain ironical flourish. The unthinkable had happened. I had been selected for a school hockey team. Several girls were ill, and school honour required a side to be fielded. I was the only remaining girl who had experience in goal. The team list had gone up when I was reading in a rhododendron thicket in Richmond Park. When they tried to find me for special practice, I was being sexually assaulted. When they rang home, my mother thought I was in school and had no idea of my long career of infirmity. I was not, quite, expelled, but it was made clear that I was unwelcome. After my O Levels I left, and my parents faced trying to find another reasonable school for a girl who had no maths or science O Levels.

There was one corollary to my disgrace. One of the subjects that had suffered from my loathing of games was history which had unfortunately been timetabled on the same day as hockey. As the punishments were being doled out, Mrs Anderson, the history teacher, came up with something novel. She didn't put me in detention, she didn't make me copy out texts or learn two pages of dates, instead she gave me a book, Cecil Woodham-Smith's *The Reason Why*. 'Take it away, read it and review it for me', she said. I had no idea what a review was. 'Well,' she explained, 'you discuss how well it covers the topic, how successful the argument is, what its failings are if any.' It was the first time anyone had ever suggested that anything in a book wasn't unassailable fact and impregnable just because it was printed. There were books I didn't enjoy and books on a scale of worthiness which placed Enid Blyton's *Castle of Adventure*, which I had loved as a child but which was banned at school, at one end and Hardy's *Return of the Native*, my detested O Level text, at the other, and there were books that were almost in a category of their own elusive badness, like *Lady Chatterley's Lover*, but the idea that my judgement of a book might be something to be encouraged, and the book might be worthy but still not good was shocking and exciting.

It took me a week but I loved the task. I was seduced by the title for a start: we had, of course, learned Tennyson's *Charge of the Light Brigade* by heart, and it had only a modest quantity of s's and r's so was one of my favourites. But I was also fascinated by the rights and wrongs of the military action and the task of writing a review felt a long way from punitive. When she gave it back to me Mrs Anderson said, 'You're a very clever girl. It's your choice really. You can go on messing up your education or you can decide you want to use your talents. I think you could get to Oxford if you made that your ambition.'

It was just that there was so much else that was distracting.

My uncle and aunt were back from Italy. They now lived permanently at the Manor in Fairford. There were parties. His books were hugely successful, his recent screenplay had won awards. Their lives were incomparably glamorous, sensual and uncertain compared to home. My mother never appeared to be envious of her younger sister who had the figure, the money, the stays abroad; but I felt sorry for her and, in my heart, cross that she was fat. Actors, pop stars, novelists, film producers all arrived at the Manor clothed in a special incandescence that seen through my eyes left my own life smudgy and indistinct when they departed. One, a patrician actor in early middle-age, already famous for playing royalty and military officers, took me with him, back to his house in Little Venice. Again I found myself wrestling, this time on a sofa, but with the impediment of my hair piece which I had added to give me maturity and allure and which resistance threatened to reveal. With the hairpiece I might continue to appear twenty-three, as I had claimed, without it I thought I would instantly be exposed as the schoolgirl I actually was. 'Can you *please* keep your voice down; the nanny and the baby are trying to sleep', he said, irritably, as he fought to get his hand up my skirt. I obediently kept my protests to a whisper as he explained the sort of thing he had in mind.

The au pair's fiancé was another one. My aunt and uncle had the au pair for their four small children. When we stayed there, the fiancé, a naval officer, would sneak upstairs to the room I shared with my thirteen-year-old cousin. Again a tongue came snaking into my mouth, this time he undid my nightie buttons. I told my mother and so did my cousin. 'It's because you give off signals', my mother said irritably.

I still sat in cafés rather than the classroom but in March 1968 I joined the anti-Vietnam war rally at Grosvenor Square. I had had two serving US soldier pen friends for a while and then, shockingly, I only had one, who graphically described the death of the other. My mother actually found out about the protest and approved as she tacitly did about me missing games; it was my evasion of academic subjects that enraged her.

Unsurprisingly my uncle, so adept at screenplays, was very good at spectacles. Later that year we had grand fireworks on the gravel pit where my grandfather had built his house. The gravel pit was twenty years from its commercial aggregates life but had, like my grandfather in his own lifetime, undergone a process of transformation. It was now a beautiful and peaceful lake, where we punted in summer and everybody in the village played ice hockey when we had a heavy freeze. In spring willows trailed in the water's edge, and coot and moorhen built nests in coves and on small islands. On this autumn night it was foggy. My father and my uncle took out a punt and anchored it. The fireworks were mounted in bottles and nailed to the side. Then they abandoned it, rowing back in a small boat to light the fuses and put on Handel. All this the whole family watched from the shore. Even my grandmother was there wrapped in a car rug. It was chaos: more like a botched Viking funeral than the Royal Fireworks. On the second attempt they dropped their torch in the water and it sunk down, shining through the murk. It was still shining the following night while blackened cardboard rocket tubes bobbed on the water.

Six weeks later, four days before Christmas, I had a final screaming row with my parents about whether I could gatecrash a party. While my mother served chops for supper in Wimbledon and I packed my bags, intending to run away in the morning, my uncle was drinking with Peter O'Toole in Soho. Life was good. He set off home to Gloucestershire in his sports car. My cousin was staying overnight with us. We were all in bed when the telephone call came to say he had had a heart attack on the M4 at Slough and crossed the central reservation before dying in a head-on collision. He was forty years old. 'Slough,' said my aunt, 'SLOUGH for God's sake. A mortuary in Slough.'

We drove down that night – I took my already packed bag – past the crash site. It seemed as if we would never be the same again. We would never be happy or silly or spontaneous or safe.

On Christmas Eve, I sat next to my mother and assailed the great pile of Christmas presents around the tree, removing packages with To Daddy or To James with love. I don't know what happened to them. Perhaps they went to charity. The funeral was a couple of days after Christmas. I wore a black Chanel suit of my aunt's; it was the first time my mother had ever let me wear black. I had never felt more beautiful as I walked into the church behind the coffin. People looked. I saw Susannah Yorke – an actress whose blonde prettiness could only be enhanced by her deep black coat, but now pink-eyed with weeping. There was Christopher Plummer, a nice man and a handsome actor who had felt the full force of my seductive skill and never even appeared to have noticed, and numerous other figures still luminous with celebrity despite the circumstances. I hoped my uncle's gardener was there to see the suit. But it was different watching the coffin lowered deep into a wet hole under a bleak sky, and at night I cried in bed and dreamed of steering wheels impaling me while I remained all too alive pinned to the seat in the snow.

Oxford and the idea I might go there had somehow become part of a different world. The possibility once expressed and my failure to do anything but sabotage the idea had only made my mother sad and cross. I reverted to truanting type. I left my new school after only one year in the sixth form, although I took English A Level before going and got a grade A and even passed maths O Level and a subject called human anatomy, physiology and hygiene, which was science for people with no scientific ability at all. We drew plans of lavatories and plotted the life cycle of flies.

I worked as a nurse for a year or so; my plan was to go straight from qualification to Vietnam to work in a field hospital with wounded GIs, and I took A Level French, but it was clearly not going anywhere. I was a good nurse but even in nursing I disappeared when the going got tough. I fell in love with a patient, a young composer with TB. Our tendency to gaze at each other in troubled intensity was not always to our mutual advantage. One day looking into his eyes while injecting him, I stuck the needle through the skin between my thumb and forefinger straight into his thigh, pinning us together. It was more nauseating than romantic. But I was confused about everything: about him, about the suffering and deprivation that was all around me and about the revealed possibilities of sudden, arbitrary catastrophe, and I was too undisciplined and too physically clumsy to comply with all the professional rules. My aprons were grubby, I boiled the thermometers, I tried to smoke in the sluice and was sick, the stiff collars gave me a rash, I sat on patients' beds at night and chatted, I mistook shrouds for theatre gowns, I ate the ward's discarded puddings, I lost my hairgrips and my caps hung off. Given my feelings about blood it had never been an inspired career choice.

Three years to the week after my uncle's funeral, I married. I was twenty years old, and it was meant to make everything all right.

Chapter 7

England 1940s

Every time we say goodbye I feel I die a little.
Every time we say goodbye I wonder why a little.
I wonder why the gods above me
who must be in the know
think so little of me.
They allow you to go.

Cole Porter (1944)

The 1940s. Life is busy. The guns are out. Game birds drop from the sky to the Gloucestershire earth in a flurry of copper and soft brown feathers. On the third anniversary of the outbreak of war, in the first week of September 1943, a house-party and four days' shooting bags five hares, thirty-two-and-a-half brace of partridge, three pigeons, one corncrake, two stubble-cock and a rabbit. In Warsaw the Germans clear the ghetto, in Madrid Franco ousts the Falangists and in the USSR, the Germans are moving towards Stalingrad and have reached the banks of the Volga, north of the city.

There are movements at home too. My grandfather has been keeping another book to prove the fullness of his life. This time it is the record of his new existence at the Manor House, Fairford. It is a classy item:

sea-green padded Morocco leather, paint-washed endpapers, gilt-edged pages and fine blue lines inside. On the outside in a swirl of gold letters it says:

Visitors Book.

Family, friends and supporting players cross the pages and fill the rooms like the denouement of an whodunit. Jolly cousins, elderly parents, half a dozen Poles helping as beaters on the shoots, RAF officers from Hullavington, bevies of nurses and a trio of Yanks: Chandler, Harold and Walt, who are joined later by Steve from Three Toots, Idaho, and Rosalind from Granite City, Illinois. Chums with names like Rotter Randell and Bubbles Beatty and Potts-Lee dance to the band.

Buried among the columns of visitors are rare appearances by my grandmother. Dick is away at school, the girls are further away still, yet my grandmother is still returning to my grandfather long after their divorce is made absolute.

I have only seen a suicide letter once and it was long and eloquent. Every 'I' was not just lower case but so tiny it was scarcely more than a comma, an accidental mark on the page, a flaw in the paper. There was no more first person in that life; in the tiny i's an individual had already erased themselves from the record. I assume at some point my grandmother had written suicide letters, but as her attempts at suicide were officially termed unsuccessful, her written farewells, not required for any coroner's court, probably became an embarrassment to be thrown away. But there is something of the suicide in my grandmother's entries in the visitors' book; she has retreated even further; she only once refers to herself as 'I' at all.

My grandmother came and went like a ghost, writing herself in pencil among the egos of confident ink. She rarely left her name; usually she referred to herself in terms of absences: 'Homeless, nameless'; 'No tears'; 'No fixed abode'. Perhaps the woman whose beauty had been burned away, who had left her home and children, who had served in a foreign army and whose lover would eventually leave her for his wife and country, could only think of herself as an outline of nothingness. Without a name, she is only recognisable by her handwriting.

A flood of Americans and sophisticated London friends with four figure telephone numbers are soon ringing to fix a weekend in the country. In the country telephones have only arrived at two numbers.

'This is Kensington 8563. Can you get me Fairford?'

'Hello. Hello?'

'Trying to put you through, Kensington.'

'Hello, sweetie, it's Verna. How's the new house?'

'Oh wonderful. Marvellous. You should pop down? How's life in town?'

'London? Oh, quite impossible at the minute. We're dying to get away.'

My grandfather is desperately provisioning himself against a day on his own.

A friend from the Air Ministry signs in: Holborn 3434 ext. 806. Another gives an address at Durrants Hotel – these are restless times. Perhaps they are all joining Eric's poker school. Unwise of them as Eric is very good at poker. He is only bested by the local Catholic priest who has been trained since the seminary to keep a straight face and whose presence disarms the innocent.

Gerald Howard is now approaching his ninetieth birthday and undeterred by his daughter's departure enjoys a long weekend's free hospitality in October 1942. 'No fixed abode', he writes in his still proud hand, echoing his daughter's lament. Perhaps he likes it better without her around. Could he have been unaware how much she disliked him? Now he sits, a bearded Victorian patriarch, in the best chair, draped in his tweed cape. The Manor in war-time is not a warm house. His youngest daughter, Blanche de Rin, comes and goes, fleetingly, bringing his granddaughters to see him. At home her husband's life ebbs away.

Eric's siblings too enjoy their stays with the new man of property. Stuart comes with his latest fiancée, and Gwynneth returns from Bermuda; she is now living with Sidney at 26 Half Moon Street (Grosvenor 1575).

'Eric, it's Gwynnie . . . no, no, we're quite happy to share a room. Are there twin beds?'

There are fifteen or so for the Christmas holiday and Sally the dog and some seasonal pups. 'A fine house for a family man. Fully recommended for all waifs, strays, inebriates, lunatics and that ilk. Turkey, wine, whisky but shortage of gin', writes one of the guests.

A fine house for a family indeed. A dream of a house for a dream of a family. Eric has mislaid his wife, two of his three children have been in Rhodesia for three years and the third is at Wellington.

By January Stuart is back with a wife, and just after Easter there is a covey of cousins from the Sarson vinegar family in residence. The oldest member of this party signs his address 'Home Forces', the youngest, in careful loops, 'Teddie's school Oxford'. They bag five snipe, four partridge, twenty-four pigeons, two hares, seven pheasant, four rabbits, one plover, three teal. It is the twenty-fifth wedding anniversary of the cousins – '!congratulations!' – scribbled across a ditty and the picture of a jolly church:

> Wilt take this woman for thy wife
> Asked the marriage parson
> Why sure old bean – she's mine for life
> Said Henry Smalley Sarson.

For life, thinks Eric. Whatever that might mean.

In summer 1944 while the Allies battle down France from the beaches of Normandy and up Italy towards Rome, the HMT *Andes* comes into Liverpool docks. On board are my mother and my aunt. The girls have not been summoned back to England rather to their surprise, indeed there have been fewer and fewer communications since their father told them he was buying a much bigger house in Fairford and sent them a picture of himself looking very handsome, in a middle-aged sort of way, in a uniform. Still, after four years, they meet surprisingly little resistance from their hosts when they suggest that it is time to go home despite the fact that hostilities continue. Berths on a troop carrier heading from Cape Town to Liverpool are found for them, and a Miss Balmforth, returning to England, agrees to act as escort. A friend's mother takes them out and buys them clothes but apart from these they leave almost all their things behind. Nobody comes to say goodbye at the station as they start home, reversing the journey they made with their mother when they were little girls.

Partir, c'est mourir un peu – I think *not*, says my mother.

The troop ship, painted in camouflage grey, has none of the luxuries of the one-time cruise liner *Capetown Castle*. There is no first-class, dressing for dinner, bridge fours or stewardess service. Crammed into bunks, when they are not being seasick they are falling in love. Miss Balmforth is prostrated with *mal de mer* which leaves them free to put on lipstick and explore.

The city the girls return to is not the city they remember four years earlier. But then the girls are not the children they were earlier either; my mother is nearly sixteen. When the haze on the horizon turns incontrovertibly into the coastline of England they cry. They have dreamed of this moment for four years. Around them on the deck others are cheering and weeping: whatever lies ahead, they have finally come home.

Liverpool is grey. It is not just the cloudy day and the dull, dark sea under the overcast sky, the paint on the battleships or even the visible bomb damage after nearly seventy raids. The whole mood of the city has changed from the sparky, nervous excitement of the early war when they left it. War is now a way of life and the people, shabby and resigned, go about their business economically. There is no band this time, no waving crowd on the well-guarded quayside, in fact, for the girls, nobody on the quayside at all.

It is late in the day when they berth. They have their minds firmly fixed on Fairford where their parents have yet to know they are back. How surprised they will be. The only hotel they have ever heard of is the Adelphi so they go there and take a room, although they are not quite sure they can pay and there they make the telephone call to leave a message for their father that they will be home the following day. They have to ring his office as they don't have his new number. They turn off the lamps and peer out of the blackout curtains at the shocking darkness of Liverpool. Cape Town had sparkled with light at night. Cape Town had smelled green. Liverpool smells acrid and oily and of drains.

The next morning they scrape together the money to pay and go down to the station. The train is delayed by an air raid en route and they stand all the way.

Hours later the train comes into Oxford station. There are milling crowds on the platform and only when passengers and those meeting travellers have cleared away do they notice one man, an unfamiliar man, left standing by the station buffet. He stares at the two brightly dressed, badly made-up young women. They peer at the man who is, of course, too old to be their father. Soon they are the only people left on the station. Finally they move towards each other, my mother starts to cry in anticipation. 'Come on,' he says, by way of a greeting, 'quickly, I've got the wrong sort of petrol.' It is not the homecoming they had dreamed of.

My mother and her sister suddenly pop onto the page of the visitors book – 'Back from Bulawayo!' – the difficulties of their arrival home indicated only by them rightly locating themselves as guests. They have never seen the house before, or the housekeeper. The sleeping arrangements are a bit of a mystery. None of their things, none of the toys they left behind in 1940, have been brought to this grand Gloucestershire house. In fact there is nothing familiar at all. Nothing of them. Noticeably nothing of their mother. They have a photograph of her in the uniform of a Polish Officer – with medals – and they are proud she is doing·war work and they get a dog to compensate for other losses; losses the extent of which they have yet to discover. 'Riffle, his mark', my mother writes next to a large inky paw print.

Finally Eric gets my grandmother on the telephone at the Polish rest-house at Scarborough. He covers the receiver with his hand as he passes it to my mother. 'Persuade her to come home, old thing', he says.

It is two years since their divorce, not that the girls will find this out for another year. Eric has never quite managed to make life work since she left. He tries, but he gets the details wrong. In order to ingratiate himself with the local families of note, he distributes nylons to their womenfolk. This only clarifies, for those who had any doubt, that he is a black marketeer, and places him in the same league as the American soldiers from the base, importuning for sexual favours.

A few years later, when my eighteen-year-old aunt is longing to go to a dance but has no boyfriend, her father goes down to The Bull and solicits a partner from those drinking at the bar. He finds her a middle-aged RAF officer who happens to be passing by. But now, in 1944, my grandmother can plead her war work and everybody else is vague. The girls go to visit her in Scarborough and meet lots of handsome and friendly Polish soldiers.

Soon they will be packed off to boarding school. They will be placed in a special house with other girls from the colonies, so that they may re-learn being English. My mother hides her lipstick in a rolled-up pair of games socks.

And 1944 is the year of drama in the capital cities of Europe. Headline making, emotion stirring, as the war finally turns in favour of the Allies. They enter Rome on 4th June, marching down the ancient route of the returning Roman legions, the Appian Way. The following day General Mark Clark climbs the Capitol and addresses the city. On 25th August there is an outpouring of joy when Paris is liberated. Brussels is reached in early September, Athens freed on 14th October. While Paris celebrates, Warsaw, once called the Paris of the east, burns and her people are cut down in her streets. The Nazis are back in control by 3rd October.

News of the Warsaw uprising and its brutal suppression filter though to Britain only slowly. The Allies had been repeatedly entreated to aid the Polish Home Army but had done nothing. The Russians had sat within a day's travel of the capital but refused to move forward. The enormity of the news is too much to take in and most British disregard it; the war is progressing forward on too many fronts and most Englishmen couldn't place Warsaw on a map. It is the thrill of seeing the liberation of Paris that preoccupies the British press and lifts the hearts of the Allies. Even some Poles have their doubts. The city razed to the ground? The whole city? Why, yet again, did no one lift a hand to help them? They had done their bit to help Britain and Mr Churchill, God knows.

My grandmother and Wotzek climb the cobbled streets and walk along the Scarborough cliffs. The day is fine, but the autumn wind is cold and she wraps Wotzek's scarf right round her head; what with the thick layer of wool over her ears, the noise of the wind and the wheeling seagulls it is impossible to have a conversation. Now that they rarely talk at all about anything important, it seems funny that once they never seemed to draw breath. Once they stumbled in each other's language, desperate to communicate; now that they are fluent they are silenced by events. To talk now is to be on guard; the minefield of incendiary topics has stretched to cover too vast a territory. He still relaxes when she plays the piano but he seldom makes love to her and when he does he simply takes what he needs. Guilt and anger are strange, although hardly unfamiliar, bedfellows. She thinks of herself as at least half a Pole. He thinks of her as at least half the betrayer – they now know Britain and America agreed to a deal with the Soviets as early as 1943.

She travels south just before the war ends. Her father is finally dying, and she comes to see the children at school.

On 6th August 1945 an American plane named Enola Gay in a tribute to the pilot's mother drops an atom bomb called Little Boy on Hiroshima; two days later the Allies drop another bomb on Nagasaki. On 14th August Emperor Hirohito of Japan broadcasts the Japanese surrender. In Britain, it is late summer and in between the bombs and the capitulation which marks victory in the east, the shooting season begins. Eric reports that the weather is very hot, the company good and birds are plentiful (the Scrivens brothers, keepers, have ruled by fear and cunning throughout the hostilities and are still using Poles as beaters). Two Americans join the party. Fifty-five birds are shot. My grandmother returns briefly. Mother and children are united. As the long summer's day fades into a hazy, dusty evening, a harvest moon rises, and Stuart and his friend Tom go wild-fowling. Or so they claim. The narrow Thames curls out across the fields westwards from Lechlade between muddy banks and reed beds towards its source. Over the shallow Coln the willow trees reach across the stream, and half-submerged branches form jetties around which the current eddies. In the stagnant water of the crumbling old canal the rotten lock-gates, immobilised by briars and elder, still creak at the least wind. There are water birds a-plenty on this perfect night. Nevertheless, no bag is reported.

Over. It has all come to an end. Still, my grandmother sits down by the waters and weeps.

One day her ashes will be scattered over these little rivers and marshy fields where the ducks still cry mournfully as night comes.

It takes Helen, mistress to two generations, nominally French, to reflect the emotions of the world outside when she writes her entry that autumn when the weather has finally broken.

'Here are the dripping trees and all the green beauty I so longed for during the German occupation when our hearts were as parched as the country we lived in.'

Gerald Richard Howard, born right at the start of the Crimean War in a handsome house in Princes Gate overlooking Hyde Park, finally closes his eyes forever just days after the end of the Second World War. He dies a few miles north of his beloved Compton Place but he is not taken back to be buried with his parents in the churchyard at Chatsworth.

Princes Gate, Hyde Park, London

1946

Well before Christmas in 1946 it started to snow. The frost was so severe the week before Christmas itself that the windows were iced up every morning and the flagstones in the hall too cold and damp to walk on, even in socks. My grandmother comes back again for Christmas.

Eric throws a party. Like the girls, only with considerably less justification, Eric has persuaded himself that she might be back for good.

There are calls for the Poles to return to rebuild their homeland. Wotzek is bewildered by indecision, by a lack of any information, by standing at a crossroads with such a dislocation between his future and his past. But to support my grandmother and to reassure her he comes back to the Manor with her, to confront her life, to meet her children, to make Eric realise that she is gone for good, that, when they can, my grandmother and Wotzek will marry.

Eric has bought her a special Christmas present – the scent she used to love – and has, as usual, circumvented rationing by borrowing the girls new dresses from the shop. There is a wonderful Christmas tree right up to the ceiling. They are all eager to see her. But when she arrives nobody has expected the tired, sad-looking man with her. That night there is the worst row she has ever known. Having drunk the better part of a bottle of Scotch, Eric finally loads his shotgun, the girls shriek, Margaret tries to phone the police and Wotzek, already at the end of his tether, leaves. My grandmother runs out into the biting winter's night, trying to throw herself in the river. My mother, still a teenager, follows pleading and crying. A row of GIs sitting on the wall outside the pub shout cheerful encouragement. My grandmother slips on the bank of the Coln and sits down heavily in the mud with just her feet in the water and my mother sits down, next to her but never touching this loved and inconsolable stranger.

There must have been some resolution between them, at least in Eric's head because his wife – his *former* wife – is still there at New Year. He doesn't postpone the party. If they entertain together that could be the start of something new and at least they will be seen as a couple. Eric lists all the guests. In a different ink from the other names – perhaps he waited until afterwards when he could be sure she had been there – he adds, Joan, Eric and the band.

She is back again the following Easter and in the first person: 'Hullo and goodbye to Fairford I passed this way but left no mark. The Manor wasn't sorry, and so, perhaps, I earned its gratitude.'

The following year, in June 1946, comes the *coup de grâce*. The Victory Parade in London. A nine-mile column of troops who won the victory for the Allies: everyone from Americans to Greeks, Arabs to Australians, Czechs to Fijians. The air is cold and drizzly, but the thousands who march and the two million who watch are jubilant. They have survived. Victory is theirs. The Poles, however, who had fought so bravely on land and sea, who had suffered so greatly and done so much to help Britain win the war are nowhere to be seen. Not the pilots who brought down a third of the enemy planes in the Battle of Britain, nor the paratroopers who fought at Arnhem, nor the gunners who played a crucial role at Monte Cassino. Churchill has banned the Poles from attending the parade for fear of enraging his Russian allies. Poland is now within the Soviet sphere of influence, dominated by the men who, however much they have been silenced in speaking of it, the Poles know wiped out its officer corps in the Katyn Forest. Probably including Wotzek's younger brother and his two cousins. Churchill says if the Poles want to march they should do so in Moscow. They are all allies now, after all; they have all fought for the same cause; they are all rejoicing to the same end; they all have the same vision for Europe. It is time, the politicians all agree, for the Poles to look forward and go home.

Most Poles resist the inducements of the politicians and the opprobrium of large sections of the press and stay put in England. They are trapped. Their public popularity is declining now that they are out of uniform and out of Spitfires and competing for British jobs, but they are nervous of a return to a regime which is not so much unknown as all too well-known for its brutality and the summary nature of its justice. So they stay, trying through every channel to find out what has happened to their families. Some are found in North Africa – several thousand are in camps there. Wotzek hears a rumour that his wife remained in Poland but went to live with her parents. A few months later some Poles choose repatriation. Better to take their chances in Poland than to be despised and unwanted in England. After the Victory Parade Wotzek makes his decision. He will return to Poland

My grandmother and Wotzek, 1946

and see if he can sort out his marriage. But first he has to find his wife who has been silent for four years. Surely my grandmother can understand, as a parent herself; he must know what has happened to Tadeusz. They had been at a concert that night, Chopin, indifferently played before he told her, and she had found herself trying to head off any conversation because she already sensed the enormity of what was to happen.

He leaves by train, and she never hears from him again. He returns to a Poland that is a different place from the country he left and, like so many, he simply disappears. Sometimes she wonders if it was all just an excuse and he is still somewhere in England. Either way he is lost to her.

A month later my grandmother is stood down. She folds up and returns her uniform but tucks her medal in her case. She kisses her boys, who had become her family, goodbye. Romek, Pavel and Jan will now fight a bigger battle to start resettlement, as they call it in England and Scotland. The Poles will go it alone. Well, apart from the couple who are marrying nice Scottish girls and are young enough to have a whole life in front of them to shape as they will. She too is all alone and is only prevented from absorbing the frightening reality of her position, her isolation, her lack of any future, by the numbness she feels after Wotzek's departure. She aches and aches for him. For months she waits for a letter but none ever comes. But then he wouldn't know where to find her. *Partir, c'est mourir.*

Her marriage is long over, her home is gone and the war finished. Her children are all at school, her lover has left her, even her old father is dead. She is also well into her forties. Without a war she has, quite simply, nowhere to go, nothing to be. She goes to stay temporarily with the widowed Blanche. Blanche has meagre funds and is living in a tiny flat in Watford with her children. One day, while Blanche is out and Blanche's two girls are at school my grandmother carefully folds two tea towels, puts them on the bottom of the oven, removes the racks, lays down her head and turns on the gas. Like everything else she tries, it doesn't quite work out. Instead, Blanche finds her and is furious at her selfishness. My grandmother lies with her face to the wall in her tiny bedroom until the doctor arranges her admission to the psychiatric ward of the local hospital. They raise her dose of sedatives. When she is discharged she finds a job through one of her better connections and becomes housekeeper to a titled family in London. It is a good thing, she thinks, wryly, that her father didn't live to see her in service. Sometimes one or other of her children comes up from Oxford to see her and they go to a concert, or she makes tea in the basement kitchen.

On better days she is calm but often she is panic-stricken or muddled. People make her frightened. She is getting thin and she cries a lot and although by day she is exhausted, occasionally she wakes up at night, and for a while she feels an electric sense of hope. She goes to see a private psychiatrist, and he gives her intravenous injections that induce a sort of fit. Often as she lies recovering in his consulting rooms she is sick and her hands and arms are always bruised from the needles.

Sometimes when she lies between sleep and wakefulness she remembers the tombs her father took Rachel and her to as little girls. It was a long journey. On the top the tombs were shiny black marble and had statues and armour but underneath were the figures of withered corpses, their shrouds fallen apart to expose the stone worms, the collapsed ribs, the bone fingers, the awful empty eye sockets. These are the Cavendishes, your family, your ancestors, he said. And that was my cousin Freddy – he indicated a plaque on the wall – murdered by the damned Fenians. Rachel nodded as if she knew who the Fenians were and agreed they were without doubt damned. Their grandma and grandpapa weren't in the church; they lay outside in the churchyard. So did the bad duke, papa's uncle. As they walked out across the grass Rachel saw a poor dusty worm and threw it at her sister; when my grandmother squawked Gerald gave her one of his looks. I shall be here, said her father, pointing vaguely at a tree somewhere in the vicinity of his mother's grave. My grandmother thought he might be a magpie, looking quite fine in his feathers as he hopped along the branches but not always very nice in character.

Now in her narrow bed she positions herself like one of those memorials. She lies on her back with her arms folded, her toes together. Wotzek always said she made so little noise asleep that sometimes he panicked thinking she was dead and woke her up. She takes the tiniest, shallowest breaths, she pictures the blood slowing in her capillaries, her extremities becoming cold, her heart just trembling. Perhaps if she just lies there she will simply cease to be without any further effort on her part. She will slowly turn to stone.

She takes chloral at night but it gives her violent, nauseous dreams and the mornings are worst of all, dragging her from furthest sleep to another day of desperation. As consciousness seeps back, dread and despair flood in.

She tries again. Dying is not as easy as she'd imagined. This time she uses her pills and she is admitted to a mental hospital: St Andrew's at Northampton. At St Andrew's it is not just a matter of containment and sedation. They are determined to make her well again. Nothing will stand in the way of recovery. They have many post-war psychological casualties on their wards, but she is iller than most. For the first time she is properly diagnosed, not with 'nerves' but with manic depression. This means, says a kind young doctor, that it is really not her fault. She was just born this way. He asks her about Geraldine, Ethel and Rachel and he writes it down busily; he seems almost excited, though he tries to be solemn. They give her barbiturates to make her sleep for some days.

When she wakes up they propose to try quite a new treatment on her. This treatment, the doctor explains, may seem a little frightening, but they have seen some very impressive results, and she is in good hands. She must learn to trust them. This is hard because earlier the doctors tried insulin treatment on her, and it was so awful she thought that she would die. Indeed she did nearly die, sweating, nauseated and thrashing around while she was being put into a coma, and they hastily had to bring her round. This new treatment is called ECT. She lies on a bed with straps around her middle and a rubber gag in her mouth. Two nurses soothe her while the doctor places some paste, then a device with a band round her head. Then – bang – and her world is blown apart. It seems as if she comes back a long time later. Her arms and legs ache and she has dried blood and saliva on her chin. They do this to her three times a week.

My mother at Oxford, 1947

All three children are now at Oxford. Dick is at Oriel, my mother at St Anne's, Susie at the Ruskin College of Art. Meanwhile my grand-father is making things better the only way he knows how. He is controlling the planet. Specifically, he is digging. It is not enough to own land and farms; as far as he can see (at least if he stands in the right place to obtain this gratifying view) he needs, like a decadent Roman emperor, to change the very landscape he inhabits. Under his fields there is gravel, and now he begins the wide-scale extraction that will bring us all, even me, as yet unborn, a comfortable life. Not all his tenant farmers are as excited by this as he is. They would rather keep sheep and pigs and sow barley, but post-war there is a great demand for aggregates; new roads, new housing, repair of cities, expansion of airports and docks. It is almost a public duty to provide it. If there is some irony in his setting himself up against the backdrop of his family's agricultural roots and then destroying the very land he has used to create his identity, he does not appear to see it.

The top layer of grass is peeled back. The earth is set aside, and then the wet gravel is scooped from the ground, deeper and deeper. Where once there was a river plain of ragged pasture and small woods, wide areas of water spread east. As each lake is scoured of its minerals, the process begins again in a new field. The newly created lakes have dangerously steep sides and are greenish white and still. A teenager on a tractor passing too close falls in and is drowned. The main road is also plastered with white mud and from it skeleton-like conveyors project above the trees. Despite this, my grandfather has become a character in local eyes. Many of them are fascinated by him. He is rich. He is eccentric. He paints. He wears cravats. He has a big, glistening car and sometimes young women. He is a brilliant raconteur. He is tall and broad and fond of shocking the timid. When my mother and my aunt bring smart boyfriends to dine at the Manor he says, regular as clockwork, 'I made my money peddling ladies' knickers down Watford High Street, you know.'

This new man, this post-war entrepreneur, has no need of a Morocco leather-covered visitors' book, and it is abandoned in 1950.

Two of the last visitors are a puzzle. One weekend in July, Willard Price, ostensibly a travel writer but thought by many to be an American spy, and Sir Esmond Overy arrive together to stay. Overy uses his formal title in his entry. They do not fish, they do not shoot, they do not dance. Perhaps they came to play poker at The Bull.

My grandfather is willing – wealth is more lustrous if garnished by conspicuous generosity – to assist his sister-in-law Blanche, whose widowhood has left her very hard up, even though he has lost hope of repossessing her sister. He employs her in the shop and offers to buy a fine Italian painting which had belonged to her late husband. He doesn't let sentiment divert his business sense, however, and picks it up at a price he can hardly believe. He congratulates himself all the way home; it's not often one can feel good about one's motives. The eighteenth-century carved frame is, if anything, more beautiful than the painting, a fact that has not passed him by. He cuts out the oil and spray-paints the frame gold and uses it for a witty display of shoes in the Watford store.

One month after she was twenty-one my grandfather walked my mother up the aisle. My father was not one of the smart boyfriends nor was he the sort of clever, pushy man my grandfather admired. He was simply ordinary and rather nice. My mother had waited until she no longer needed the permission her father had refused to grant. She had left Oxford without her degree. She made her choice. In the photographs she is walking up the path where one day forty or so years later, her coffin will be carried on an equally fine day. Shopkeepers stand outside their premises as the big cars glide up the marketplace; women hover outside the church for a peek.

Snap, and they are caught for ever just outside the church.

In October 1949 my mother looks abundantly healthy with a shy smile and thick, dark curls. My grandfather too is smiling widely with closed mouth: more Clark Gable than Dr Freud on this occasion. He

My mother's wedding, 1949

looks slick, strong, in control and magnanimous. He was not often forced to hand over his property to other men. As they paused in the porch he whispered to her, 'Don't worry, my dear, you're not getting yourself into anything a good lawyer can't get you out of.' He congratulates himself on changing his will to distance his money from the new couple. My mother's brocade dress with sweetheart neckline, her froth of veil and headdress had all been borrowed from the store in Watford. Her single string of pearls was a present from my father.

They returned to the Manor for the reception. The following week the local paper reported it all with delight: the bride's grandmother, Lady Fanny, was a sister of the Duke of Devonshire (my grandfather had compressed two generations in the interests of clarity); her uncle was the well-known artist and cricketer; her aunt, the Countess de Rin, had given her some priceless monogrammed linen; the couple were to honeymoon in the south of France (another imaginative excursion of my grandfather; they were actually staying in Newcastle). Titles, men in uniform, expensive presents; it was a post-war dream. I have the cutting. On the reverse is a report of the trial of a Captain Peel of Charlton Kings for the murder of his wife. Considerable understanding was evinced by the court on hearing that the captain was suffering from schizophrenia following his wounding and shell-shock during the war. He was ordered to be detained during His Majesty's pleasure.

Unreported by any paper, the bride's mother lay on a bed on the top floor in what had once been the maid's bedroom throughout the proceedings. She had come to the wedding; she had bought a new hat and her old lamb coat, but had not managed to hold everything together. By late morning they had to restrain her and call in the doctor. While her husband and children left for church and when her eldest daughter returned, a married woman, to celebrate two floors below, she slept, heavily sedated, in the company of a nurse. She only woke once to wave giddily from the window as my mother came out in her going-away outfit and my father drove them off. Nobody looked up and saw her.

Chapter 8

Berlin

My mother came to stay when my son was born in Berlin, and we invited my grandmother along. She was surprisingly adamant in her refusal. After the operation she was rarely forceful about anything. But she knew she didn't want to see Berlin divided. Later she did come to visit me when I was living in a pretty medieval town in West Germany. It appeared that she no longer spoke or understood German. My mother, at school in the war, never had; her repertoire was confined to the language of film Nazis. On the third day my grandmother, now in her seventies, fell over inside her locked hotel room. My mother flailed at the reception desk: 'Mein Mutter is kaput' and then, when they were slow to respond, 'Oh Donner and Blitzen', exasperated, 'Mein. Mutter. Kaput. En haut.'

But this time my grandmother was unequivocal. She didn't want to see the ruins and she didn't want to hear about new architecture and young spirit; to her Berlin was gone. For once quite animated she described travelling in Germany between the wars and the graceful beauty of Unter den Linden, the great thoroughfare that ran across the city, edged with limes, and with the handsomest of the city's buildings running along each side. She talked about taking a boat on the Spree with German friends on a breezy spring day.

None of this could be seen in 1972 when I arrived into the Cold War, seven months married and seven months pregnant. We had travelled only once as a couple – on our honeymoon to Paris, four days before Christmas. It rained, and we went to see *Diamonds Are Forever*, in English. The high point of my honeymoon was the wonderful smell of the hotel soap. By the third day I was so homesick, and money was so tight that we returned to England. Still, I was already pregnant by then.

Coming in to Tempelhof Airport, next summer, the plane descended to pass down the Berlin corridor at the prescribed height, at which level it lumbered about between blocks of flats where Berliners tucked into their evening meal behind rows of pot plants. If my first sight of Berlin was its citizens at that most universal activity: eating; the second was a fascist masterpiece, the long, tall airport hall, designed by Hitler's architect, Speer. I had seen it in staccato newsreels, with long banners bearing swastikas and the sound of cheering troops. Then we were off through the streets to the British officers' club. That first night was intensely humid, and I gazed out of the window at the monument of the eternal flame, burning until the city was re-united. This felt momentous. Here I was with my soon to be born baby on a hot night at the troubled heart of Europe. In the early hours of the morning there was a storm and during it the freak rainfall put out the flame.

Home. Berlin. A place where ideology was a spectacle. Where the complexities of post-war settlements had woven a sticky web of rules and myths and demanded set-piece dramas in which we all played a part. Home. A solid semi-detached house in Spandau in a middling kind of street, with plane trees and cobbles and an air of quiet respectability. There were regulations about car-washing, bush-planting, tree-pruning, radio-playing, snow-clearing and days prohibited for hanging out washing. I always thought that it must be intolerable to be in an occupied city, with the occupiers lording it about in uniform, with money and bad accents, imposing their regulations, but perhaps it helped that Germans were already so adapted to a life of rules.

Berliners now only in middle-age had heard the rallies, joined the party, fought on the eastern front, bombed Coventry, been widowed, lost their sons, been boy-soldiers in the last desperate defence of the city. They had seen their capital destroyed by bombs and heavy artillery, carved up among the victors. Soviet troops with long memories and vengeance in their hearts were the first to enter the city, and in the last terrible days of the war the fate of thousands of Berliners, particularly its women, mirrored the fate of the city of stone.

Berlin had been punished for the sins of a nation. The new capital was at Bonn. But western Berlin had been patched up; it was an evolving city with exciting new quarters and a young population enjoying the financial inducements to live there. There were a few awkward memorials, it is true, all the more powerful because of the indecision about their future: the large deserted mansions, their drives overgrown, their gates secured with hefty chains, which fell, decade by decade, into desuetude, waiting for absentee Jewish owners who might still appear, having survived against all odds, to claim their property, and a speckle of shrapnel marks on the few surviving pre-war public buildings, but mostly it looked energetically forward.

The place where I spent my first night was Theodor-Heuss Platz. From 1933 to the end of the war it had been Adolf-Hitler Platz. Other streets still bore the names of the long-gone Prussian court. There was Hohenzollernring and Friedrichstrasse and quiet leafy Fürstenweg in Spandau, the street where we lived. Spandau was dominated by the prison, spot-lit by night like a castle on a Bavarian crag. It had been built for 600 miscreants, but now only one prisoner lived out his days there, guarded in careful rotation by officers and soldiers of each of the four Allied powers. Humanity demanded that the partially demented old man be kept in kinder conditions; economics certainly did, but the right to control the prison in turn suited all the Allies: the Russians crossed from the east to share the duty with the British, French and

Americans. Rudolf Hess, once Hitler's deputy, had been there for thirty-one years and it would be another fifteen before his death, allegedly by suicide.

There were protocols. Russian spy cars with dark windows circulated around West Berlin just as ours, equally recognisable, drove around the east. Fighter planes buzzed the suburbs, and every day a junior officer boarded the train to the west, a train with no purpose beyond maintaining the right for it to travel those long kilometres across eastern Germany. 'Do not put your head out of the window', notices instructed. On Friday crates of rations were delivered to every military family, not because food was currently limited but to disperse stockpiles maintained to prevent a Soviet blockade, as they reached their storage limits. The blockade of 1948, only broken, at some cost, by a prolonged airlift, had provided lessons in precaution and paranoia.

I spoke German, and though I was rarely spoken to *by* Germans I could eavesdrop around the city. But what did the Germans think now? I never knew. Some nights there would be massive military exercises. Berlin was waiting for the Russians to cross over the border with their tanks and sweep up the little enclave of West Berlin, so prosperous, so confident, so western, sitting 166 kilometres on the wrong side of the iron curtain. Our whole way of life was predicated on this, and the armies of three nations were kept ready. In the early hours of the morning when there was an exercise, an armoured car would rumble through residential areas, calling in troops: 'Alert. Alert. Rocking Horse. Rocking Horse.' It passed over the cobbles with an accelerating roar still broadcasting as it passed into other, distant roads. 'Alert. Alert.' In the bedrooms of military quarters men jumped into uniform and were off. Arc lights, engines, heavy vehicles, formations, arms, trucks; everything went on the move grinding through the dawn streets. In their bedroom my two babies would cry. They had nightmares about marching monsters called Left Rights for years and years. But away from the barracks each time there was an exercise some troubled German would think it was the Russians again for real and jump to their death.

And then there was the wall. Getting lost in Berlin was an impossibility; every wrong turning eventually led to a cement and wire dead-end. One hundred and ninety-two streets were cut short by the wall. The majestic Brandenburg Gate, surmounted by its chariot of winged victory, was no longer a gateway on Berlin's finest avenue, but a fortified barrier. Beyond ran a now dreary stretch on Unter den Linden, minus the Linden themselves which had been destroyed during the war. At checkpoints the political chaos found its Babel voice; signposts displayed a mantra for the city.

> ## YOU ARE LEAVING
> ## THE AMERICAN SECTOR.
>
> ## ВЫ ВЫЕЗЖАЕТЕ ИЗ
> ## АМЕРИКАНСКОГО СЕКТОРА
>
> ## VOUS SORTEZ
> ## DU SECTEUR AMERICAIN
>
> ### SIE VERLASSEN DEN AMERIKANISCHEN SEKTOR

I never knew why the local population only merited small capitals but the notices were redundant anyway; the barbed wire, guns, uniforms and fortifications made it clear that you were approaching a significant spot. Going West to East without papers was more or less impossible by the 1970s. Before then, before the actual brick and wire wall went up in 1961, if you strayed into the Russian sector from the West it meant arrest and imprisonment and release on payment of a fine. Going East to West was always another matter. It was simply forbidden on pain of death.

By 1970 there was a routine. If you had military status, and that included wives, you could put in for permission from your HQ. You drove up to the American checkpoint in a car with a driver. The Americans processed foreigners travelling east. Papers and permits were checked, advice given. The gate was lifted. You drove up to the East German post and then, as the armed border guard half-heartedly signalled the car to stop, you drove on. The Allies did not recognise the DDR – the German Democratic Republic; the East German guard, who knew that was how it went, stepped back into the warmth of his guardroom. Day after day pretending to stop cars. Further ahead was the Russian checkpoint. An officer stepped out. The car stopped. You held your passport up to the window and as he indicated with a right to left movement of his hand, you turned over the pages. On my second journey, the Russian signalled that I should get out. 'Nein', said my German driver, who had won a medal on the eastern front. Or let the window down? 'Nein.' My driver kept gazing forward. The officer stepped round. He bent over. He must to speak to the passenger. 'Nicht möglich.' Behind him a young conscript was trying not to laugh. A stand-off. I smiled. At everybody. As always. 'Strichjünge', muttered my driver, very quietly, despite the medal. Our breaths on the windows started to condense. Every time I looked to the left, there was this chest a few inches from the glass. Eventually I wound my window down a few inches and cold air knifed in. He put his face, rather awkwardly, side on to the crack and his breath smelled of beer. 'You are very beautiful, Madame', he said. He had a magnificent great coat but young grey eyes and chapped cheeks under the low brim of his hat. He stood up and waved us on.

Of course except for officials, the process the other way – East to West – was lethal. There were platforms on the western side where you could look down on it all, presumably so you could count both your blessings and the cruelties of communism: no man's land, barbed wire, dogs, electric cables, mines, watchtowers, armed border guards and the wall itself; virtually impregnable, ninety-six miles of it enclosing West Berlin. Those few who made it across were the stuff of legend as were the extraordinary contrivances which assisted their crossing: gliders, hidey-holes in petrol tanks or under fake floors in lorries, rafts, diving gear, cars without superstructures. Those who failed also entered a kind of immortality on the western side. In Bernauer Strasse in the French sector the wall was made by the frontage of an apartment building, bricked up overnight on 13 August 1961, so fast that curtains had been caught in the interstices of breeze blocks and mortar. As the soldiers thudded upstairs shouting and plastering, some occupants leaped out of the windows, often to their deaths; deaths marked by plaques on the street which lay in the west below. People, usually young men – who had been children when the wall went up, to whom life in the free west was an ideal not a memory – were still trying to get across in the 1970s. When – rarely – they succeeded, a bell was rung in the American sector. When they failed they died. Despite the evidence of fantastic exhibits in the museum at Checkpoint Charlie, they were not all killed trying in ingenious disguise or trying to climb the wall or crashing through checkpoints; many were drowned, or shot and subsequently drowned, trying to swim the River Spree, the Havel, or the Teltow or Britzer Zweig Canal. Two fell through the ice on the Griebnitz Lake on a bitter December day. The last person to die simply left a little too soon; soaring upwards in a home-made air balloon before tumbling to his death in March 1989. Eight months later the wall came down as suddenly as it went up, again catching the world asleep and a way of life, an immured, small world of suspicion and containment, of watching and being watched, came to an end.

Berlin was surrounded by water: huge lakes and small rivers. The city may have been largely destroyed in 1945 but the water and the forests remained Berlin's great beauty. In the late nineteenth century members of the prosperous German upper-middle classes had built great summer villas here, with pleasure gardens running down to the water. Some of the most successful of these merchant families were Jews who lived in greater numbers in Berlin than any other German city. Now, at weekends, Berlin took to the boats on the Havel, as it always had, bobbing about in small flotillas or following the banks with a picnic; it could be chaos on a hot day as families escaped the heat. Escape in the east held a different meaning. The eastern banks, as green and pretty as the ones enjoyed on the opposite shore, were deserted. The eastern stretches of the Havel were still and empty. A row of dark buoys marked out the border.

The Glienicke bridge, repaired after the war, crossed the Havel and the border. It always seemed long and narrow, its rusty metal struts familiar from numerous spy films. When I think of it now it is in mist and monochrome, such is the power of the cinema, not the browns, greens and greys of reality. But real spies crossed here too, stepping out from under the East German flag and starting the long walk to the west with guns at their back as others stepped forward and began their journey home from the Federal German Republic to the German Democratic Republic.

On my first trip to East Berlin I went to a winter fair, where wooden nativity scenes, tin pans and rabbit hutches were on sale. I dressed as the films suggested I should: as a cross between Anna Karenina and Catherine the Great. Red fox fur coat and fur hat. It was a good look in my Spandau bedroom. It was a good look walking to the car while snow squeaked under my boots. Over the wall I stuck out like a sore thumb. I was a target for American speakers everywhere. 'Hi, heated lady', said a man selling roasted nuts, in a conversational tone of voice. '*Toller Vorbau*', his friend muttered from a doorstep. 'Crazy horse', shouted a group of teenage boys and then 'Elvis Presley' as an afterthought. There was little to say in reply. I sat in a park and waited for black marketeers to come and offer me an illegal currency exchange. We had been warned. Nobody came near though some shouting continued. No black marketeer worth his ambitious Ostmarks would approach such a glaringly obvious trap.

There was, famously, opera in the east. Western diplomats and army officers would pass through the checkpoints in evening dress and through the unlit night streets of the east in their chauffeur-driven cars. It was easy to feel smug in the possession of street lamps, garages and bright advertising hoardings just half a mile away. The opera house was aflame with lights and the reds and golds of mess dress; the rest of the eastern city was dark and bleak. Blocks of utility flats, *Plattenbau*, constructed out of pre-fabricated sheets of concrete, looked to the future but all around were the piles of bulldozed rubble, vacant, burned churches, crags of once great buildings looking to a much nearer past. From a western perspective it was as if virtue resided in tidying up the war and that the poverty of life in the east was revealed in their carelessness about living in the ruins of a battle lost.

In the west they had their own memorials but they were those of art and sentiment, contained and respected. In November 1943 Allied bombers had destroyed one of Berlin's most famous churches. Now the inside the ruined interior of the Kaiser Wilhelm Gedächtniskirche – the memorial church – was one of the most peaceful places in the heart of West Berlin. In the remaining tower images of Prussian royalty in burnished gold and rich-coloured mosaic gestured upwards to where the decoration fused into charred masonry.

Once a year we had grand Allied dinners. The Russians were not invited. At one, in the French sector, I sat next to a smiling German Luftwaffe officer in late middle-age. He spoke first-class English and I asked if he had visited Britain. He loved Britain; he had been to the Lake District, Bath, Glastonbury – 'I think it comes from Germany your story of King Arthur and his knights' – Hadrian's Wall, Scotland, and London. 'Well,' he corrected himself, 'that was my second visit. The first time I go to London I bomb it.' He smiled. Perhaps I looked surprised. 'Ah', he said. 'I think everybody else has told you they were away on the eastern front'. They had. 'Believe me,' he said suddenly very serious, 'nobody who talks about the war in the east was ever really there. If they were there, they do not speak about it at a dinner party.'

'Do you mind – about all this – about us, I mean?' I asked clumsily, indicating the room with a vague wave. I could have meant having to go out to dinner in a hot uniform and eat boeuf bourguignon and cherries jubilee, but he understood. 'Well, we have had twenty-seven years, four months and – uh,' he did a quick calculation, 'thirteen days, to get used to it.'

The Wives' Club was another army institution. In keeping with the mood of the city, the club element in the name, implying a certain recreational and voluntary element, was deceptive. For an officer's wife, however young and disaffected, it was compulsory. My mother's faint exhortations that, given my history of protest, I might not find military life entirely congenial, were at first redundant. It was all fascinating; it was fascinating to watch this society within a society and it was fascinating to watch myself in it. For someone who was not yet quite out of adolescence it also presented undreamed of opportunities for rebellion, cheaply, easily; the simplest prop would do. The *Guardian* taken into the Mess and read idly; a miniskirt and bare legs. I said with careful nonchalance that I didn't think I could accompany my husband on a posting to South Africa or the southern states of America because of apartheid. It introduced a certain coolness into the room, but I trembled as I spoke. In the Wives' Club I was third in command. First came the CO's wife, then the adjutant's wife, then me. After that, but really in control of the whole project, was the sergeant major's wife. She came from a service family and was trained to drive a truck should the Russians come. After that were the soldiers' wives with their babies and their domestics and their homesickness. More stories were told in the Officers' Mess of soldiers, their wives and their sexual adventuring than of any battlefield glories.

From outside they seemed to fall into two categories. There were the small, under-nourished sort, who got into trouble, largely after drinking, lurked about holding cigarettes between finger and thumb and had fearfully young wives who looked pale and bewildered.

Unmarried, these were the soldiers who, it was said, asked for postings to the Far East when they found themselves with a handful of local girls all pregnant at once. Mother and daughters were a favoured variant. It was widely believed that when they went on exercise the wives put OMO packets in their windows to signify they were On My Own. They never *were* on their own, of course, what with the other wives in their closely packed flats and the pushchair loads of children and the SAAFA welfare officers. Less Trojan in their intrigues were the fit career men who spoke in acronyms, did sport, and bought tax-free cars and large stereo systems. These had trim wives who used the PX in the American sector for value and had sons with cropped hair who were already being toughened up.

I was eight months pregnant with my first child when the Wives' Club went on its late summer outing. The heat had lain heavily on the city for weeks. Some afternoons I simply lay in a bath of cold water with a book balanced on my large stomach and lime cordial standing on the soap dish. The Wives' Club had decided to go to see a historic monument. They had done the seventeenth-century Charlottenburg Palace, they were too nervous of an incident to go east, George Grosz was in exhibition at the National Gallery, which ruled that out, and anyway there were the children, and the zoo had been widely condemned two years before as being less good than the one in Glasgow. So they chose the Plötzensee Prison. To be followed by a finger buffet.

Where else? This low brick building set in pretty gardens had been the site of execution of scores of opponents of the Nazi regime, many women, some very young. Among numerous others were protagonists of the attempt on Hitler's life, hanged with piano wire and filmed for Hitler's later viewing. Usually the condemned were guillotined. Flowerbeds surrounded an urn which contained earth from each concentration camp, with the names of them all inscribed on the outside. Inside, the building was cool after the August heat. A large, high room, with arched windows, was the execution chamber. It had been left as it had been in use and in appearance fell somewhere between a medical facility and a factory. Horror, for me, resided as much in the clinical half-tiling and small hand-basins as in the meat-hooks still suspended from a beam. I felt light-headed, sweaty and rushed out to be sick among the memorial flowers.

If I was not a great success as a member of the Wives' Club, I was probably even less so as a wife. I had one child after nine months of marriage and another a year after that. My husband was away in Northern Ireland and slightly older officers would drop by of an evening to see if I needed help with the boiler. If the British Army had wanted to protect the virtue of regimental wives, they could have done so simply by installing modern boilers. Ours stood vast and unpredictable, wearing its gauges like campaign medals in its own room in the cellar and another room was full to the ceiling with damp coal to feed it. When my husband was on exercise I was too scared to go down to the cellar and I kept the door locked so that nothing could come up. By day I would walk in the Berlin Grünewald – the green wood, with my daughter sleeping in a pushchair and my son stamping in puddles with shrieks of pleasure, or running through drifts of fallen leaves, or excited at the sight of a red squirrel. Most days we would end up at Toc H and have a cup of tea.

But as winter drew in I became more lonely. My husband was away, the days were short and cold. I had become very thin after my last baby, and I always seemed to be tired. I woke up early every morning but sometimes I never managed to get anything done all day. I felt oppressed by the house, by the city, by my life. The wall around me seemed to get higher and higher. One of the agreements of the Allied occupation was that they should employ civil workers. I had a *Pützfrau* – a cleaner – for six hours a day. This felt more like surveillance than help, although she was a harmless, round, short widow with four adult children. Her soldier husband had been missing since the Battle of Stalingrad but she believed he was still alive. Sometimes she thought he was a prisoner of 'those verdammt Russians', other times that he had been ensnared by just one Russian – an Olga or Svetlana who wanted a good German husband of her own. Getting the house untidy enough for her to clean was an uphill task, even with two small children, especially as I was so often out in the woods. The cleaner really wanted to look after the children: she was very keen on my older child, a large blonde boy, but much less interested in his rather fragile, black-haired little sister.

Regulations meant that I had to get permission to leave and that I could not hold a bank account. To shop in the city centre or have my hair cut I had to use a chauffeur employed by the garrison. Increasingly Berlin felt like a prison not a dark adventure.

One day in January 1974 an East German border guard took a fellow guard hostage and attempted to get through Checkpoint Charlie. He was shot. In spring an escalation in tension between the superpowers brought MiG fighters screaming over the western city. My daughter wailed in her pram every time one swept over the garden until it was easier to leave the pram in the dining room. On some days I found that I hadn't got round to getting dressed, but my Frau was happy and encouraged me to lie on the sofa listening to *Rhapsody in Blue* while she dressed my son in strangely formal clothes she had brought from her home. When my husband returned it was to a wife who had retreated. I never knew myself how I would feel from day to day and for him I had become unpredictable and inaccessible. Unsurprisingly he took to spending evenings in the mess. The CO's wife came to see me and explained in firm but kindly terms that I was missed at the Officers' Club: 'Some of the Wives are asking after you', and that as an officer's wife I was supposed to set an example and that it was generally a bad thing to let my husband believe he was single.

Roles were so prescribed in army life that as long as you continued to fulfil expectations, more or less, nobody noticed anything wrong at the core of an individual. Just one friend had suggested I needed help. I went on a visit home and saw my mother's doctor who instantly saw there was a problem. I was, for a start, terribly thin. I also couldn't stop crying. 'Post-natal depression', she said. 'In your case, given what you've told me: two children within a year, second one with worrying health for a time, largely absent husband, far away from home, it could hardly be considered an abnormal response.'

I started anti-depressants, and this time the weariness and sense of danger lifted within weeks. When I returned to Germany, or what we called the Zone, we had an order to move.

We were moved to western Germany to a provincial town on the Weser. I already knew about the Weser from my poetry-reciting days in the Lower Fifth. Even by my early twenties, it was Eliot and MacNeice, Larkin and Donne whom I read for pleasure, but it was school fare – poetry to run an empire by – that was ineradicable. '*Hamelin town's in Brunswick near famous Hanover city / The River Weser, deep and wide, washes its walls on the southern side / A pleasanter spot you never spied.*' It was, of course, being set up as a place where something so bad would befall the town's children in 1284 that it would pass into myth. Minden, our new home, was twenty miles further along the river from Hamelin but it too was a pleasant spot, although it too had history: it was best known for a date in 1759 when 41,000 British and Germans fought 51,000 French and Saxons in battle. Other times; other alliances. Minden was also in Nordrhein-Westfalia, words that I enjoyed saying to myself. One of the first things I did was to buy a long painting of the Weser snaking through reeds and rough fields that looked like the River Coln at home.

The children were thriving, and we would bump along Minden's cobbles, throw bread for the ducks and eat sticky, cream-filled pastries in the little Konditorei. I made friends, other slightly reluctant army brides. But my marriage was in trouble. He played sport, went on exercise, was an extrovert. I read books, stayed at home and was endlessly introspective. He liked pubs, rugby matches and his army friends, I liked churchyards, old houses and woods. If he had little inner life, I rarely escaped from mine.

My parents took us on holiday for marital repair. They chose Portugal. It was not the best of choices as it turned out. We arrived the month of the revolution. They were very pleased to see us because all the hotels were empty. It had been a tense, though bloodless, coup, but the violence was in slogans: every wall was daubed in red, but there were rallies and armings and sometimes waiters serving breakfast were far away lieutenants in the people's army by dinner. The beaches were soft and blue, and yellow fishing boats were drawn up on the beach with eyes on their prows. As far as the marriage went, it too fell bloodlessly. We were staying thirty miles from Cape St Vincent. Another place I knew of from the Lower Fifth. *Nobly, nobly Cape St Vincent to the north-east died away / Sunset ran one glorious blood-red / Reeking into Cadiz Bay*. At the time the reeking blood idea had made me feel funny, but since then the sense of drama prevailed. I was desperate to see the fiery elegiac landscape of Cape St Vincent. He was desperate to play golf. I never saw Cadiz Bay – whose topography could never have lived up to poetry, anyway. But as I lay in my hotel bed I knew the distance between us was too great. I had occasionally asked myself if this was all there was and now I had the answer.

In summer 1976, I flew home. Like all unwilling exiles I had kept a sentimental picture of home in my head. The place I would see as we finally descended over England: villages and spires, great and old cities on their glittering rivers, fields of wheat and oceans of barley, all bounded by leafy hedgerows and farmsteads, sheep grazing in green and undulating pasture. My fantasies could have been set to music. As we crossed the French coast at 20,000 feet with my three-year-old running his toy car along the back of the seats, to the annoyance of the people behind and my two year-old, pink and round, slumped in my arms, asleep, I was trying hard not to cry with love and relief. But what came into focus below was a foreign land. We lost height and circled out over the South Downs. Under us the landscape was earth brown. As we dropped further, fields of sparse yellowing stubble could be seen lying between dry, grey hedges, and some woods were already bearing the copper and gold foliage of autumn. We flew over a reservoir, its pale clay sides exposed and a puddle of dark water at its bottom and then an area of burned black heathland with faint wisps of smoke still rising. As we raced along the runway dead grass and bare earth passed beside us and when we stepped out even the tarmac was sticky.

It had not rained for weeks and the earth's crust seemed to be cracking. Fissures appeared across the beaten earth of what had once been prized lawns. Great trees suddenly tore themselves out of the ground and fell cracking and splintering, revealing caves under their roots. A Drought Act had been passed, and water supplies were intermittent. The trains were dirty and unwashed, lavatories un-flushed, and wilting flowerbeds watered perfunctorily with a bowl of washing-up dregs. There were standpipes in back streets and on village greens and spies watching for hoses or shining cars.

But it was hard not to respond to the long days and blue skies. My children were soon brown and dusty, including their scalps as my son had found some scissors and given his sister and himself a patchy crop. I bought a very old open-topped car, and we crammed into it to drive to the seaside. My son sung the first two lines of *I've got a Brand-new Combine Harvester* round and round and round, and I hummed *Good Vibrations*. All over Britain something seemed to change for ever that summer; the old order melted away as the temperature stayed close to ninety degrees for day after day. Men appeared in shorts on city streets, their legs white with shock, cafés put up outside tables, and families sat talking under night skies in their back gardens while children's bedtimes evaporated. At night couples lay naked and hazed with sweat on top of their beds. One time I was sleeping in a friend's flat in London and, restless, heard crying in the night. When I got up to look through a window into the central well of the flats, I realised it was simply a woman having sex, her cries and exhortations rising up the well from another window flung open to the airless night. And then I realised that other, silent people were at other windows all around me.

That summer I was divorced. I had no qualifications, no money and had never lived alone. Now I did so, first in a to my mind picturesque, but actually squalid, cottage which was soon afterwards condemned, and then in a tiny modern house. A starter home. It was appropriate. I was back in the village where I started. Where I had been born. My parents lived in what had been my grandfather's house on the gravel pit, my widowed aunt lived in a bigger and better one on the newer pit next door. My father always said that the village was no good for us, and I always thought that was just him but much later I found a letter in some files, written just after my uncle was killed which showed that other people thought it too. On behalf of the directors of the gravel extraction company it wished to offer the family its condolences and extend the hope that the misfortunes that had dogged us were now at an end. They were not, of course.

My grandmother was lodged in a genteel old people's home in Cirencester. She had fallen over one time too often in the dark medieval cottage where I had lived as a baby and she had lived in old age. Arthritis, scars, shingles and poor eyesight had made her as physically fragile as she had once been mentally, but she was razor sharp on one thing. When she saw my mother or my aunt she'd ask crossly, 'Do you know what day it is?' Knowing what was coming they'd stay silent, and we'd try not to giggle at the familiar routine. 'It's the six hundred and thirty-first day since you put me in here', she'd say. She was still unaware that they had sold her house.

Where her brain had been modified with ECT and then a leucotomy, now her body was undergoing surgical procedures to rid her of failing tissue. Her foot was filleted and toes amputated. Her pain receded but she still tended to fall over. It seemed hard that a woman who had been slightly reclusive should end up in a home. She had her own room but still, it was a publically lived life. Although she was not the sad and troubled woman she had been decades earlier, there was always a certain brittleness about her. She had a clipped accent that now dated her as a late Victorian and her slightly high voice was always modulated at the same pitch. She was incapable of raising it in anger or, in public places, lowering it in discretion. Her small, but rarely flattering, views on other people were therefore broadcast unequivocally. A particular ordeal was taking her out for lunch. She would insist on calling nursing home staff and waitresses by their surname only. Apart from this she was undiscerningly polite; she appeared to have no other register: children, nurses, window-cleaner, other residents, all elicited the same response. She had no interests herself and little sense either of other people's. What warmth was in her was displayed, in fairly short snatches, to her children, but she still had a sweet smile. The television was the background to visits and telephone calls, so her attention was never quite with visitors or younger grandchildren who were paid to go and see her. Her favourite programme was *I, Claudius*; it was, she said, quite, quite unsuitable. She knew; she had watched the original showing and the repeats.

In a triumph of selective memory she also disapproved of my divorce. You would never have been able to return to the village in my day, she said. No one would have received you. In fact the only person who had made it quite clear that He would not receive me was God, or God's representative. The Vicar of Fairford, an elderly man, a descendant of the famous Keble of Oxford, had decided he could not, in conscience, give communion to divorcées. I had never been confirmed, though very tempted by the crocodile of white-veiled boarding school companions, because of the whole blood as wine thing, not to mention our traditional atheism, so my exclusion was not as painful as it might have been. My grandmother, now considered a deserving unfortunate, and her mind focused with age, had the Host brought to her in her room.

I was not to stay unmarried for very long. I probably should have. By 1978 I felt strong and hopeful. With a degree of naïveté I wrote to two local papers for a job, and one of them commissioned a piece on a church and one on a pale spinster Sister at the local hospital who wrote steamy Doctor and Nurse romances. 'Cut and thrust' was my headline but they chopped it. Still, it was the first occasion on which I had been paid for writing. The rest of the time I worked in my aunt's restaurant and had tangled love affairs with various customers. My children lived on crab mousse and After Eight chocolates. The fact that so much chaos obtained in the emotional life of one village might have made me reconsider my views on marriage but I was a romantic. In fact it was being a romantic that had made life so untenable at times. The deep, wide gap between literature and reality could never be closed but I could never quite give up hope.

My second marriage was to a reserved, kind man. He had much to commend him; he had none of the qualities suited to army life, he didn't vote conservative, he had a very nice dog, a regular income, liked my family, needed me, and he was local. No more moving. His father had been a pilot in the RAF and had survived the war briefly only to die rehearsing for an air show at the age of twenty-six. Dying in a rehearsal somehow made it worse; dying once the war had finished did too. The step-father who followed was a controlling bully and, for a time, when they lived near us his step-father would drop round of a morning when I was alone. Then I would see his intellect and predatory charm with the throttle off. For the rest of the time he dissipated his boredom and disappointment with life by crushing the spirit of my gentle mother-in-law. My new husband was determined to be a better sort of step-father to my children and a far better sort of husband.

Meanwhile my mother had found Freud. Her conversion was absolute; she was now in training. Penis-envy dominated breakfast and a paranoia specific to hard-line Freudians dominated her conversation. Jungians were regarded with wary affection but the Kleinians were an ever-present threat and vigilance was essential. When she eventually died the Kleinians came to the funeral en masse, but we were suspicious of their motives.

We bought a cottage near the Round House. My children went to the village school. Every day they would walk down a long flagged walk in the deep shade of yews by the church singing 'Brown Girl in the Rain'. 'Ring' I would say, twenty times a day. 'It's not rain; it's Brown Girl in the *Ring*.' 'Brown girl in the *rain*.' 'Brown girl Down the Drain', they'd sing back. If they were early they would play hide-and-seek behind the table-tombs. The church was perpendicular, my brother's headmaster had told me when I was seventeen, between ardent kissing sessions. They would pass the tomb where I was laid when I fainted at a family wedding and where the long-dead Stuart used to sit, a monument to atheism. On the wall by a walk was a quotation by Shelley who had once been here too:

Thus solemnized and softened, death is mild
And terrorless as this serenest night
Here could I hope, like some enquiring child
Sporting on graves, that death did hide from human sight
Sweet secrets, or beside its breathless sleep
That loveliest dreams perpetual watch did keep.

Some time around then I had a bad experience with cannabis. After all, neither of us even smoked. My husband claimed to have had a few years of mis-spent youth working at Fenwick's near Oxford Street with a dope-toking founder member of the modern IRA but if he had it was well out of sight now. When I was a student nurse I had taken token breathy dips at a joint before it was whipped away by my deep-inhaling friends.

A friend – an actor – gave us the seeds as a present. We planted them in our tiny cottage garden. A site apparently made for them as the plants flourished in a way we had never achieved with sweet peas and love-in-a-mist. Soon they were looming over the hollyhocks and becoming a potential embarrassment. Our neighbours were all pensioners so unlikely to be bothered by the exuberance of the frondy hedge now waving over their fence; the vicarage and the tennis courts were a few doors up, but the roughest pub in town was a few doors down, and various mouthy friends who whiled away the domestic round with a joint and their morning coffee would want a share.

We cut it down, fitted it, just, into a black plastic bin-liner and hung it from a rafter in the attic. Many weeks later in the Easter holidays while the children were playing downstairs, I went up to look for a box of books. I opened the bag, smelled – it was overwhelming – and took a twig out. It was not promising. Later that morning I popped down to the village shop, bought a packet of cigarette papers, feeling that my forehead was branded drug addict and went home to roll up my stash. I couldn't combine it with tobacco as tobacco had always made me throw up, so I crunched it up, leaves, stick, seeds – were there seeds? – well, that's how I remember it – as tightly as I could and lit it. I took several deep puffs and felt giddy. I lay back in a chair and inhaled in a more measured, more knowledgeable way. After half the joint I could face no more and anyway, I needed to put the washing out. My ears felt funny. The children and a friend from over the road were tumbling and yelling in and out of the garden.

I was trembly and clammy. I felt odd so I went upstairs but the stairs had become unfamiliar. Waves of fear rose, were suppressed and returned, stronger. I crawled into bed. From outside boughs of trees spread probing fingers towards me, and a tentacle of climbing rose tapped insistently on the window pane. I squeezed my eyes shut. I could only think of the branch which would pin me down and slowly pierce my chest, while my eyes opened wider and wider exposing first the whites and then the glistening red network of tiny veins, and all the while the rose – it was *Gloire de Dijon*, a beautiful rose of torn, parchment colour petals, tightly packed into the bloom – tapped insistently for entrance. I went to the window with my eyes squeezed shut and closed the tiny space open at the top. I pulled the curtains and hid under the bedcovers. I knew the back door was open and I could not even protect the children. I was icy cold and felt dreadfully sick. My legs shook even when I placed my hands on my thighs to quiet them. Even with the thin curtains closed I could see the silhouette of the trees glowing darkly against a colourless sky. Each time I opened my eyes, I measured their distance. With my eyes shut I could still see them and the lacy pattern of blood vessels in the membranes of my eye. I knew what time it was if I looked at the bedside clock, but time itself had become distorted. I knew that I had to survive two hours before my husband would come home. I prayed that the mother of the children's friend would not come and fetch him as I knew I could not open the front door.

For two hours I was overwhelmed with terror.

I had never seen anyone have a bad reaction from dope, so I assumed I had quite simply, if rather abruptly, gone mad. By the time my husband arrived home it was diminishing slightly. Sanity flooded in; the buds and the twigs and the branches and the trunks and boles retreated into themselves. The rose was a rose. By supper time I got up. Some days later I told him what had happened. Could it have been the cannabis? He was sceptical. He was calmer and less fanciful than me; he would try some. He rolled it with tobacco.

His transformation was so quick that at first I thought he was winding me up. He started rushing from room to room – not far in our tiny house – in a frenzy of agitation. He lumbered into the furniture. He flung a door back and it crashed against the wall behind. Plaster dust floated to the ground. I asked him to be a bit quieter as the children would wake up. He started to swear: this mildest of men, reticent and unaggressive, drew himself up to his full height, stuck out his chest and pounded it. Something I had only seen in a documentary about apes. It was nearly funny. He marched towards the door.

'Out.'

I pushed the bolt into place, I danced to one side, out of range and dropped the keys behind the bookcase. He looked puzzled and tore open the top of his shirt. He started to try and raise the window. It stuck. His eyes were intensely focused on something I couldn't see. I had this vision of my gentle husband, a young professional man with a career and reputation to nurture, standing in the marketplace, bellowing his curses, and doing his orang-utan routine. I stood across the door, knowing that all this they shall not pass stuff was ridiculous, yet aware – the first time I had ever considered it – that he was bigger and much stronger than me. It was a miracle that the children never came down.

We burned the cannabis in our inglenook fireplace the next night. You could smell it all down our road.

When I finally had a breakdown two years later, the trees came back.

Soon after this, things started to go wrong. My parents' marriage, which appeared to have reached an accommodation in its thirty years, fell apart in a very emotional, very un-English way. Though its tensions and flaws were obvious from the outside to the slenderest acquaintance, and my mother's love affair with Freud played its part, his role and all the other tensions were and remained invisible to my mother. She had, by her own lights, been a good wife. She had tried to be everything her own mother was not. Unwilling to address the enormity of what was happening she was first vocal and bewildered in her protest and then finally silenced and abandoned. For a big woman she was suddenly very small. She simply couldn't understand what she had done or failed to do.

My father by contrast was at his wits' end; he knew all too well what he had done and was almost immobilized with guilt. Then my sister, young for her age, much-loved as the baby of the family, was sent down from university in the advanced stages of anorexia. Fragile as a baby bird, with her huge eyes, downy hair and skeletal arms covered in cold, rough skin, she returned home to the nest where there was now a vacancy. There they lived with a shared interest in food: my mother able to surrender to her weight, and my sister counting every molecule, gramme and calorie.

Within weeks my mother was trying to make the best of things, which she had always been good at, in the very village which my father had always claimed was unlucky for us. His was now the victory in this argument. Having fled to London he was, if anything, in a worse way than her. She, at least, had a role to play. She could occupy a substantial area of the moral high ground. 'Well', she said one evening as we were sitting in the garden. 'I have to say your grandfather would have been pleased. He always said your father had no initiative.' My father, now reeling from initiative, was unable to move forward into a new life because he was so shocked at having left the old one. He wasn't eating, was anxious and depressed, and I worried for him. They would both ring to talk to me, going over and over the same ground, and sensible conversations would soon liquefy into tears. The children would hover round, anxiously, as I wept; for some reason these calls always came as I was trying to cook supper for them. I would stand by the stove afterwards stirring sticky or burned food, blinded by tears. I would feed the children but could not eat myself. It all felt infinitely more painful than my own divorce; the difference between disassembling four years and disassembling a third of a century, and I experienced my father leaving my mother as a bereavement. If listened to Brahms or Sibelius, which had played as a background to my childhood, or if I stood in my parents' laboriously well-kept garden, I would cry as if he were dead instead of mowing perfect stripes in another place.

That summer the newly formed 'we' went on a family holiday. I was three months pregnant when we arrived in an austere *gîte* in the Dordogne. We had been trying for ages to have another child. All I remember of the holiday is that it rained a lot, we played demon poker incessantly and I lost the baby. The local French doctor after a period of misunderstanding contingent on my mother's French during which he thought I was attempting to procure an abortion, sent me to the nuns, but nothing helped and we ended up driving home early with the pregnancy over. I went to the doctor in Fairford, who was an elderly locum. He looked at my records, saw that I'd had a termination in my late teens and passed on the medical wisdom that people who messed around with their fertility often found this sort of thing happened: that they lost babies subsequently. Sometimes they were quite unable to have children. 'You can't just pick and choose your pregnancies', he said, smugly. Indeed not. This was of course ignoring my exuberantly healthy children.

We were asked by my husband's employers to move; to the east Midlands. We declined. Then we were asked a bit more forcefully and finally we went. We chose a village on the same long spur of limestone that cut north-east from the Cotswolds and in some ways, if you ignored the absence of hills, it looked like home. There we settled in a simple, square semi-detached cottage with a simple, square garden.

My husband struggled with a new job. Things were terribly on the line for him. In the autumn I lost another pregnancy, very early on, perhaps because I was scarcely eating, and I swooped downwards into the worst low I had ever experienced. My childhood had been a lie, my future was as a stranger, there was only now, and now wasn't tolerable. I was desperately homesick. We were in many ways both completely adrift. I didn't know anyone, and although some people made overtures of friendship, I was so mired in loss that if the telephone rang or there was a knock on the door, I would stay upstairs quiet and stiff as a shop dummy except for my crashing heart. Soon I would get the children off to school and then go back under the covers in bed. When they were home I tormented myself with the thought that I might hurt them. That madness might overwhelm me and in some fugue-like state I would commit some terrible atrocity. One night I got up and threw the worst knives and the meat tenderiser into the shrubbery at the end of the garden. I would see my son and daughter and love them and yet be frightened to touch them and would know myself a hostage to a dreadful fortune. My grandmother had never shown any sign of violence to her children but then she hadn't had them for very long before war threatened them with a violence of its own and then parted her from them. I cried for hours on end, sitting at my cheerful kitchen table, bent forward with my head on my arms, next to the fridge where the childrens' paintings and dentists' appointments were stuck on with ladybird magnets. I had taken off the alphabet stick-ons as they had started to re-assemble themselves into worrying words of suggestion. Finally my husband called the GP. He was a furtive, badly dressed man who had never learned eye contact. Both he and my husband seemed rather embarrassed. He put me on heavy doses of medication. I stopped shopping, I stopped eating, I stopped brushing my hair. My weight tumbled on down; soon I didn't have any clothes that fitted but it didn't really matter as I only ever wore my dressing-gown. 'Is there anyone who can look after you?' he said. But everyone I knew was crying out to be looked after themselves. 'It will have to be hospital, then', he said.

Chapter 9

Peterborough 1980s

Into the nothingness of scorn and noise,
  Into the living sea of waking dreams,
Where there is neither sense of life nor joys,
  But the vast shipwreck of my life's esteems;
And e'en the dearest – that I loved the best –
Are strange – nay, rather stranger than the rest.

John Clare (1793–1864), *Written in Northampton County
Asylum.*

November. The trees breathe dampness; the piebald plane trees look
diseased. The traffic and trains roar by and this is Peterborough. This
a car park in Peterborough on an early winter's day, and the condensation rolls down the inside of the car, and the rain spatters unevenly
on the outside. Inside, next to my husband, I am leaning forward and
my head is resting on the dashboard. My face is wet too. I no longer cry
noisily, muscularly, but just empty. All is sorrow. If I am awake I cry.
There is no time for anything else.

The hospital is square and tall. If I go in they will be expecting me.
That's what my doctor said. Just a week in hospital for a rest. Six

nights. And how I long to sleep, to be warm and lost and dry. In fact when I am free again, from another place than this, it will be spring: Easter, the skies will be watery blue, the trees will have blossom, the hedges will have a green haze of early buds. England will be facing another war. My life will have changed for ever. But I do not know that now or I would never go in.

I had become so frightened of everything. Of real things – car parks, journeys, meetings. Of completely unreal things: that harm might come to my shining, happy children. That a motorist or a microbe or some other killer might take them from me. I see them in film-like loops, thrown into the air by a car bumper, falling off high buildings, thrashing against an undertow. I cry at this prospect, of never being able to smooth their soft, straight hair again, never smell them warm and true. Never hear them, distantly, laughing in the garden or at a cartoon on the television or squabbling in the kitchen. That *I* might hurt them. I am hurting them of course, in my crying. I do all this, as they play around me, curious but self-absorbed.

A few months before my descent into fear and doubt, I remember being on a small boat following the coast with my mother in the prow, my daughter with her head in my lap, flushed and fast asleep, my son trying to catch the spray as we cut through small waves. My mother had taken us away for a few days for me to convalesce from my miscarriage. There was the boat's captain and my husband by the wheel. Even off shore you could smell the wild thyme, and my lips were salty. I was suddenly overwhelmed with joy.

I recalled a quote – from *Romeo and Juliet*:

If it were now to die
'Twere now to be most happy.

At the time it seemed portentous. It wasn't; it wasn't even *Romeo and Juliet*. So much for the exquisite accuracy of these epiphanies. Everyone I loved was there on this boat in the late afternoon sun. I felt as if my whole chest would burst with it; I could feel, smell, breathe, hear, see the world broken down into tiny fragments of energy and light.

Later I would come to recognise these phases of hyper-sensitivity and contentment as not necessarily being a positive sign. Rapture as precursor to despair. It came to mean I couldn't trust happiness.

By October, loved faces suddenly have the lineaments of menace. It is quite subtle. I look at their features, and they shift imperceptibly and become ugly and utterly strange. I can't really recognise anyone, not with certainty; it is that moment in science fiction when a familiar trusted head is raised and the eyes which glare out are of a different person hidden within.

Then there are the phrases that go round and round and round in my head – patterns nothing will take away – I exhaust myself thinking of other phrases to stop them coming in. I see my thoughts like a ticker tape. Spewing out aggressive letters. *Felo de se* was one of my nasty phrases. I didn't even know what *felo de se* meant; I had to look it up, though I guessed it wouldn't be good. What demons send messages in foreign languages? What if I hadn't owned a dictionary? 'I have promises to keep and miles to go before I sleep', that was another. I hate American poetry.

Worst are the *unreal* things proceeding from *real* things: messages hidden in the titles of books, on advertising hoardings, on lists of ingredients. **DaI**sy Mill**Er**, DIE. **GoOD** Hou**S**ek**EE**ping, GOD SEEING. I don't even believe in God, I think. I reverse the joke I heard a vicar tell the atheist: 'Well, he still believes in *you*', said the vicar with a smug beam. I wonder what if I believed in Him but He didn't believe in *me*? Suga**R**, **E**ggs, **D**airy chocolate . . . RED. Red is always a problem and is everywhere. Red is blood. Blood frightens me most of all. It always had since I first fainted when the dog bit me in Highgate. Aztecs, Dettol, tomato juice, butchers' shops, strawberry sorbet. It would all be funny if it didn't scare me so much; if I could stop my mind doing it. **Rays**: rays is RAZOR.

The car radio is playing as I cry. First it plays *The sun'll come out tomorrow*. I weep harder – if silent, motionless tears can be expressed with more vigour – probably I simply increase the fluid that pours out of me. Then they play the theme tune from the television series that everybody is watching. They are, they say, glued to it. The programme is *Brideshead Revisited*. Shot at Castle Howard.

I am so tired.

Getting out of the car is an act of extreme courage. I have scarcely got out of bed for weeks. But here I go. He and I exchange looks – we are rather awkward with each other. All this drama was not how it was meant to be. I have let him down, and he is letting me down and we know it. Then I am in a lift. The lift is terrible. Three floors, then the ward, two doors, not locked, no one waiting. Then an office with people, and one jumps up and comes to see me. I am trying not to cry, to make a good impression. But then I am saying goodbye to my husband who knows me a bit and am alone with people who know me not at all. But perhaps it is a relief. They have no expectations of me. I have a bed at the near end of the ward, and it is a bit like school. Mine is the bed by the door which I like because it means I don't have to walk past other women to get to it. On the other hand, the shower rooms are down the other end.

I wonder what the children are having for supper. I gave them sweets when I left. In the car I remembered that my father gave the dogs a Mars bar when they had to be put down, and I wish I'd given them a toy. I'd been going to buy them new underwear but I couldn't get to the shop. Will people think I am a bad mother because their underwear is old and too small? My daughter gets overexcited when she's tired. I have their pictures wrapped up in my bag but I don't dare unwrap them because that will set me off – my lost babies. I just keep my hand in my bag and hold them very tightly.

I go into a little room with a kind nurse. We discuss things: the silly facts that have dissolved the glue of my life. The children and my parents and my sister and losing babies and the sadness that has overtaken us all. She gives me the box of tissues which is waiting for patients on the table. She says it is all hardly surprising, and the doctor will see me soon and I will feel better in no time. The doctor sees me soon, and she explains that there are different sorts of depression, but I probably have depression which has just been slow to respond to treatment. I am to go onto two new sorts of pill, and they will make me feel calmer and then I will start to feel properly better in a couple of weeks. She asks me about my family history. When I tell her about my grandmother and some of the others, she is interested. She writes it all down. She says that sometimes there does seem to be a genetic component in these things, and it is just possible I have another sort of depression. I know all this. Have known it for years, but I try to look interested and not to snivel, though I am well aware that trying hard not to look mad, not even to look nervous, is ridiculous in a psychiatric ward. She says it will be useful to observe me in hospital for a little so they can be certain of their diagnosis.

When the doctor comes I read upside down. I am obsessed with his diagnosis. This time it says unipolar affective disorder. The words I dread take six weeks to emerge. Bipolar disorder. But there is a question mark by it which I hang onto like a child in a picture in one of my books long ago who dangled from the moon. The gap between me and my grandmother has not yet closed. Unipolar is just one of those things. Unipolar is depression and might go away for ever. Bipolar is a curse. Depression is something you get. Manic-depressive is something you are. A destroyer of lives.

That night I am tucked up in bed in the dormitory and it doesn't seem too bad. I hope the children won't wake up in the night. I hope no one will wet their unfamiliar bed. I hope their schools will be kind. I hope my mother will come.

It has been dark for hours. The pills have made me sleepy. There is one nice woman who went with me to the washbasins and who has been in here with obsessive compulsive disorder and a fifteen-year-old who is thin and scarred and gets the other women to help her wash. The day nurses give way to the night nurses. The ward gets quieter.

The staff nurse introduces the night charge nurse. He is a tall, old-fashioned, schoolmastery sort of man. Long white coat, rough wool tie, shortish back and sides, thick glasses. He smiles.

Later he comes back to see the two of us who are new. He sits on my bed, where I am trying to put my things away. He helps me gently. He tells me that it is not serious. That I need some good food, plenty of sleep, to take my medicine regularly and that they will keep an eye on me while I get better. Briefly I think of the eye on Portuguese fishing boats but I am trying not to. Which will be a week or so. This is just a break-down he says. Which is interesting as I always wondered what that meant, what actually happened when you broke down. It sounded so electrical, so final; that declining whirr as a little motor fades. And now I know, all it is is this: crying and word-madness and tiredness and fear.

So, my first night in Peterborough and as it is 5th November, there are still fireworks a long, long way away, casting their dying spurts of silver and gold across the sky; far-off explosions that have nothing to do with me.

A Guide to Arcadia.

It is hard to feel you are not acting a part in a mental hospital. All the time the dialogue goes on, exhaustingly at times, between a rational self who recognises delusions and the delusions themselves. Of course letters do not rise from book titles to create new and malevolent words. As any fule kno. But there the words are. Of course individual words cannot resonate endlessly, filling the auditory horizon, blocking out all others, refusing to move on, but it had first happened to me when my governess had taught us French when I was only seven: *règle* was the word. My only defence was to giggle and soon we three little girls were all giggling if we saw *règle* appearing sentences below where we were on a page.

And then there were the gloriously extravagant antecedents. I was if anything over-prepared by a diet of books and films. Mrs Rochester raging in her attic, the disintegrating wife in *The Yellow Wallpaper*, the rebel in *One Flew Over the Cuckoo's Nest*. Laura Glyde falsely imprisoned. I recognised and played bits of all of them. As for my grandmother who had herself been locked and sedated in an attic while my mother set out on All Souls' Eve, a fine autumn afternoon, to marry at the village church: the only time I had seen her having psychiatric treatment was when surgery had suddenly made her respectable; when she was a proper patient, with flowers at her bed-side, not a neurotic. When the family were waiting to see if she would awake serene and welcome from her leucotomy into a new self. It would have to be a new self as she had never really had a contented old self to return to. She lay flat, quite silent in her bed in the long ward – unconscious, I thought at the time. Now I knew that she might just as easily have been awake but that in silence lay her only power.

Because of the films, and having been good at art at school, I drew deliberately disturbed pictures in art therapy. Oily seas in which crea-tures writhed, ivy curling round a classical tomb which owed a lot to Poussin. This established me, I thought, as better at art and having more cultural references than my peers, but it was also intended to please. In my head it was anyway, at least at first. The large and kindly art therapist seemed oblivious to the message but gratified by the results.

Apart from this, a terrible boredom descended. It was boredom exacerbated by the dazed fatigue of the heavily drugged. There was tel-evision, endlessly, and there were the squabbles and dramas of the patients. On Tuesday and Thursday there was, for a selected few, ECT. A tired and pale housewife called Joyce, given to occasional outbursts of tearful rage, an elderly man who never spoke or moved or had any expression on his face, and a skinny young man who was a day patient all disappeared behind patterned curtains down a passage at the end of the ward. On those days they skipped breakfast but a couple of hours later were guided out by a nurse and given toast and jam in the day room. They weren't right all day. Joyce, in particular, would look a little puzzled, as if she had lost something.

I was acquiring privileges for good behaviour. In the second week, the night charge nurse, who had taken to sitting on my bed for a little chat each evening, secured a single room for me. 'You don't want to be out here with these women,' he said, 'they're not your sort of people; it's not what you're used to.' Fortunately he was right. Now I had a room of my own with a view, through a sealed window, of a further wing of the hospital where people came and went and climbed stairs and lifted linen on and off shelves. Anguish was replaced by inertia, the insatiable delirium of words by experiences to which no words were attached. The grief of being torn from my children and my home sub-sided. That was another life and this was now.

There were no grotesques in this mad scene. Even the charge nurse who came to exact his price for kindness within days, only wanted what every other man in my life had seemed to want. But his arrangements for this were so uncomplicated, required so little derangement of clothing or time, that sometimes, on his nights off, it seemed as if it might never have happened. Afterwards he would give me my medication. Everyone had medication; it was a favourite topic of conversation. Doses, side-effects, horror stories, new, old, changed prescriptions, mistakes. Lunch and dinner came with rattling plastic pots of gaudy pills. The really big cap-sules were haloperidol; if you had one of those you were at the top end of the madness scale. The nurses stood over you until you'd swallowed convincingly. Hoarding was one of the few serious transgressions in this new world. I had brought in forty paracetamol in my forlorn and untouched make-up bag. I had never considered suicide but I needed to feel I could regain control. The only medication I cared about was the transparent amber oval capsule which made me fall into a dreamless sleep at night. They had poetic names these drugs: chloral, welldorm.

Chloral, Chloë, chlorine in the Wimbledon baths, stinging the eyes, floral, my mother's dresses, floral tributes, aural, sounded like it rhymed. A joke.
Well dorm. 'Sleep well, darling.' My mother singing Golden Slumbers.

Sleep well but briefly. For they did not put you out for long enough. I would wake, sudden and alarmed at 2 am. My new protector would double the dose. Extra medication was his gift to me; a gift given, he explained, as he buttoned his white coat, at considerable risk to himself. Later, at Christmas, he brought me a furtive box of Milk Tray too.

This is how it would be. I had stopped reading. I had stopped being sad. The seasons had stopped. The calendar had stopped. The day as people outside knew it did not exist. Where others marked their day in hours, we had drug rounds. Having lost a baby my breasts were still swollen with un-needed milk. I leaked. I felt hot and unwell and punished. Still he returned.

Joyce, stupefied for much of the time, occasionally alerted herself to the possibilities of the real world by stubbing out cigarettes on her arm. She wore long sleeves but she showed me her decades of scars, climbing up her arm like the family height lines we had in a doorway when I was growing up. In order to emulate this panacea, I had to take up smoking which made me feel a great deal iller. Everybody smoked here. I had tried to at eighteen but with no great success but this time I was properly motivated and I began to burn. Everywhere I could press the red tip of my cigarette I pressed. It was no secret. One night a kind nurse knelt at my feet dressing my wounds. She had tears in her eyes. 'Why are you doing this?' she asked. 'Your skin is so beautiful.' I think, for a few minutes, I felt she loved me. He, too, in his way, and undeterred by the dressings.

Joyce was discharged, officially better. That wasn't the way she saw it. She turned on me: 'They think I made you do this crap – that it was my fucking idea.' She had tears in her eyes. 'I thought you were my mate but guess who gets thrown out, not you, oh no, you're posh, you stay. I'm the one who always gets pissed on.' It has never dawned on me that I had any friends here or that for some people inside was a haven of sorts, better than out there.

Psychiatric wards are remarkably competitive places. The next day I was told that a madder woman than me was being admitted: a young Indian new mother who had subsided into post-natal mania. She was noisy and needed the single room. I was to be returned to the general ward. I went into the day room and threw a vase at the window. It smashed, the glass didn't. They were quite calm but they went through my things and found the paracetamol. I said I was going to discharge myself. That evening I was taken into a small room with upholstered chairs. A kind nurse held my hand as a young and harassed registrar told me that I was being sectioned under the 1959 Mental Health Act. For twenty-eight days. It would end on Christmas Eve. Then I would be re-assessed. He made fleeting eye contact. Nobody thought I was of any potential harm to anyone else, the nurse explained, but they believed I was to myself.

The trouble – well, one of a sea of troubles – with mental illness is that any response to its pressures and dramas which would be seen as legitimate outside its fragile and sometimes brutal world, immediately confirms the diagnosis. I started to protest, calmly, trying to explain that I would never, ever kill myself because I had children, but it escalated into me begging and eventually wailing for my children who had, as I saw it, no one but me, however inadequate, and who were, in turn, all that I had. The registrar wrote busily on his forms; the first signature was the consultant psychiatrist whom I had scarcely seen, the second was my husband. On the information he had, which was slender, what else could he have done?

Christmas. The Indian woman had pulled her mattress off her bed and sang, cross-legged, all night long, however much medication they tipped into her. The charge nurse had got in the habit of waking me up and taking me, stumbling with sedation, for brief trips to the ECT suite or the guest lavatories. The nurses were mostly happy and full of enthusiasm in their extra duties which involved stretching twisted crepe and tinsel across the day room and tying a plastic Father Christmas, with shrouded sledge and jolly reindeers leaping for the ceiling, along the corridor. There was an exclusion zone, discovered only by testing, in the area near the ward entrance where those who were sectioned were forbidden to go, so I never saw it, but they had, apparently, put a gold and red banner over the doors to the ward with Happy Xmas in huge letters. It was only looking back that I came to realise that the biggest difference between films and books and the reality is that there is no sense of irony in a mental hospital.

There were carols and Morecambe and Wise on the television, and I was allowed home for the day. Outside a bitter wind was blowing and grey clouds raced across the sky. I could smell the sickly scent of sugar beet which always hung over the city. I could smell everything, new and strange. The cold was colder than I had remembered. With my husband I went to church in Peterborough cathedral where the heating had failed, and the congregation huddled in the choir hardly able to mutter the responses, their breath rising in an ascetic cloud above the pews. I had put on my make-up and a navy blue dress which was now far too big for me. I wore gloves because my husband hated the scars.

Like my grandmother, forty years earlier, I was coming home for Christmas and my children were waiting excitedly. Everyone else was apprehensive I expect. My mother had brought me lovely presents to give to the children. She had even wrapped them, which had never been one of her strengths. But it was nice: the huge house was warm and soft, my uncle and aunt and young cousins ebullient and kind. My mother gave me a pair of tiny, perfect, diamond earrings, nestled in silk in a dark leather box and catching the light of fire. Earrings I would have to leave behind. It was familiar and safe, the old routines, the old jokes. The Christmas tree rose to the ceiling and was a tower of lights and presents. I was not part of it but I could watch and see that happiness was there and I could cuddle my children and feel pain at losing them again, which was better, much better, than nothing at all.

But things slipped away again in the longest nights of the year. I was discharged briefly to my mother's house on the lake. There I lay in bed taking my sleeping pills three times a day to stave off a tidal wave of panic.

In early January I was moved to Northampton. The hospital where my grandmother had been treated in the 1940s. The same County Asylum which had held John Clare until his death. I don't remember the journey to Northampton. I only remember being in my bed in a small, quiet room, tucked up. I was in the medical ward for patients who were far beyond talking therapy. I didn't talk, or wash, or eat, or move. Later my psychiatrist reminded me that the first few times she saw me I was curled up like a foetus or a shell, with my face to the wall, hardly breathing. Years later, when I came to Cambridge to be interviewed for a university place, I thought that the nautilus shell that was my college coat of arms was an appropriate symbol for the women who came from their curled up lives into possibility.

I was not, however, asleep. I was confused by this place. At Peterborough it was obviously a hospital; it smelled like a hospital; it had lino and uniforms and fluorescent tubes. Here there were carpets and softer lights, and you couldn't hear people coming. They could catch you out. The staff here were friendly and concerned rather than briskly cheerful. I was not convinced this was a hospital at all. But if not, what was it? I dreaded someone coming in and putting tubes in my veins while I slept. I dreaded the dark. It was hard to stay awake and watchful against a regime of high-dose drugs. Outside it seemed to be foggy most of the time. As the day slowly lightened the central lengths of tree trunks loomed out of the greyness, cut off top and bottom by the sill and the lintel of the window. As I couldn't recall coming in, it was a long time before I could make sense of what lay outside. Most mornings something passed running and panting, pounding round the building. It had all the threat and mystery of my first childhood poem: All night long in the dark and wet a man went riding by. Why did he gallop and gallop about?

In depression the things that have once been familiar and comforting and given pleasure are the first to alter imperceptibly to threat and corruption. Like slightly sour milk, they are, at first, just not quite right. The nearest thing I can think of to this is the world of fairytales, where woodland paths, gingerbread houses, soaring castle towers, medieval towns inhabited by honest countrymen and beautiful princesses under moonlit nights and bright-edged clouds, are nonetheless fragile and sinister; all are poised to darken and change. So, when you are in the blackest depression, the landmarks of everyday life shift and shriek alarm where formerly they gave automatic comfort. My own things: my nightie, my hairbrush, my watch, my hand, appeared altered in some indefinable but malign way. Even as I knew it could not be so, I feared and ruminated on the severed golden stalks that stood stiffly in Cotswold fields in August. There they stood, sharp and brittle after harvest, while the cracks opened up in the earth and tiny speedwell flowers took hold of every crumbling clod. With each tiny breath of hot wind the stalks whispered across the rise of fields. I had heard it summer after summer. As children we had crunched them underfoot or picked them to drink through. Now I became obsessed that, if it was not a hospital, lacking tubes of the approved medical sort someone might try some intravenous improvisation with these. Now it was winter and Northampton but some sharp hollow stalks still survived, bleached white in the empty black fields outside the towns of the eastern midlands.

A nice Scottish doctor came in and took some blood and then said that he thought I might like to go to sleep for a long time and how would it be if they sedated me heavily for three days. They would have to feed me a fortified liquid diet as I was so malnourished, but I probably wouldn't remember being woken up for this. No tubes, he promised, and I believed him. Then, when my body and mind were rested we would start to work on a plan to get me better. There was nothing I could have wanted more than oblivion.

When I woke up Dr L., the consultant, arrived. She must have been right at the end of her career. Very tall, very thin, with wiry white hair, flapping skirts. The nurses and junior doctors were a little afraid of her I think. *I* was a little afraid of her. She was a caricature of a certain sort of academic woman. She examined me. At the end she said, 'You are very ill but you will make a complete recovery. It will, however, be hard work. Your blood counts are abnormal, your liver is not functioning as it should, EEG shows temporal lobe epilepsy. We will get you physically well and then we shall set about getting you emotionally well. You need high doses of drugs which may make you feel sick.' None of these pronouncements permitted any element of doubt. 'I don't want your mother to come and see you.' This was a burden lifted – before she had merely *not* come, now she was forbidden. I could believe she wanted to. 'And I think it would be frightening for your children. You look very unwell, so I hope you will be very brave and agree not to see them for a while, for their sake, then they won't have to worry about what they can't understand.' This time it was the illusion of choice that sustained me.

The drugs did make me feel sick. Dr L. was without pity. Once I sat in her office and was sick into her waste-paper basket. No quarter. Another time after a sleepless night I complained about throwing up twice. 'Well, it says here you were nauseated not that you were sick, retching isn't being sick', she said. She was a stickler for accuracy. Later – many months later – when I was convalescent, out of hospital, planning a trip to Greece, I complained again about the foul taste in my mouth and my inability to distinguish flavours. 'It's hardly haute-cuisine in Greece, is it?' she said. Handing me a new and equally high-dose prescription.

There was an elegant sixty-year-old, all bones, with raven hair and white skin, dressed in couture clothes now too big for her, who was good to talk to on the rare days when she was neither stuporous with depression nor off her head with mania. Her emotions cycled so fast that she could hurtle from one to another within hours. Down, she simply sat, mute, her face like wax, staring at her lap. Up, her jacket would be buttoned carelessly revealing fine pink silk and lace under-wear. On these days she kissed everybody and gave away all her belongings. She gave me a handsome 1950s crocodile handbag. Sister suggested we all give these things back. Once this woman had had a husband, children. Nobody visited her now except a vicar. In a brief lull between poles of emotion, she explained that she was being assessed for surgery. A lobotomy of sorts. It was a desperate remedy, she said, but what life did she have. I wondered what life she would have anyway if the furies let her fall. What remained of her poor battered existence outside?

Dr L. was more careful about exposing my notes, and I was at first too ill to try to read them. When I eventually did I saw 'depressive psychosis' written upside down and underlined in black biro and I felt a great leap of relief. Perhaps the only person to do so. 'You don't think I've got manic depression?' I asked tentatively. 'I'm keeping an open opinion', said Dr L. 'You're certainly more depressed than manic; we need further observation. You may just be a naturally excitable and imaginative girl who has become very depressed.' Nevertheless she put me on lithium, the standard treatment for manic depression.

The writing on the ECT consent form was beautiful calligraphy. *Electro Convulsive Therapy,* it said in dark print. I wished it had been in typeface like the rest of the document. I was frightened by the elaboration; it seemed unreal and unmedical, the announcement of a drama. It looked a little like an old legal document; a conveyance, a king's ordinance, a death sentence.

I was too scared to sleep when I knew the morning brought ECT. I hated its well-rehearsed procedures. The nil-by-mouth notice on the door, the treatment nurse, smiling with resolve in the morning as she came on collection. I sat up until dawn hugging my knees however many pills they gave me to sedate me. A nice night nurse sat in my room and knitted by a low light. I was five again and there were shadows on the ceiling.

It was kindly done. Unlike in the 1940s. Unlike what they had done to my grandmother. You would go in, lie down and they would put a needle in your hand and pump in the anaesthetic and a muscle relaxant. After they had passed a large enough charge across the brain, so that, it was said by other patients, your extremities twitched, they would leave you to come round to your ill-matched world on a trolley in a quiet dead-end of the corridor. As your brain struggled to reposition itself, it had a cheerful morning fabric to focus on. Yellow. Yellow, *of course*, with appropriately abstract flowers. Behind the curtains other trolleys held their bemused loads.

After four sessions I woke up one morning and decided I had reached the end. I couldn't bear any more of it. I was more terrified than ever, only now my fear had a focus. It was not the going under, nor the thought of the electric charges arcing over my brain, firing across synapses, while my fingers convulsed before an audience; all that was simply unbelievable. It was the coming round I couldn't bear. The terrifying, incalculable space adrift from any reference points, the stuff, quite literally, of nightmares. It was a state of pure, disconnected loneliness. But if I had given consent I could withdraw it. I walked down to Dr L.'s office and waited. She was cross and at her most headmistressy. 'Why are you always so timid?' she asked exasperatedly. I had always thought that routine sessions with a psychiatrist were composed of long silences and leading questions; patients were never told what to do. Certainly there was no ticking off. This had never been the style of Dr L. Perhaps appropriately for a psychiatrist she spoke her mind. But I held on. I was never going to have ECT again.

Finally she indicated that I could go but as I was walking out of the door she looked up, and I looked back. 'It's worked of course, or you wouldn't be here now', she said. And as I walked up the corridor I felt the returning warmth of power.

In my early days I would sometimes try to find my old routines. I would start washing my hair, long and matted as it had become, get it full of suds and then lose energy and direction; this simple task suddenly fractured into component parts so complicated that it was impossible to assemble them in the right sequence. Sometimes my hair was still dry under the dollops of shampoo. Alternatively I would wander off looking vaguely for help with water dripping down my back and end up in the entrance hall, frightening less confused newcomers. A nurse would retrieve me and walk me back to a basin and rinse the soap out. But slowly, incrementally, I was coming in focus. Now getting up or going to bed had become automatic again. I brushed my teeth. I washed my face. I was moved upstairs; half way up was a huge paint-ing by John Piper, an explosion of dark blues and greens, of growing things and half-perceived shapes and, I think a ruined building. I came to love that painting which brought something of the outside inside. I was always grateful it was not the usual anodyne pastoral print but allowed some drama and uncertainty. The nurses knocked on my door now; the illusion was that I was less of a patient and more of a guest. I was only in bed at night. I had my own bathroom; I made a few friends. From upstairs the gardens made sense.

I began to learn things about Dr L. She had a son and wished that she could have had more children but she had not been fortunate in this. Her husband was a doctor too and worked in prisons. She was, she said, and this intrigued me, completely apolitical and unimpressed by things material, as manifestations of power were of no interest to her.

I made a friend: a young married woman of similar age and weepi-ness to me. This gentle friendship sustained me, but the friend began an all-consuming affair with another charming but very disturbed inmate. One night she tapped on my door sobbing. Dr L. had discov-ered the relationship and been furious, but among her accusations was dereliction of friendship. Elizabeth needed you as a friend she had said.

The night nurse from Peterborough began ringing me in the day room. His reasons were vague. Guilt? Affection? Anxiety at possible revelations? Could my madness still be trusted to discredit anything I said? What if I got better? I told my nurse who had overheard some of the conversation. When we then told Dr L. her anger was cold and terrifying and immensely comforting.

Dr L. believed me instantly and completely.

She probably saved my life, if not the life itself the quality of that life and its years to come. She also began to put my grandmother back in her place. 'We were on the edge of breakthroughs,' she said, 'but there was still so little we could do in the 1940s and so much illness. The

therapies seem barbaric now, but we needed to be seen to do something, anything, faced with wards of seriously ill patients. Of course the
developments seemed exciting to some.' A long pause. 'The patients
were in despair, their families were in despair, and we were perhaps the
most despairing of all.' She sat forward. 'The thing about your grandmother', she said, moving notes from right to left in a thick, faded
brown file that had been hers, 'is that I imagine she would have lived
a reasonable life if she had been born a generation later. Once she was
on lithium and noticeably once imipramine became available she did
much better. It's why we started you on them. Why we gave you ECT:
because it worked for her.' It was odd to think some of my grandmother's suffering had helped me. But Dr L. knew what I was
thinking – she usually did. 'The leucotomy was eventually judged advis-
able, I think, because of the shingles. It was the shingles that tipped the
balance for her. We did a lot of them then, of course.'

I worked out that I had been in a mental hospital for one hundred
and eighty-three days so far and that reminded me of my grandmother counting the days in her old people's home. I wondered
whether she, in her psychiatric career, had endured any of the troubles
I had, or found any of the surprising kindnesses. It would be strange if
she hadn't; she had once been vulnerable and as eager to please and
as desperate as I had been.

The claustrophobic February mornings with their fog and yellow
lights started to get lighter and soon it was March. I talked to the nice
and gently melancholy man who ran round the building every morning.
He galloped about because he wanted to be ready for the outside.
There was a grandmotherly woman in a room near mine, and one afternoon we went for a walk around the grounds; she was as small as I was
tall and with my coat collar up and with a slight wind catching the tops
of the trees, I had to incline to hear her. We talked about rivers and
travelling; she had lived in Turkey and explained that while it was quite
easy for anyone to communicate in rudimentary Turkish, for the educated it was desirable to arrange a sentence that it hung in perfect

balance about its centre. It gave me something to think about. It was the first time I had walked rather than crossed the wide spaces around me. There were great beech trees, their branches still bare, last year's nut cases crunching underfoot as we passed, but at their feet were violets. Along the paths, tiny green spikes were breaking through the earth. It was an unstable sort of early spring day but from the palest blue sky dabbed with smudges of smoky clouds I could feel, just, that the sun had a little warmth in it. For the first time in months of lethargy I recognised the feelings I had. I felt just as I did every other year, at this time: hopeful.

My father came to see me as usual, and I could tell at once that he too could see and felt change. The day he came it was raining, but we sat and had tea looking out over the wide vista of parkland through big windows. My grandmother had had a stroke and was frail he said. I thought to myself that when I got out I would go and see her. When he left for the last time he hugged me and with my head buried in his rough wool jumper I could smell him, warm and familiar. We both knew it was going to be all right. Tentative, precarious, but all right. A week later my husband brought the children in. They were shy for five minutes but soon they were chatting away, and other patients were talking to them and giving them sweets. Soon I was sent out for a day return to try home again.

In April, I left for good. A rack of cloud covered and then uncovered the sun. I had been in hospital for half a year. Nobody had ever needed to bring me different clothes, and take away the ones I had arrived in – the thing I had dreaded as marking the beginning of a new season and confirming a life in an institution. I never looked back. For years afterwards if roads brought me to Northampton, I avoided letting my eyes drift to where I knew the hospital stood in its park. It was ungrateful, really.

The effect of mental illness on a marriage is very like adultery discovered. However determined you are to rebuild, to forgive, trust has been destroyed. Who knows whether there will be more straying, and the simplest actions take on significance that before the betrayal would never have been noticed. With the best will in the world the guilty party cannot promise not to weaken, cannot make things the way they were. Anyway, like the most adept adulterer, I now knew a few tricks; I had learned quite a lot about dissembling and power.

In the throes of depression it is impossible to believe it can be better. Now I knew that it was possible to escape. Now I knew that I could survive anything, that, I thought, I needed nobody. What had happened to me would never ever happen again. I had been vulnerable, and the word came from the Latin *vulnera*, wounds. My wounds were healed. I trembled at my anticipated recklessness, existing somewhere between invincibility and dread.

My husband's father had survived the Battle of Britain and service with the Chindits in Burma before dying in the air show accident. Another plane clipped the tail of his Meteor, and he fell from weightless grace to a fireball on earth. My husband's mother never really recovered from this early widowhood. For my husband, a man who had also, much later, lost wife and infant daughters in a painful divorce, my defection to madness was one abandonment too many. He was as apprehensive about my return as I was. Mostly he coped with it at first by pretending I wasn't there. He had retreated into his own shell. We were two quite different people, our weaknesses terribly and embarrassingly exposed to each other and to ourselves.

Coming home. I had longed for it – held on to this small memory of safety and privacy for so long. In reality the world outside was a very different place from the one I had left. It was dazzlingly bright, noisy and fast. The pace felt like an assault. I had been stationary for half a year. It had never been necessary to do more than one thing at once and even those had defeated me for a while. Dressing, eating, walking; that was all my life had been. Now I was a slow coward in this brave new world. My senses were exposed to so many stimuli that I emerged into an almost continuous state of panic, quite unable to filter those sounds and sights that should affect me from those that I could ignore.

From morning to night I was overwhelmed. Days were so intense, people so loud, movement of men and machines impossible to respond to. Cars and lorries hurtled passed; everybody seemed to shout. Spray, hooting, metallic plates, echoing an unbounded world of huge sounds. I could not coordinate preparing a meal or take on the washing, drying, folding and selecting clothes for a household. Crossing the road was impossible. A week into my return a friend took me to a new shopping centre. It had been built in my absence. Round and round we drove in the multi-storey car park. I was giddy and terrified and kept my hand on the door handle ready to jump. On the way home we passed a lay-by; I longed to tell her to set me down in the darkening day and let me walk home. Or, better, walk away.

I felt safest by night although I lay, a stranger to the man I had married, gazing at the rectangle of light that was our window. Once I had woken up alert with terror while my brain raced to remember perfectly familiar surroundings and make sense of them. Now the familiar was strange; I could not just lie straight, trying to breathe calmly and wait for consciousness to let recognition extinguish a bad dream. There were layers of dreams. As one peeled away it was only to reveal another. My home, the people I loved, my routines were all faintly out of kilter. I was, worst of all, homesick for St Andrew's. Friends fell into two categories: those who were so kind and understanding that they had to be learned again and those who were so hungry to have me back that I recoiled instinctively at their demands.

But all around me the year was unfolding. On good days there was the hint of buds and blue skies, and the haze of green on the hedges was full of promise. Sometimes I stood on the kitchen step and felt the sun on my face. And then, like a sudden, but lethal squall, out of nowhere came trouble, but for once not for me. On 5th April as I was preparing to leave hospital, Mrs Thatcher despatched a Royal Navy task force to some small islands in the South Atlantic known only from stamp collections. What had started as the sort of diplomatic spat that either amuses or bores became troop movements, threats, the rhetoric not of sanctions or displeasure but war. In late April 1982 I started to read again. I scoured the papers, I turned on the television. After a bit I stopped taking my emotional temperature the second I opened my eyes in my haste to turn on the radio. The children would cuddle up in bed with me while I listened in astonishment. Despite life in Berlin, despite the bomb sites of my childhood, it was astonishing to find that we were a country at war. A month later we were a country that had torpedoed an Argentinian ship full of teenage conscripts. The ship had survived Pearl Harbor and its torpedoes dated as well from the Second World War. It was all unbelievable. It was madness. I watched the television and cried and, for the first time in a year, it was not for me. I cried again when the Argentinians turned the *Sir Galahad* into an inferno in June and melted, blackened men were brought home.

I took my daughter and joined a protest march in London. My mother came too.

It was the Falklands which finally helped me make the transition from illness to sanity. It acted as a psychological zoom lens. One minute I was watching my life in close-up, in tiny detail, the next I had zoomed out fast, and the whole world was back in the frame. Pity, now, was for other people. It seemed quite wrong but it was undoubtedly the case that I was rehabilitated by a war.

Chapter 10

Lincolnshire 1980–1990

It was disturbing how far you could see driving around the flat side of Lincolnshire. Disturbing because, however far it was, what you actually saw was nothing. Three years after my recovery we had been moved further north and further east. It had been gently done; people were still cautious about my reactions to change, but although very different it was not as much of a culture shock as everyone about me had feared. I had a new daughter now. I never had a hint even of post-natal blues. It brought us all closer together and the older children were fascinated. By the time we moved I had a tall, fair-haired, twelve-year-old son, a beautiful daughter, a year younger, fine-boned with a fall of smooth black hair, and now an exuberant two-year-old, with blonde curls and eyes of palest blue.

Slowly I began to see that, just as I loved the hills of the west, the beech woods and the wild garlic of the limestone escarpments, the streams and linen-fold valleys, those who loved the east cherished the width and distance across which the eye could roam, the horizon vast: a line of grey with nothing to break up the landscape of light and soil but the occasional thin church spire. Even in spires, I never really adapted from the square bell-towers of the Cotswolds, although the fine eastern spires, lonely on any faintly rising ground, were more clearly about sweeping the hopes of earth to God and marking out man's path. In the west our towers were all too obviously interchange-ably defensive positions, or raised by merchants; our churches and our earth were golden limestone, the one sprung from the other, often the great glory of a west made wealthy and lovely by wool. Around the churches the clothiers' children and the poorest ploughboy had been buried in the woollen shrouds forced upon them by law, as a faltering wool trade sought out new markets to conquer.

Now it was black-earthed counties of the east, rich in subsidies, that were the agricultural treasure house. In Lincolnshire, sugar beet and kale and the bright chemical rape stretched flatly and efficiently across the landscape. What were marked as rivers on the map were more like canals in reality. Raised, treeless banks kept the water in and they ran straight for miles delivering water it where it was needed. Power resided in the Drainage Board where local worthies puffed on their pipes in an upper room on a dreary winter's afternoon and made the crucial decisions about sluices and allocations that kept the land rich and safe.

Square farmhouses in that liver-coloured Midlands brick with win-dows which reflected the sky looked every bit the small industrial units they were but younger farmers with aspirant wives planted three lines of leylandii around these homesteads to mark them off from the flat-lands around. The dark, fertile reclaimed soil brought forth a harvest that the brashy, weather-blighted Cotswold plateau had never dreamed of. The impossibly inaccessible hillsides and sodden valley folds of the west were a fecund tangle of willow and ash, but they were a barren landscape by comparison with where I lived now.

Next to our house was a pig farm whose pigs were housed in cor-rugated metal shelters, while on the edge of town behind our house chickens were processed from life to deep freeze, in a hangar, and on the road out of town fields of sandy Trent-side soil were periodically blown across the road, creating a dune and considerable delays on the 'A' road to Scunthorpe while they were retrieved, but mostly men in blue overalls and the best, biggest, brightest machinery beet could buy, worked every acre of the land. At weekends they left the prairies, put on cowboy hats and went and played country and western music in a club on a roundabout near Lincoln. Villages around here had muttered names: Scawby, Thealby, Kexby, Wrawby, Osgodby, always with the last syllable pronounced as a triumphant, explosive 'beh', or villages like Grayingham, Willeringham and Winteringham with the g said hard and adenoidally. Hagg, Brigg and Scotter summed up the hard, unsentimental spirit of Lincolnshire life, but there were strange names and monuments that could have come straight from a Gothic novel: Warping Head Drain, Owsby by Spital and Kimond le Mire.

Our house – not our house, of course, but the landowner's large house in which we lived – was gentrified within. High ceilings, flagged hallways, an Aga. An Aga, of course. But outside all was blight to my eyes. If there was a single issue that marked out my years in Lincolnshire it was the fence. There was no fence. There were two gate posts where in cosier times a gate had hung but now only a cessation of grass mowing and a rim of muddy ruts marked where home ended and fields began. I longed and importuned for a simple boundary marker that would keep the house enclosed and the business of the fields away. When we first arrived there were a range of redundant farm buildings opposite the house; low brick outbuildings of squalor and charm. More charm than the metal grain store which soon came to replace them and which hummed night and day drying the corn. Only the beet clamp interrupted the view of the grain store from my bedroom window. Inside the bedroom floribunda roses, lace curtains and a white-painted Victorian fireplace won the age-old farmer's wife's battle of refinement versus the soil.

All the time I was in Lincolnshire I waited for the symptoms of depression, symptoms that had, after all, pre-dated any diagnosis that that was what they were and had always popped up in my life when faced with certain combinations of event. The flatness, the isolation, the lack of a home of my own, should all have been precursors and homesickness fatal. But nothing happened. Instead, a tremendous calm descended. In my large house, far distant from my friends and the rest of my family, surrounded by a garden I couldn't be bothered to control, I gathered my breath with my husband and children. It was a protracted emotional convalescence. Life was small and un-ambitious and comforting. Even nature lay low. We lived in a town called, deceptively, Gainsborough: it was not a place of eighteenth-century elegance and landscaped gardens where the shades of silken, wigged grandees might loiter in ghostly nostalgia. It was a failed light industrial town, with exiled Londoners and Glaswegians housed in large estates with no work. It was on the Trent and was famous for two things: record levels of under-age pregnancy and the Aegir – named after the Norse god of the seashore. This was a tidal wave which sometimes tore up the Trent at equinoxes, appearing at its most dramatic at Gainsborough. It was said to have been a model for the flood in *The Mill on the Floss*. It never so much as rippled in all the time I was there.

But then there was a series of strange events. I can't call them premonitions because I didn't experience them like that at the time and, anyway, I would have to dismiss them as a – mostly – rational person. One late afternoon in winter, driving along the Scunthorpe road, I saw one of the small abrupt farmhouses on fire. Flames leaped at the bedroom windows, but when I rounded the bend with my heart racing, preparing to stop, it was just an illusion of the setting sun, an illusion that left my arms trembling on the wheel. The real fire came weeks later, when I was again returning home, and there were no flames, just smoke and a shocking, unforgettable smell. In the long field running down to our house – black shapes lumbered about. There was something terribly wrong with the scene but my mind struggled to make sense of it. There was a police car and two small figures in overalls ran up and down the perimeter fence and then slowly I took in the greasy black smoke and heard the cries: of humans in distress, of mortally injured pigs. The spark from a jump lead starting a broken-down tractor had ignited straw bales. In seconds the barn housing the animals was ablaze. For a while the pigs were trapped but then in terror they broke out through the side, horribly injured. The police were preventing the farmer from despatching them with his shotgun. The law required they wait for a vet and a humane destroyer. I sat in my car cold and shocked. The always smiling farmer, who had no children, wept, and I wished I hadn't seen him laid low by grief.

The same winter a motorist skidded on the icy road and, trapped in his car at the end of the drive, was incinerated while onlookers were beaten back by the heat.

Then, one evening, my mother rang. 'There's been a fire', she began. Indeed there had. She was out at the time doing her psychotherapy in Oxford. Faulty wires under some boards in a spare bedroom had ignited dust and smouldered for days. Finally a fireball burst through the floorboards, underlay and fitted carpet. It leaped up the walls, caught at the curtains, licked across the ceiling. It spread into the neighbouring bedroom where windows faced three ways. The panes shattered in the heat, and the oxygen that was sucked in turned the fire into a force able to blow a great hole in the roof.

The beauty of the house had always been its isolation and the proximity to water. Now its remoteness meant that it was a long time – too long – until a rising plume of smoke was spotted, and the great expanse of water was useless to extinguish the flames. Fire engines arrived from Gloucestershire and Wiltshire. Pulling down the walls they tried to create a fire break but by the time my mother turned down the drive, seeing the blue lights twinkling in the inlets of her lake, it was all ablaze in the winter gloom. A kind policeman took her into a car where to a background of radios, falling timbers, shouting, and, at one point the lifting out of a crate of beer for the exhausted fire men, she rang to say that her house, my grandfather's house, the house that would have been my brother's house, was gone.

Now she really had nothing, just the clothes she was wearing. Two days later we returned in daylight. There was something elemental about the destruction. There, still, stood the house, on bare earth, its immediate garden gone, trampled by firemen. The charred structure was surrounded by spoil heaps of burned debris beyond which the water of the lake was smooth and untroubled. The gable end stood singed but intact, so that if you approached it with your eyes half shut, it looked like home. On the ground floor, the lavatory was the one room of the house that remained inviolate. Inside the stairs still went up filthily to the top floor, above them the sky and ruined joists. In my mother's bedroom her bed – a black slab – was still recognisable.

In a linen cupboard the vaunted Cavendish linen was still folded on the shelves as were sheets monogrammed with the Cunard Lines crest. Yet all was soft, burned and crumbled away at a touch. The walls which remained were saturated and the floors squelched underfoot. A wall of jars in the kitchen still stood, their contents intact but the glass cracked and blackened. Old Henry's solid Arts and Crafts furniture, the trappings of his early success, came through, in the hands of experts. After the fire we were finally able to decide that the bigger pieces were hideous, although we briefly reconsidered when it all went for auction and the bidding reached unexpected heights. I kept his coal box and umbrella stand, though. I have them still, singed leather and all.

My mother's papers, her photographs, files, our school reports, her letters, were all gone. I was glad I had been pilfering family items since childhood; among the many small things I was able to return to my mother was a chipped white china elephant with clover on his sides and his trunk at a cheerful angle. It was a start.

The effects of what should have been a dreadful set back were not quite as one might have guessed. My mother had been abandoned by my father in that house and it was where my step-grandmother had lain in agony while she died, slowly, of cancer in her early forties. Not so long ago, at my maddest and most desperate I was hidden away in one small room up there with my terrors, deeply sedated, waiting to be moved to St Andrew's, while in another my sister had struggled with a shrinking world of anorexia. This time, despite the apparent violence, no one was hurt. Even the dogs and cat had escaped. Just as there had been an atom of excitement in seeing the immediate, smoking devastation, so as the days and weeks passed we could gaze on the ruins with a nugget of relief.

After a bit we discovered strange survivals. A copper vase my mother had had since she married, a handful of pictures which turned out to be retrievable behind opaque, cracked panes, my mother's jewellery box in the sludge. She had never had jewels but she was glad to see the box; it had always signified hope. Some family papers were not so wet they couldn't be aired out. We began to be excited by small finds – trying to remember where things had stood to look for them. It was mostly hopeless, of course, and soon a fire officer arrived and chivvied us out; the water tanks were delicately poised on damaged beams ready to pulverize us as they fell.

But help flooded in too. My mother, always so strong, had been divested of the means to be irresolutely independent and had to accept the care of friends in the village and, like her mother before her, to live with her sister. She said with a degree of wonderment that she was surprised how little she turned out to care about her material possessions and that she felt free. It was always good to find out you were a nicer person than you'd thought, she said, and for the first time in her life she could buy clothes that matched; clothes that would be more in the spirit of accessories, than separates, and furniture that she actually liked. The jokes we had made about Thornfield Hall, the doomed house in *Jane Eyre*, and the fact that the family house was called Thornhill Waters had taken on a deliciously uncomfortable significance. Life seldom followed art so assiduously. My grandmother had been locked, raving in the attic at Manor Farm, now my grandfather's house had burned almost to the ground. But the fates had been fairly forgiving. Nobody was dashed to pieces – it only had two low storeys – or blinded in redemption.

Most of all, the last trace of my grandfather's influence and taste and the links to my mother's own sad childhood had been expunged. The many items he had taken as souvenirs from his winter cruises, hidden in his weighty cabin trunks, were all gone. I personally regretted the Queen Mary footstool, which I had often considered re-housing myself. His gold-yellow carpet – which, like Midas, he laid everywhere he lived, was black and soon smelled of decomposition; the pages of his books on socialism, sex, Impressionism, Freud, war, car crashes, water lilies and opera would never, *could* never, be turned again, if they ever had been in life. Those that weren't destroyed smelled of soot forever afterwards. This included his *Debrett* where the corded silk bookmark still plunged between the pages to his hard-won resting place in the bosom of his former wife's family.

His Maria Callas, Tom Lehrer and Edith Piaf records (demonstrating a simultaneous appreciation of both high, alternative and foreign culture), his self-designed bobbled glass kitchen units, the inlaid wood dresser – quite valuable before he made holes in the back, wired it for light and converted it to a cocktail cabinet; the charts marking his years of daily weigh-ins and the elaborate head-high scales upon which this had been accomplished, had all disappeared; the quilted pin-boards with their pattern of tumbling game-birds were reduced to ashes; his own, heavy-handed paintings, somewhat in the manner of Utrillo, had melted, the oils sizzling down the wall.

He and all his works had, finally, gone up in smoke.

Outside, the gardens were largely destroyed, but the willows still stood at the edge of the water and if for a while it looked more like the gravel pit it had once been, and from which our wealth had been dug, but nature was soon disguising this reality again. The insurance company proved strangely obdurate over the matter of the downstairs lavatory. There it stood, not a mark on it in its breeze-block bunker and there they insisted the room must stay, valued at £4000. So it was that when the new house rose two years later, it did so with a small lavatory at its centre. It was a sort of shrine to survival.

The new Thornhill rises on the rubble of the old

My mother did not want to tell my grandmother what had happened; she was declining in health and who knew what horrors fire still held for her.

In the time I knew her as an adult my grandmother appeared to have left strong feelings, strong desires, behind her. Mostly she complained about this and that in a gentle way. But it turned out there was something she wanted to do and she was quite insistent, and so it was that she set out on her last journey. With a nurse she embarked on a cruise to Norway where she saw the fjords, the ice, the snow, the mountains, the forests and glaciers – all the things she had loved as a girl; the sort of terrain she had once mastered. Finally she ended up in the furthest north at Tromsø where she saw what she had come for: the Aurora Borealis. The Northern Lights. The Northern dawn. She stood unsteadily on the deck and she watched the flares of green and gold and the curtains of blue and indigo wash from the sky and quiver over the hills and then she came home.

She died one night in January, seventy years after the party at Villa de Giez, near Lausanne. It was a century after her eldest sister Geraldine had been born, sealing her mother Ada Curtis's relationship with Gerald Howard and the direction of this strangely troubled family.

My mother and aunt were ten miles away when my grandmother died in her unloved old people's home. She died as she had lived, alone. She didn't have anything to leave anybody, but my mother gave me a little wooden box of hers that I had loved as a child. It was cedar wood and was very smooth outside but inside the lid was a creature who was called an ouroboros, my grandmother had told me. He was a fat snake curled up like an 'O' and eating his own tail. Now it was my mine.

My grandmother's funeral took place in Fairford, Henry's birthplace. The funeral tied her inexorably with Gloucestershire and her former husband's roots; she had, despite the celebrated social connections, no roots of her own. Her family had always been isolated and blood was their territory, as they clutched the remnants of their monogrammed silver and linen, always looking back to Chatsworth and Holker and especially Compton Place, as some golden age of inclusion from which they alone had been expelled. It was probably no coincidence that first Gerald and then his children always hovered around a variety of seaside towns.

In our family burial was the tradition, but my grandmother had been so very unhappy at times in Gloucestershire that actually interring her in the churchyard seemed a little unkind, so in death her ashes were scattered alongside the swift-flowing River Coln near the Round House. This was in its way a reunion; it was the river she had tried hard to end her life in forty years earlier but it was also where she had fished on summer evenings in better times. This last dispersal was more appropriate for a restless, homeless spirit than a burial. We planted a rose for her in Fairford churchyard instead but it failed to prosper. Eventually, nearly a quarter of a century after her death, we arranged for her name to be added to my mother's gravestone: '*and remembering Joan Edith Barbara Edmonds, née Howard*'.

My grandfather, on the other hand, who had built up his respectable persona as dynastic gentleman farmer and landowner in Fairford, was finally taken back to Bampton churchyard in Oxfordshire, where *he* could be re-united with the first woman to desert him: his mother, who had died when he was six.

At my grandmother's funeral, her Polish Star and Grand Order of Merit lay on her coffin. Around her were her three children, ten grand-children and two great-grandchildren. Several had my grandmother's great ability with languages, others her love of cooking. Many came to share her ability to create gardens. Some were fine skiers, one or two had the alleged Howard chin. None of her grandchildren had lived through a World War. Of her large number of siblings only Blanche outlived her.

And did the brain surgery finally give her some peace? Well, depending on how you looked at it, she was either cured or lost for ever.

Chapter 11

Home

In hourglasses the grains of sand increasingly rub one another smooth until finally they flow almost without friction from one bulb into another, polishing the neck wider all the time. The older an hourglass the more quickly it runs. Unnoticed the hourglass measures out even shorter hours.

Ernst Junger 1895–1998

My mother only outlived her own mother by a decade. Where my grandmother died at a respectable and, given her history and intentions, rather surprising, eighty-three, my mother, who embraced life, was twenty years younger at her own death.

In the years after the fire I realised that the mood swings which had once elated and frightened me had smoothed out. The landscape of my mind had changed with the landscape of my surroundings. I could have moments of sentimentality about losing my childhood home, but I was not scarred by it. I was sad for my mother but not obsessed with guilt or grief. In time my father was a far calmer, fulfilled and more enquiring man in a new marriage. My sister was putting on weight and returned to university and then to marriage and babies. My brother had his large family of sons. My own children were settled and happy.

By degrees I stopped taking the pills I'd been on since I was in hospital. Nothing changed. Words stayed on the page.

My mother too was moving on. She lost quite a lot of weight for a while. She went out with a couple of men in a half-hearted way. Her new house, built on the ruins of the old, though much simpler, had a consulting room for an increasing body of patients. It was filled with her own things, furnished in the present not the past. It was so close to the lake that when you lay on the bed reflections of light flickered on the wooden ceilings like watery clouds. She began to read much more widely as so many of her patients were Oxford academics and she needed to keep ahead, she said. There were books on every subject from religion to gynaecology, from history to poetry, novels and plays on her new shelves. She moved into provinces that had been my father's: classical music was the main one, though she also went to exhibitions and brought modern prints to hang on the walls. In art she seemed very keen on green. She even took up riding again and coerced me into accompanying her up and down old bridleways, picking the biggest blackberries from the better vantage point of a horse.

The Americans were still up at the base in the village. After the war they had never left. In spring we walked; her, the children, with my youngest in a pushchair, and my aunt to protest against the bombing of Libya. She and my aunt were energetic, vocal and persuasive. Large numbers turned up. That autumn she decided she would return to South Africa. My brother, a school-teacher, was taking a group of pupils and she decided to go along. There were so many issues she needed to resolve, she said.

Since her training she was keen on resolution and reconciliation. She no longer discussed masturbation or got into squabbles about penis-envy; it had all moved on a bit. Now she simply corrected people who said 'subconscious' rather than 'unconscious', talked a lot about transference or wrote papers about 'the fugitive libido'. Cynics might see in the structures of psycho-therapeutic training, a remarkably clever self-sustaining system: all those dishing it out had, simultaneously, to be in therapy themselves; as a business there was no way it could fail;

guarding the guards lay at its heart. But there was no question that she was on a long, difficult and brave journey into her own past. She had always told us in caricature accounts of the awfulness of evacuation, of missing her mother, of being unwanted, of having her childhood snatched away, but now she started to remember the colours, the smells, the brightness and the wide spaces. She was looking forward to the trip. She took my teenage son. It was a huge success.

But not so long after her return she began to lose vigour. We went to France to see her sister but first she seemed to have flu and then exhaustion. Walking round Nice in the heat, she trailed behind, and eventually sagged onto the steps of a hotel, her eyes closed and her head against the cold stone. None of us knew it, but it was the last time she would see the town. When she left France, with some relief this time, it was for ever.

From then onwards she had fleeting fevers, often she was cold and shivery, most mornings she woke up feeling sick. She was diagnosed with diabetes. She was sleepy and grumpy and either not herself or, worse, she was rather *more* of herself: dogmatic and judgmental, but without her customary wit. For a year or two all these changes were intermittent. Her rather obsessive cleanliness was replaced by a careless disregard for cleaning at all. She refused to wash – as opposed to rinse in cold water – coffee cups, her clothes were slightly stale.

After my father's departure, she had changed sides. She began to occupy what had been his space in the matrimonial bed, and her own space was the one vacated. The fire turned the marriage bed to ash. Not long after her new house was built, she was attempting to sleep in that side of the replacement bed without disarranging the other side at all, so that it took less making. There were other odd housekeeping short cuts. She ate the same thing day after day. She refused to use the washing machine on anything but cold cycle. Her linen got dingier and more stained. When she went out, my sister and I would rush to put her towels through on a hot wash, or rinse her cups in bleach. In the old days she would have noticed and been outraged.

A few months later I had a call: my mother was at the Round House with my sister and her family and had 'gone a bit peculiar'. When I arrived she was sitting very upright and slightly forward in her chair. She was talking nonsense, some of it very funny and, not having seen her for a couple of weeks, I now noticed that she was slightly yellow. Her hands were very cold but then it was winter. She was muddled about who was who and looked worried so I put her in the car and took her home to the lake while she delivered a long monologue about members of the royal family, previously below her field of vision and irredeemably tainted by their association with Geraldine, but who she was now calling the royals. The doctor came and she was admitted to hospital. After he had rung the ambulance he walked around the lake with me for a while. My mother had presented at the surgery a few months earlier and she already had advanced liver disease. She had been slow to complain and, by the time they saw her, she was dying. She was too ill and too overweight for a transplant. Her failing liver would cause periods of mental confusion and personality change. They could treat her this time, she would be put on medication and she would have good periods, but the end was in no doubt. She had perhaps two to three years left. It was probably a virus caught in Africa but it could be genetic; Stuart had died of a similar illness. But Stuart had drunk and my mother never had. The doctor reeled off a list of possibilities. Nobody ever quite knew.

That summer we went to Turkey. We had taken a house not far from the sea, nervous about whether her illness would be affected by the heat she usually loved. In the event she flourished. As a matriarch she was a respected figure; here she was with her two daughters, two sons-in-law and five of her grandchildren. She was large and dignified and looked well, her jaundice disguised by her tan. We had a hot little stone cottage with un-English hollyhocks and geraniums by the door and a dusty path which zigzagged downhill through great plates of rock. In the morning there were cicadas, and when we returned home at the end of the day the dry grass crackled as small tortoises shuffled off under the shelter of our steps.

We saw ancient tombs standing like rocks in the clearest of seas. We saw mountains that close to were honeycombed necropolises. At Patara the finest sand had engulfed all but the tips of arches, temples and aqueducts. The only building standing free of this dry flood of sand was a granary, empty for millennia. We stood in the ruins of ancient Greek theatres, and my mother's voice projected from the stage to the back rows. The ruins of the Letoon, once the greatest sanctuary in Lydia, lay half submerged. Here Leto had turned the villagers into frogs for not letting her and her twins drink from their pool. The frogs were still here, chirruping in the rushes, while terrapins basked on fragments of arch. It was a monument to maternal vengeance. It was the most extraordinary and incomprehensible country I had ever seen.

In water my mother had always been in her element; playing or swimming, pushing the water behind her with firm strokes, she was always graceful. Brought up by rivers, seas and gravel pits she was weightless and in control when she swam. She had strong and shapely arms and legs. Her handsome face was unafraid however deep or rough it was and her hair curled tightly when it was wet making her look younger. Only as she emerged from the water onto land with the wet draperies of her large bathing costume unkindly clinging to her was she turned back into a fat woman, who became breathless when walking uphill.

One morning we joined a small boat party and sailed out into the bay from islet to islet, stopping to swim, to barbeque, to pick our way between broken potsherds and clearings of olive trees around mosaic floors. On the way home, the sea was calm and deep and clear. My mother dived in when we stopped in a particularly pretty bay. We were so used to her being the best swimmer of us all that we scarcely bothered to watch her but she had got tired, and when we swam back to the boat she couldn't pull herself up the rope ladder. She got her feet on the lowest rung, her arms grasping each side above her. But her sodden swimsuit adding to her own weight defeated her. She simply couldn't raise herself and between efforts to do so, there she hung, like cargo, waiting to be hauled in. She was grey-faced and she strained until her knuckles were white, biting her lip. My sister and I reached down and touched her hands but we couldn't get ours around her slippery wrists. I lay down and tried to reach the back of her swimming costume but she was too far below me.

The other English passengers looked embarrassed. We were embarrassed for her and anxious. Two young crew members ran over. The boat, mortifyingly, dipped heavily to one side. She was lowered nearer to the water. They reached for her; she, now white beneath her tan, reached up for them, let go and fell. There was a horrible crack as she hit the water. This time she was not, as she had always seemed when swimming about, weightless; now her weight bore her down with surprising speed. Shocked or resigned she made no attempt to swim upwards. My sister and I gazed over the edge where she sank beneath us, her brown arms and legs out, her hair wide from her face, her bright costume, sinking away from us, clear under the water and yet already far away. It was a moment suspended in time.

The look my sister and I gave each other was one of knowledge that this was the moment that we would always share, always remember, when we watched our mother drown on a family holiday. She was already too deep for my swimming to reach her. But then one of the boatmen, less susceptible to the dramatic moment being recorded forever, was in the water diving to fetch her in. He dived, cut downwards, almost vertically, with two or three strong strokes, and then had her in his arms, he and the water bearing her up and then two pairs of strong arms reached down, first of all just managing to hold her hanging above the water. They made a last burst of effort and they landed her: first one arm and leg, then a second leg and finally all of her was delivered glistening and flaccid on to the deck. It was probably the moment at which she gave up fighting.

She lay along the benches and just occasionally she whimpered very gently. When she moved a little the planks had left long marks along her skin. Despite the heat, and her pink shoulders, she was cold and her lips were grey. We covered her with damp swimming towels. I could not fit beside her on the narrow seat but perched at the end with her feet on my lap, like the small dog under the booted heels of some knightly tomb. I stroked her cold toes. Some time between the bay and the shore, she said 'Don't leave me.'

I did not leave her. But from that day I knew that she would leave me.

When we went back to Lincolnshire I knew that I had to act. My mother was dying, my children were growing, the years were rolling across this flattest of counties. I had no job, few friends within 100 miles and no qualifications. That year I decided that rather than go on waiting for depression to find me, I would take action.

I started to think about what would come next. My mood swings and the dramas of my teens and twenties had occupied so much of my energy that suddenly I had time on my hands. I decided to go through the few papers I'd rescued from the fire, and the diaries and documents already in my possession and try to organise them. I had some vague thought of one day going to university and thought it might make a project to buttress my rather insubstantial A Levels. In novels tremendous mysteries were unravelled in posthumous explorations of unknown caches of paper. Sometimes there were fortunes to be found.

At heart there were things I hoped I might understand. What made my grandmother mad. What made *us* mad. Why my mother ate. Whether we were in fact Jewish as my mother claimed. I'd always escaped by reading and now I thought I might read my way into some kind of personal enlightenment. Anyway, although at weekends I returned to what I still called home and spent time with my mother, during the weeks in the east I had long, silent days to fill, now all my children were at school.

I made a list. It went something like this:

1) why mad?

2) Jewish?

3) where did Gerald meet Ada?

4) where did the money come from?

5) where's Rupert?

To begin with I was just trying to understand the previous generations of my own family: why some had unconventional lives, others were more obviously disturbed, and a few lead calm lives of probity and good sense. I was trying to understand whether what had happened to me had been inevitable. I had begun to be drawn in by my detective work and my archive seemed to expand quite swiftly as other members of my family handed things over. I already had the diaries, but the main body of papers were in a Gladstone bag and a tin cash box. Both had belonged to Henry Edmonds and were stamped with his initials. They were appropriate containers for Henry's twin poles of existence: gentleman of means and successful merchant.

There was several things that were curious about these papers. They were both carefully and carelessly assembled. For a start they often represented both sides of a correspondence; so someone had bothered to retrieve their own outgoing letters and save them. Then, despite the inclusion of papers that were shocking or inflammatory or simply extremely unflattering to the individual identified, there were major family events of the period which went completely unrecorded. Also, somebody had torn off virtually all the stamps and, in their eagerness either to sell them or to furnish a stamp album, took with them a corner of every letter inside the envelopes. But it would be disingenuous of me to express shock; I only noticed when it occurred to me lying in bed one night that there might be valuable stamps on the correspondence and I went down to check.

The range of what else had been preserved was agreeably eccentric. There was light-weight propaganda for dropping from military aircraft into occupied Norway or, in Gothic script, into enemy Germany, a summons for speeding in Wales, an 1899 report on the effects of the use of soft-nosed bullets at Omdurman, a thank-you letter for a birthday present, handwritten on Downing Street paper and signed by Winston Churchill. In a large envelope were pre-First World War drug prescriptions for venereal disease made out in Paris; a 1944 cartoon strip in which Hitler is shown in despair confronting various auguries of defeat and eventually hanging himself; the stained, possibly blood-stained 1914 military papers of a French corporal of Light Infantry: Théogène Jourcin of Albertville, several photographs of a single nineteenth-century family gravestone, a Masonic handbook for the Suez Lodge, and typewritten letters from my grandfather beseeching the authorities to give him a medal.

I picked out an envelope at random.

From the Hotel de l'Univers et du Portugal, 10, rue Croix-des-Petits-Champs, Paris: '<u>SIR YOU ARE THE ACE OF CADS</u>' began the letter inside. It continued in angry ink for four sides before ending, tellingly, 'I'm sorry I ever went to the Legion dance.'

These were Henry's bags but there was a lot more in them than Henry's things.

Where my grandmother's dowry of silver and linen had attractive provenance – it had its well-worn family monograms – all the wealth of the family was made by her father-in-law, Henry. But despite the numerous stock transfers, share portfolios and deeds in Henry's box, where the money came from was a question that was to remain unanswered. His father was a small-scale farmer, his mother and grandmother were gypsies, there were several older sons than Henry, and when Henry was growing up in the 1870s there had been a series of disastrous harvests. Farms were failing all over the west, and poverty ravaged farming communities. Henry cannot have had an easy childhood. Yet by thirty he had become a very rich man. Presumably he made some lucky investments, or, more likely, some very wise investments, showing early the business acumen that made him a man of some substance by the First World War. But where he got the money to invest in the first place is a mystery.

Henry Edmonds, my great-grandfather, 1927

While pursuing Henry's money, Henry's alleged enlightened Fabianism was the first piece of family history to unravel. The bag was stuffed full of political letters, newspaper cuttings, pamphlets; sympathetic accounts of the anarchist assassin of Empress Elisabeth of Austria, gleeful reports of industrial arson, of impending uprisings abroad, lists of unions susceptible to encouragement to strike, membership papers, political donations. Henry, as it turned out, was not a Fabian but a British Socialist, a communist, a man every bit as paternalistic in dictating to the lower classes, every bit as determined to assert the right of working men and, at a pinch, women, as the more respectable Fabians, but far more willing to contemplate extreme means of achieving this. And far more able to finance what he could not undertake himself. In politics he was Brother Edmonds but in business he was Edmonds Bros., London Stores. Henry's unsuccessful attempt to hire the Royal Opera House for a political rally is followed by success in booking the Royal Albert Hall. Henry wanted anarchy. Henry hoped for revolution. Henry wanted the House of Lords to be 'utterly cast down' one way or another – he wasn't choosy which. Above all he loathed the bloated capitalist whose figure stalked the wad of bitter and shocking cartoons he had cut from the *Daily Herald* and filed. A capitalist not unlike the man he was becoming.

Henry wrote pamphlets. 'Women': <u>No Objection to Women as Women</u>. 'EDUCATE TO AGITATE' scrawls Henry in a draft. It is 1912. Henry knows he is supposed to want women to get the vote. But he has problems with this ('No training. No experience. Do not read.') How could women deal with instituting compulsory military service, launching Dreadnaughts, he asks (himself) in tiny writing? How many of them, he wonders, finally, have read Homer.

On the whole I was finding further questions rather than answers to the questions I'd started with. But while I was trying to assemble the past out of these scraps I was also laying down foundations for the future. I decided the time had come to go forward. I sent for university brochures. I started filling in forms. But I was still doing research, and one line led me in a surprising direction.

It was easy to find Gerald and Ada's marriage and birth certificates but there were revelations there too. Ada, or Ada's roots, had been just down the road all the time I was thinking about her.

A few years after I had left Lincolnshire never to return, I went back. Lincoln cathedral with its great buttresses and steep roof can be seen from miles away high above the flat lands. Falling away from it are the steep cobbled streets, which pass the castle, the ancient Jew's House, then continue down to the chain stores and the river of people. Over the railway line and the houses get meaner. Here in the county I had considered to be so alien, my great-grandmother had been born, schooled, sent off into service and had returned in disgrace in 1881 to give birth to a little girl, Geraldine; the first of her illegitimate children by Gerald.

It turned out that Ada's family had never left. Only Ada had been snatched away by love in the shape of the importunate Gerald. Her ancestors, her family, *my* family, had been here for generation after generation. They had their own dynasty going back generations in the same place doing the same thing. They were still butchers; prosperous ones now. I must have passed them, unknown in the street, eaten meat from their shop, even as I longed for home in the west. I met my fourth cousin. *Their* story of Ada was quite different. But their information threw some light on the Howard family's ostracism of her and why Gerald might have waited until his mother died to marry her.

Gerald had met Ada when he employed her as a housekeeper-cum-maid of all work. She was his servant; by the social standards of the time, it should have been an unbridgeable gap in status. The Curtises implied the blame lay with Gerald. Ada had been a nurse, they thought, before Gerald took her into his household and then ruined her. She had simply wanted to escape a father who drank and when in an alcoholic rage would cut her bonnets up and stuff them down the lavatory.

It was odd to have to delete butchers' shops from my decreasing list of phobias now they were family. It wasn't sawdust and the smell of blood now I discovered, but I hadn't been inside a butcher's shop for decades.

Stuart's wife had described the family as Jewish in her 1930's *roman-à-clef*. My mother believed that it was Ada who was Jewish. She thought that lay behind the Howard family's antipathy to Gerald's bride. It now seemed unlikely. The fact that Ada had been Gerald's servant, the illegitimate children, the butcher father, would have been cause enough to ensure the disapprobation of one of England's more self-regarding families. The maternal line of Ada's family had come from Jamaica in the early nineteenth century and there were no records of them anywhere. They had dark hair and dark complexions. Probably not Jewish then, but different; just as, on my grandfather's side, Henry's mother, the gypsy, was different. In the long run perhaps Ada found the disapproval of her husband's family didn't matter to her. She sits, big, strong, her thick hair piled up, at the centre of family holidays in photographs forty years later and there she is in the last picture I have of her with the Howard coat of arms and a large feather worn on her hat.

Ada in her hat with coat of arms, c.1913

Madness as a heritage turned out to be as elusive as Jewish ancestry. Some years earlier, when I was pregnant with my third child, I was sent for a psychiatric assessment. 'I'm surprised you thought it wise to embark on another pregnancy', said the psychiatrist, who had never met me before, as he scanned my notes. 'I imagine you'll be sterilised afterwards?' I had often worried that my depression had cast a shadow over my older children's childhood, but nobody had ever suggested

that I should never have *had* children. I tried to get him to expand. Was
it my own maternal skills that were in doubt or the genetic heritage I
was passing on? It seemed to be mostly that he thought I was jeopar-
dising my recovery. 'But of course you know very well, there's a familial
element to these things', he said. 'I understand there are other members of your family with serious depressive illness.' I cried on the way
home. I had thought my children were my one success. The two people
whom I loved completely. The thought that I might have passed the
bleak gift of mental illness onto them was one I had tried hard to avoid.

But the more I explored my grandmother's life, the less straightforward the connection became. My grandfather's family were
unconventional and my grandmother's were insular but there was no
line of lunacy shrieking through the generations. My grandmother was
simply born at the wrong time. The last decade of the nineteenth century, which might have appeared to be the apogee of British influence
and achievement, was, as it turned out, the worst of all times to be born
even with a precarious toe-hold in the upper classes. She was a casualty
first of the peculiarities of her parents' marriage and the stifling and
unforgiving mould of Victorian social attitudes, then of a terrible and
disfiguring accident, and finally of two World Wars in which her losses,
though less than some had to endure, broke her spirit as well as her
heart.

Probably she inherited a rather labile personality. From whom
rather depended on your political views. The Howards, thought my
father, Ada, said other members of the family. Three of my grandmother's sisters, my sad trio of older great-aunts, were clearly deranged
to some degree. Only the youngest seems to have found happiness and
that through a short but happy marriage. The boys did better because
they broke away – a long way away – young. But it was history as much
as genetics which made my grandmother's life so difficult.

Nevertheless, among her thirty-six descendants there are, unequivocally, a number who have had their struggles with depression or manic
depression. They are spread out across the family but those who have

it have mostly been blessed with some talent in art or music, acting or writing. Some think it is worth the price.

While I was still exploring my small archive, I applied to a polytechnic to read English. They accepted me, so I upped my hand and applied to a good Midlands university near home. The interviewer told me that he would offer me a place but suggested that all I seemed to have done was read and write since I left school, had I ever considered another subject? A fresh, new subject. He thought I might get bored. It was a strange thing to suggest about his own life choice I thought.

I considered – strongly – history but then I kept returning to memories of Turkey and the fascinating, incomprehensible muddle of ruins and further back to the gravel heaps and the fossils. When my grandfather had been digging holes in Gloucestershire they came across burials from time to time and tiny Anglo-Saxon settlements. All work stopped while these distant lives were exposed in neat trenches marked with pegs and lines. The best bit was when they found skeletons. My grandfather would fume at these interruptions to the smooth flow of minerals and money but then adopt a proprietorial position to the acquisition of knowledge and walk around the site, pointing out its salient features – as explained to him earlier by the archaeologists – to his guests as if he had personally stripped the field simply to benefit the historical record.

A few months later I put in my application to read Archaeology and Anthropology at Cambridge. In December I went up for interview and an exam. I didn't tell anybody. The city was still and frosty, the grass and trees white, and the sky brightest blue. I sat in a taxi looking at my hands – I couldn't bear to see something that I wanted so much and might not be able to have. It was the nearest I had ever experienced to love at first sight. That night I couldn't sleep for excitement.

The offer arrived on my birthday in January.

She saw me go to Cambridge. On the first day I sat on a bed too small to sprawl on, gazing at my empty bookshelves and large desk, wondering what on earth I had done. I missed my children. There was a large bunch of flowers waiting on the desk and a small card. On the card it said 'At last. M. x'.

The last year of my mother's illness is marked in my memory by set pieces. The day when the doctor gave her the first clear intimation that time was now running out quite fast, we had seats booked for the play about C. S. Lewis, *Shadowlands*. My mother had bought a copy of Lewis's *A Grief Observed* to assist her in observing the grief of her patients, and I had been so excited by *The Lion, the Witch and the Wardrobe*, which she had read to me as a child, that the whiff of a purple crystal mothball was still as laden with possibilities as any tuberose or ambergris. So we went. To change our plans seemed to acknowledge news too momentous to be absorbed. We found ourselves watching a brilliant, unbearable explosion of suffering, loss and grief. There was no moment in our relationship with her illness when things were been more clearly laid out. In Act One we sat stiffly, slightly embarrassed. In Act Two, finally, we both cried. By Act Three we were smiling, relaxing into the awful appropriateness of it all while all around us discreet English sniffs were dabbed away with handkerchiefs. Outside my mother had to prop herself on the windowsill of an eastern airline to recover. Behind her a globe turned slowly, its destinations illuminated like stars. 'I hope it turns out to be a wasting disease', she said.

It wasn't; she died as large as she had lived, but it was quite quick.

It all ended just before my first-year exams in June. I had walked back from a supervision on a hot dusty Cambridge day in late May. I was hoping I might get a First in Part I. I had hardly unlocked my room when the telephone rang. She was in a coma in hospital in Oxford. She had seen her patients in the morning. Evidently something about her condition had alarmed her but she had not rung any of us or her friends, simply called a taxi. On arrival at the John Radcliffe Hospital, she was just about lucid. By the time she got up to the ward she was confused, half an hour later she was unconscious, a whole month later – she was, after all, not very old – and her heart was strong – she was dead. It was typically efficient but also sufficiently dramatic to make a fitting end. My father returned to sit with her as things moved inexorably to their conclusion. She would have liked that too.

In the last days, when she had sunk deep into an irreversible coma and her kidneys were failing, my sister and I sat in my mother's room going through her things, knowing we would soon be dispersing them. By her bed was her cassette player and various tapes piled up to be played. There was Strauss's *Four Last Songs*, the mournful *Scottish Fantasy* by Bruch, and Mendelssohn's *Trust in the Lord* (she didn't but she liked the idea). It was a wonderfully excessive soundtrack to a terminal illness lived to the full. There was one further tape, already in the slot. My sister pressed the knob and we waited to weep. It was *The Best of Richard Clayderman*.

My mother had eaten for comfort and to pass the time. Under the seat of the car and in every coat or apron pocket were Mars bar wrappers and the odd forgotten chunk of hairy chocolate. She ate clotted cream on French bread. She ate jam from jars. But she seemed to be a stranger to any kind of overt depression. Genes for mental illness appeared to have passed her by as had any literary or artistic ability. She read words but could not compose them, and the drawing of a stick man was the limit of her capability. But madness had its role to play in her life. Instead of *being* mad she made a career out of judging who else was and became a psychotherapist. You would have thought she'd had enough of that at home but of course treating the disturbed gave her an element of control over damage and anger that had once been beyond her power to resolve.

She specialised in people who hid their faces from the world: nuns – breakthroughs occurring when they finally removed their veils – and anaesthetists: 'Ooh, you wouldn't let an anaesthetist put you to sleep if you'd heard what I hear', she said. The more worrying alternative didn't seem to bother her. But when mental illness came back into her own life, her own home, she flailed. My own battles with depression were too threatening, too reminiscent of her childhood, I think, and she withdrew to her camp on the heights and waited for the cover of dark. Only much later did I come to see that she had used psychotherapy to try and make sense of her family just as I was now using history. Still, even her lack of problems was not quite the truth we had accepted. After she died her woman consultant admitted they had assumed at first that my mother's advanced liver disease was a result of heavy – though secret – drinking. She fitted the profile. But tests had shown this not to be the case. 'Of course your mother's addiction was food', she said ruefully. I mentioned the metabolic disorder. 'She didn't have a metabolic disorder,' said the consultant, 'she ate to heal her wounds.'

My mother, towards the end of her life

Not long before this final decline she took us to another play in Stratford one fine summer evening. She still wished she'd been allowed to be an actress and we went to the theatre a lot. Again the play had been chosen with minimum sensitivity: *'Tis Pity She's a Whore*. We ate a large dinner watching the swans after which she felt too uncomfortable to sit through the second act and I reeled out shortly afterwards when the protagonist appeared brandishing a dripping heart on his dagger. A real heart, though possibly not human, with gouts of blood which stained his wrist to the elbow. While the others stayed to watch the finale I went to find her resting in our car, the seat tipped right back, and we talked in the dark. It was always in these corners of our life that she would concede things were not turning out as she'd hoped.

Where I am most often reminded of her is at Harrods. If I go there and go up to the fifth floor, I see her hovering outside the restaurant in some would-be elegant navy blue jacket and smart shoes well on their way to becoming shapelessly comfortable and a scarf round her neck tied and re-tied into defeat. When she sees me her face is full of excitement. It is the treat. The treat was the 15/- smörgåsbord lunch we had three times a year from when I could be trusted not to bite circular chunks out of the glass, cut my lip and faint, until I had my own children. Smörgåsbord was new and stylishly Scandinavian in 1960, though the pianist still rippled medleys from the Warsaw Concerto or songs from the great musicals.

For a family of atheists, Harrods held the function of a church in our lives. Rites of passage, consolation, celebration; comforting ritual, transcendence. There was a library and a bank, both of which my mother used. She ordered cut flowers there, she sent wreaths to funerals. She had her bras fitted, she had her watch mended. There I bought my first hamster and had my first haircut. When I was a bridesmaid I had a special hair appointment which included my ear being seared with curling tongs. The primrose garland which balanced on my tidy waves also did so on my blister. As I grew older I graduated into Ladies' Hairdressing. When I went to boarding school, we ticked off the items on the list; a dark red cloak, a felt hat, worsted suit, three Viyella, two poplin shirts. Ties, gloves, grey socks, garters, six white inner pants and two grey outer pants (there is a potential anthropological treatise on the codes of middle-class English schoolgirl underwear in the 1960s), a dusty pink silk frock for best. After I became engaged we ordered the wedding stationery – I cut my finger on the bevel-edged invitation, selected a Wedding List, and then, finally, at a moment when I was almost paralysed with doubt, we went to choose my dress. I stood on a vast white sheet, all alone, the folds of heavy cream shantung falling from a tight Brussels lace bodice, held together with tiny fabric covered buttons. Behind me the long train opened out. Around the edge French seamstresses with mouths radiating pins knelt altering my life, while a junior stood holding waterfalls of silk veiling, as fine as vapour. Far away my mother sat on a gilt chair that was dangerously inadequate for her, watching them go about their work.

I had a trousseau too. Beautiful Swiss lawn nighties, broderie anglaise underwear, a quilted dressing gown with violets on it. Three months later we were back to the first floor for lilac maternity trousers, a sea island cotton smock, a nursing bra and two voluminous cocktail dresses. Another half year and we were buying a layette in the baby department: perfect and perfectly unwashable lacy matinée jackets, rich cream merino wool vests, Viyella nighties with intricate smocking, tiny ribbonned bootees. A shawl like cobweb. It was another world.

It was where my mother and her sister had one perfect memory: of buying pretty straw hats and summer gloves with *their* mother in the first summer of the war.

When I was five and my mother was expecting her second child, she took me to see Father Christmas. It was free at Harrods, unlike at Selfridges, which meant that it was not vulgar. This was convenient because things at home were tight. Father Christmas sat in a sort of drawing room with slightly arctic overtones and discussed the year's behaviour. Little children sat on Father Christmas's lap, bigger ones on a chair, knee to knee. Girls were assumed to want a doll, boys a train. Delivery was promised on Christmas Day. Because it was free there were, sadly, no mysterious packages to be handed over right away.

*Me (front right), bridesmaid at my aunt
and uncle's wedding, 1957*

But downstairs everything shone and promised. Piled up in one of the glass counters were pirate chests with filigree bags of gold foil-covered chocolate coins. I dragged on her arm. I went back and looked again. I asked nicely for a bit and then fell back into whining. 'Daddy's ill: we haven't got enough money', she said. She patted the large bump that contained my brother, in emphasis. We knew who to blame, then. As we went into the lift to go up and find the lavatories, a woman in a fur coat rustled in, followed by her chauffeur, carrying her parcels. As she got out on the first floor she handed me a tiny sack of coins. 'Happy Christmas, my dear.' My mother was furious. 'Who does she think she is?' I was ecstatic. I even kept the wrappers and the gold net after I'd eaten the chocolate.

Harrods. A new heaven. For a woman whose paternal fortune had been largely built on London stores – a fortune that allowed them to achieve acts of impressive social mobility – and for the child she once was, who had been happy buying a hat, it was not surprising that it was a place of potential transformation.

Only recently when visiting her sister, my aunt, in the depths of rural France, I got lost. Eventually having turned at the right set of rubbish bins, I saw a gate. On the mailbox, waiting for the postman, was a handwritten envelope: The Fabric Department Harrods, Knightsbridge, London SW1, Royaume-Uni. I knew I was in the right place.

After she died, my sister and I were trying to piece together my mother's last days. Had she felt ill? Or worse, been frightened? Alarmed by florid precursors of death? (There was a very fine but unmistakable spray of blood in the bathroom. I wiped it off quite calmly so that my sister, who had a month-old baby, would not see it). Then the bill arrived from Harrods. The weekend before her final collapse she had managed to get to the station, get on a train, visit her brand-new grandchild, get in a taxi and set off to buy several items of clothing in the outsize womenswear department, all of which she had left for alteration. Harrods had followed her even into the afterlife. They were, appropriately, forgiving and let her off the bill.

My mother had two lines from a poem that she quoted cheerfully, if insistently, from when I was a child.

O fat white woman whom nobody loves
Why do you wander the fields in gloves?

She said it so often that it had become meaningless. She only had to say
'oh fat . . .' and we would all join in. Long after she was dead I finally
collided, painfully, with the whole verse, a poem by Frances Cornford.

To a Fat Lady Seen from a Train

O why do you walk through the fields in gloves,
    Missing so much and so much?
O fat white woman whom nobody loves,
Why do you walk through the fields in gloves,
When the grass is soft as the breast of doves
    And shivering sweet to the touch?
O why do you walk through the fields in gloves,
Missing so much and so much?

The clearest single picture I have of her is back in Gloucestershire.
We decided to go out to a pub in a nearby village for supper. It was one
of the last times we did this and the shadow of illness was still faint. She
insisted she remembered a short cut, bypassing the main road on land
she claimed, as always, her family had owned. I looked on a map –
clearly there was some sort of track between the fields. We set off. The
lane was narrow with high brambles and hazel. Soon the tarmac died
out but we bumped on. The sides got closer and the centre of the track
alarmingly more substantial; solid tufts of grass thumped on the under-
side of the car, clods hit the exhaust. We reassured ourselves that this
was, obviously, still a lane, a lane meant for vehicles: there were after all
deep furrows either side of the central vegetation. We went through a
gateway and came to a halt. A great sweep of gentle hillside fell away
from us in evening light. Near at hand was a solitary stand of trees.
Birds sung, sheep stood. On the other side was the village with the pub.

Between us and it were large fields whose apparently thin, stony soil nevertheless supported pockets of thick mud in one of which we were now stuck. We revved up to a smell of burning, spinning the wheels into the mire. We got out and put my cotton jacket under the wheels. We looked at each other: her hefty, in a skirt and her best shoes, me too thin as always then but in my jeans. It was obvious which one would have to shove and which one steer. Finally the car came out with a violent wet lurch, its rear wheels suddenly spinning, covering her in thick mud. We had done it. We were no nearer dinner, but we were free.

Epilogue

Much later, I tracked down mid to late-nineteenth-century Cavendish and Howard portraits, hoping to see an image of my great-great-grandmother, Lady Fanny, whose influence resonated three generations beyond the grave. I never found a picture of her, but those of her brothers and other family members displayed chins that were invariably strong. Later I learned that these chins were matched in strength by intellect, and in particular an ability in mathematics and physics. Blood, it appeared, would not always out.

However, I did find out what had happened to her grandson, my grandmother's brother, my great-uncle Rupert. It was the only question on my list to which I received an unequivocal answer.

Rupert Howard had disappeared, it seemed without trace. We all knew that he had died in the First World War. Geraldine had that picture of him in his uniform although that was now lost. But he was never on any of the Howard family trees. I checked the censuses and tracked him down aged 15 in 1901 at a rather second-rate boarding school, and this provided his date of birth. Part of the answer was eventually revealed in his birth certificate. He was illegitimate, like his two older sisters, so only Ada was named as a parent and he was not a Howard at all. His parents' subsequent marriage could not legitimise him at that time.

But what of his death? Geraldine had been so pitifully precise in naming the very minute of her loss: 'Our Darling Rupert killed in France 11.45, September 2nd 1916.' I checked the records of deaths in action. Nothing. I checked with the extensive records of the War Graves Commission. No Englishman of the right name and age lay in their tidy care. I began to think he was another family myth. Perhaps he had done something unspeakable. Perhaps he had never died, only escaped, and the son killed in action was a story developed to add lustre to family history. Perhaps he was a deserter and shot?

Finally a historian friend found Rupert in an archive at Kew. Gerald would not have countenanced his oldest son not holding a commission but Rupert's illegitimacy was an impediment to acceptance as an officer in a smart regiment. In the end he had managed to obtain one in the 88th Battalion of the Canadian Infantry, part of the Canadian Expeditionary Forces. Empire regiments were less fussy when it came to awkward birth certificates. His papers survive in army archives. Suddenly there was his signature, clear and confident on the enlistment form, in January 1916, using his father's surname. It was the month conscription was introduced. Eight months later he was dead. He died during the Battle of the Somme and was laid to rest in the Military Cemetery at Ovillers as the aristocratic sounding Lt. Rupert Howard. The price of his name was that he was not buried as an Englishman; his corner of a foreign field was forever Canada. For the young man born Rupert Curtis the prejudice of the age almost hid him for ever.

On the other hand, of the 3,439 soldiers buried at Ovillers, only 1,080 were ever identified at all.

Thanks

I am much indebted to all those who have helped me build up a picture of a large and complicated family. I am very well aware that the story I tell will not be their story; even within a single family different members experience and interpret the same individuals and events very differently but I hope they will feel I have done it justice. Conversations with my father, with my brother, Dick Moore, my sister, Susannah Cannell, my children Nick and Miranda Bolter and Abigail Speller, and my cousins Simon Everton and Guy Kennaway have helped map some shared impressions onto this story while Miranda organised my archive of photographs and took some modern ones herself. My friend of decades, Sally Cherubini, held invaluable letters and recollections from my time in hospital and of our years in Germany.

My aunt Susie Vereker answered numerous tedious and often repetitive queries, provided some of my favourite photographs and gave me a draft copy of her book concerning the experience of evacuation and homecoming shared by her and my mother as children. She also provided some insights into her mother and we jointly investigated the war-time experience of the Poles.

Victoria de Rin, daughter of Blanche Howard and Angelo de Rin, helped with information about her parents and memories of Gerald and Ada Howard, her grandparents.

My uncle, the late Richard Edmonds, his widow Sarah and my cousin Anna Rankin, allowed me access to the rich archive of letters and documents which, added to diaries, papers and photographs already in my possession, helped me build up a picture of the contradictions in the early life of our family.

One of the bonuses of writing this book was that I met Neil Curtis, my fourth cousin, a link to the elusive Curtis family of Lincoln, who provided invaluable background material for understanding Ada's life.

I could not have written a book covering such a breadth of events without a researcher. Karen Hore slogged up and down to the record offices in London and Kew and made breakthroughs where I had been unsuccessful for years. I am extremely grateful to her for her expertise, enthusiasm and stamina. Catherine Hopkins and Louise Foxcroft provided invaluable information and insights into the legal, social and historical ramifications of illegitimacy and Dr Richard O'Flynn on past and present psychiatric treatment. I am also indebted to Andrew Pettit, the archivist at Chatsworth House for advice on the Compton estates at Eastbourne and to Charles Noble, the Keeper of the Devonshire Collection, for advice on portraits. Val and Ivor Neal of Derbyshire, whom I only know through the Internet, checked local records to confirm the burials of my great-great-grandmother and great-great-grandfather at Edensor, Chatsworth. Broad-ranging discussions with some of my Cambridge creative writing students have made me re-think certain aspects of my book.

I have been immensely fortunate in my agent Georgina Capel and all at Capel Land and the team at Granta and, above all, my patient and assiduous editor, George Miller. No writer could ask for more.

The support, ideas and feedback provided, as always, by Caron Freeborn and Louise Foxcroft have been central to this enterprise and I am indebted to the President and Fellows of Lucy Cavendish College, Cambridge, who made possible these precious friendships and other transformations in my life by admitting me as a mature undergraduate.

Were my mother alive she would undoubtedly wish to point out that Lucy Cavendish herself was her first cousin, twice removed, by marriage.